San Mateo County

A SESQUICENTENNIAL HISTORY

MITCHELL P. POSTEL

PUBLISHING COMPANY, INC.

BELMONT, CA 94002

PUBLISHING COMPANY, INC.

BELMONT, CA 94002

WWW.STARPUBLISHING.COM

Library of Congress Cataloging-in-Publication Data

Postel, Mitchell.
   San Mateo County : a sesquicentennial history / Mitchell P. Postel.
      p. cm.
   Includes index.
   ISBN 978-0-89863-285-9 (hardcover : alk. paper)
   1. San Mateo County (Calif.)—History. I. Title.

F868.S19P675 2007
979.4'69—dc22
                                        2007022462

ISBN: 978-0-89863-285-9   *Printed on acid-free paper.*

Printed in the United States of America

0 9 8 7 6 5 4 3 2 1   •   20 19 18 17 16 15 14 13 12 11 10 9 8 7 6 5 4 3 2 1

Dedication: For Al and Pat

Contents

Introduction for San Mateo County:
A Sesquicentennial History

*I*n 2006, the residents of San Mateo County are celebrating the sesquicentennial of its political creation. San Mateo County was not one of the original counties in California when the state was admitted into the union in 1850. Rather, it was born out of political compromise surrounded by intrigue and corruption. That it has risen from those times to become one of the most desirable suburban communities to live in on the planet is a remarkable story.

This sesquicentennial history is not a comprehensive, chronological, blow-by-blow account of the people of the peninsula. Instead, it introduces certain themes of local history that have helped to make the county what it is today. It is meant to be easy to read, but it is not a puff piece either. Much thinking went into each of the three parts of the book. Since 1994, the San Mateo County Historical Association has been planning the exhibits at its new location in the Old Courthouse in Redwood City. In order to plan those exhibits, the museum's staff spent long hours with scores of community members and other historians crystallizing what we view is the essence of the county's history. Much of that thinking manifests itself in this book. I am most appreciative of all the staff and advisors have been involved since that time to help to tell this history.

The book is laid out in three parts. Because this is the sesquicentennial year, a discussion about the county's political beginnings makes up the first part. In this portion of the book, I have made an attempt to look at original primary sources and draw conclusions not put forward before. Like most historical subjects, the more I dwelled on those initial months of the county's life, the more I knew we still need to learn. There are so many unanswered questions and untold stories about the county's political history, that I hope that this volume will inspire immediate further investigation and publication.

Part II of the book is a series of essays, written as a reflection of the major exhibits being created at the San Mateo County History Museum. The subject area here includes how the natural resources of the peninsula affected the overall history of the Bay Region and the West, how San Mateo County became a leading force in the creation of the western-style suburban community, how this place became so ethnically diverse after the discovery of gold in California, and how the peninsula became a hotbed of entrepreneurial activity, particular during and after World War II.

Because much of the story of San Mateo County is so diverse in a geographical way, Part III tries to describe the highlights of the county's history regionally. It is plain that there is much divergence in the culture and environment of the coastside as compared with the bayside. North County is distinct from the south or middle parts of the county. This part of the book focuses on the local factors that make the regions of the peninsula so different.

Some years ago, when I saw the writing of this book coming, I thought that the best way to handle it would be to write in a sort of team approach. I spoke with local historians and staff at the

Admission Day Picnic at Coyote Point September, 1888. Old Maids Fraternity, Redwood City Young Ladies. Photo taken by James Van Court.

museum—alas, no takers—I was on my own! Writing the history of San Mateo County is intimidating because there is so much to consider and analyze. My greatest hope is that this piece not be taken as any last word, but instead, as a launching pad for new ideas, theories, and research projects.

Here in San Mateo County we forget how meaningful our story is. We live in the most important state in the most powerful country in the world. Our county's contributions to the economy, lifestyle and culture of California should not be understated. The county's history is significant. We should not rely on outsiders to tell us that. We should understand our own story. It will help us when we represent ourselves to others. It will help us to realize our own potential, especially this year—our sesquicentennial year.

Bay Area "Wheelers" at Coyote Point, circa 1880s. Oyster box at center.

Mitch Postel, January, 2006

Part One

The Sesquicentennial Legacy

Chapter 1

Election Day at Crystal Springs: May 12, 1856

For 22-year-old, Hungarian-born Gaza Haraszthy, the morning of May 12, 1856, must have seemed grand. It was voting day in the Crystal Springs Valley. Today, the reservoirs that provide San Francisco and parts of the peninsula with water lie on top of what was a fertile farming valley, complete with a little village called Crystal Springs. This voting day was very special, because it was the first election for the new county of San Mateo, born out of a political compromise in Sacramento on April 19 known as the Consolidation Act. Residents of the new county were to select their original leaders, choose a county seat, and begin the privileged American process of governing themselves.

The Crystal Springs Hotel was a popular stop for stagecoach travelers enroute between bayside communities and the coast and was a luxurious destination hotel too.

Gaza's father, Agoston, had originally come to the United States in 1840. He sailed with a friend, Charles Halasz, from Hamburg to New York. Agoston was 38, fleeing political persecution, and Charles was 18, lusting for adventure. They somehow ended up settling in Wisconsin.[1]

Agoston was of noble heritage. Born in 1812, in Futtak east of the Danube, he was the only son of General Charles Haraszthy of an old landed family. Following his father's footsteps, he joined the military, serving in the royal guard under Austrian Emperor Ferdinand. He retired from the guard with the rank of colonel. Later he became the private secretary of the viceroy of Hungary. His deep commitment for an independent Hungary forced him from the favors of the emperor's court, and Agoston went back to his family's estate, where he engaged in raising silkworms and grapes for wine making. He kept close to politics by serving in the Hungarian Diet and marrying Eleanor de Dedinski of Polish noble blood. They had three sons, all named after Hungarian national heroes: Gaza (the oldest),

Attila, and Arpad. Eventually, Agoston's activities as a Hungary patriot landed him in enough trouble that he found himself forced to come to America.

In Wisconsin, Agoston founded Town Haraszthy (now known as Sauk City). Here, in partnership with an Englishman named Bryant, he established a sawmill, a grist mill, a brickyard, and a general store. He built houses to rent, ran a steamboat and ferry service, raised livestock, grew corn, and started the first hop yard in the state. He donated land for a school and a church. He even tried a hand at planting grapevines for wine making—perhaps his only failure during his Wisconsin days.

In 1842, he returned to the realities of European politics to retrieve his family. It was a rough time. His lands were taken from him, later valued by his family at $200,000. His wife, Eleanor, died. However, he remarried (eventually having three more children in America) and got his family, including his father, out of Hungary and to Wisconsin.

The Haraszthy family prospered in Wisconsin. Agoston even wrote a two-volume set of books in 1844. The set, published in Hungary and, of course, written in Hungarian, was a travelogue of sorts, describing Agoston's impressions of America. It is said that the works influenced many Hungarians to come to the United States. Perhaps the only major negative aspect of the Haraszthy family's Wisconsin experience involved Agoston's battle with respiratory ailments that made him desire a dryer climate.

In 1848, Wisconsin became a state, and that same year, word came that gold had been discovered in California. Perhaps a combination of better weather, new economic opportunities, and pure adventure influenced him. By the spring of 1849, the Haraszthy family (from the 59-year-old general to an infant girl) was on its way to the West Coast.

Along for the ride was a group of Wisconsin friends, including the former district attorney for the territory, Thomas W. Sutherland. Once arriving at St. Joseph, Missouri, a traditional launching community for the trip to California, the group selected the more southern Santa Fe Trail (over the Oregon Trail) as their route. They purchased their oxen and wagons and were preparing to set out, when they were given a great surprise.

Eldest son Gaza, age 15, had been on the East Coast preparing for the exam to enter the United States Naval Academy at Annapolis. When he heard that his family had made the decision to come to California, he determined that he would not miss the adventure, so he joined his family at St. Joseph.

Gaza became restless during the slow-moving journey, however. At the old town of Albuquerque, he talked his father into using his influence to have him enlisted in the United States Army. Gaza joined Company K of the Second Regiment of Dragoons under a Captain Kerr. Gaza would spend four years with the Dragoons, participating in various Mexican-border skirmishes. He was wounded once.[2]

In the meantime, the wagon train reached San Diego before the end of 1849. Thomas Sutherland almost immediately became the village's *Alcalde*.* The Haraszthy family went up north to San Luis Obispo for a while, but soon returned to San Diego. Agoston befriended Juan Bandini, and the two formed a partnership in which they ran a livery stable, an omnibus service, and butcher shop in the old town section.

---

*Alcaldes were sort of mayors in the old Mexican government.

In 1850, William H. Dougal drew this view of a rider on a mule near today's Belmont on the "road to San Jose." Travel by stage coach from San Francisco to San Jose took between 9 and 6 hours.

In 1850, California became a state, and San Diego became a county. Agoston was elected sheriff, and his father, the general, became a judge and a city councilman. With their old friend Thomas Sutherland, they built the town's first jail. Agoston was also involved in fighting off an Indian uprising.

Late in 1851, Agoston quit his law enforcement career and was elected to the state assembly. He then moved up to San Francisco, while sending his wife and four youngest children back east for better educations. He imported Zinfandel and Muscat grape cuttings directly from Hungary in February of 1852, and in March, with son Attila, he planted the first such grapes in California on 211 acres purchased near the old Mission.

In 1853, Agoston expanded his wine-making enterprise by purchasing two 320-acre tracts of land in the Crystal Springs Valley, today open space maintained by the San Francisco Water Department.[3] On hillside property, he built a house and barn. He cleared away chaparral and, in March of 1854, planted 30 acres of grapes, including his Zinfandels and Muscats. He also planted 20,000 fruit trees, strawberries, and grain. He decided to raise cattle on the property as well.

Agoston had purchased this property, believing it to be public land. He claimed it by filing state school warrants at $2 an acre. However, in 1854, a United States land commission ruled that the acreage was part of one of the old Mexican land grants, *Rancho Feliz*. Agoston kept 385 acres by paying the owners $15 an acre in 1855. In 1856, he purchased another adjoining 645 acres.

While all this was going on, Agoston moved into the gold business, becoming an assayer and a refiner for the Adams Company. In 1854, he was appointed by President Franklin Pierce as assayer of the newly created branch mint on Montgomery Street in San Francisco. A year later, he quit this position to replace his father as melter and refiner. The general stayed on to serve his son as an assistant. With all this activity, Agoston must have been much pleased with the arrival of Gaza.

In 1853, Gaza had become restless once more—this time with the hard Army life of the Southwest. Gaza asked his father for help. The colonel again used his influence, this time to get his son *out* of the service—with an honorable discharge. After arriving in San Francisco, Gaza became interested in agricultural pursuits and joined the laborers down on his father's properties in the Crystal Springs Valley.

Gaza was thus engaged in working for his father on the morning of May 12, 1856, when he arrived at the polling station. Here he encountered part of an effort that would represent one of the most blatant attempts to fix an election in American western history.

Almost everyone in the Crystal Springs Valley knew each other. The place was mostly made up of farmers. Most accounts indicate that a total voting population of about 25 souls resided in the area.

At the polling station, instead of familiar faces, Gaza encountered five election judges he did not know. All were San Francisco rough types, including the notorious Liverpool Jack. Intimidation of local voters was part of this gang's plan. However, in Gaza Haraszthy the boys had encountered the wrong man. When he left the army in 1853 at the age of 19, he was still only 5 feet, 2 inches tall. But now he had grown to a full 6 feet. He was a seasoned soldier and a member of a prominent family. Gaza voted, then stayed at the poll to observe the proceedings. He counted 30 voters. Yet, 297 were eventually tallied.

Columbus Huffaker, who lived at W. D. Harrington's Mountain Lake Farm, about three miles from Crystal Springs, got to the poll at eight in the morning. He stayed until three in the afternoon. He later testified that nowhere close to 297 people voted that day. He saw several strangers around the ballot box—he had never seen any of them before.

W. D. Harrington had lived in the Crystal Springs Valley since January of 1851. He felt himself well-acquainted with most everyone there. He was also present at the polling place. Like Haraszthy and Huffaker, he was apparently not intimidated by what he saw, but was certain that something irregular was up. Harrington testified that after arriving at the polls and seeing the strangers, he asked them who they were. They responded that they were the official election judges. Harrington only recognized one of the men, who he had seen at the notorious Abbey House located at the extreme northern section of the new county. Certainly none of these five men were from the Crystal Springs precinct. Harrington noted that at first he saw only four judges, and he asked about the fifth. They then "pointed to one who was asleep, snoring melodiously . . ." This man then got up: "He was a pockmarked man" and "seemed to be sick." Harrington suggested that someone take his place, but this was refused. Later, another Valley resident, Mr. Moss, recognized the pockmarked man as Liverpool Jack, a well-known San Francisco character. Harrington confirmed that no more than 25 adult men lived in the valley (remember that this was before women had the right to vote). He concluded during his testimony: "It is not possible that 297 votes could be polled in Crystal Springs."[4] Gaza Haraszthy certainly agreed.

So what was all this about? What had Gaza Haraszthy witnessed? It was hardly an isolated incident. Instead, it was part of a highly organized, politically approved takeover of a new county by disreputable thugs from another.

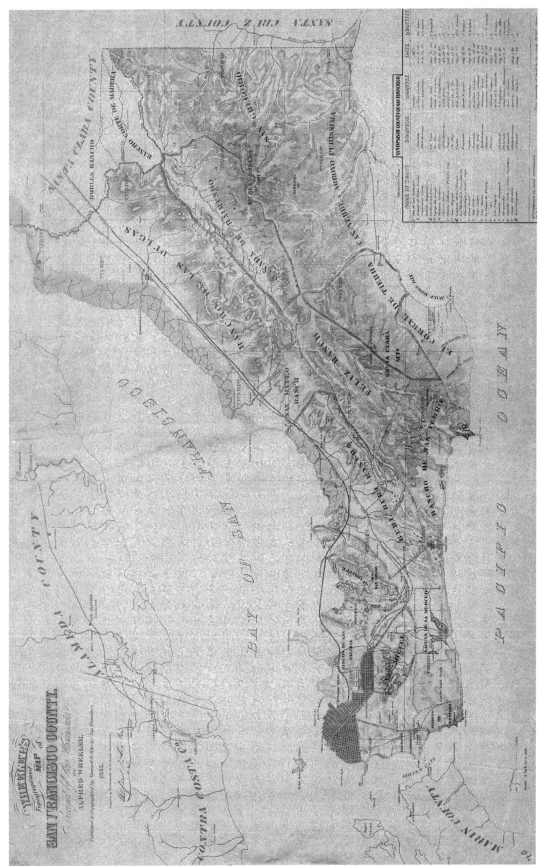

San Francisco County in 1855, including much of what we call San Mateo County today.

Chapter 1 Footnotes

1. Paul Fredericksen, *The Authentic Haraszhy Story.* Wine Institute, 1947, pp. 1–3.

2. Author unknown, "The Haraszhy Family," July, 1886, manuscript collection, Bancroft Library.

3. Exhaustive research by San Mateo County Historical Association member Stephen M. Pace has located this acreage "just to the north of the Highway 92 causeway across the reservoir on the northern face of the hill in the vicinity of the Pillaricitos Quarry." His paper can be found in the archives of the San Mateo County History Museum.

4. *County Court—San Mateo County Minutes*, Hon. Ben F. Fox, County Judge, Belmont, June 10, 1856.

Chapter 2

The Set Up: San Mateo County Born in Scandal

The muddled beginnings of San Mateo County political history has origins in the failed attempt of David Broderick to become a United States senator in 1852. Broderick was a leader of Democratic politics in San Francisco, with an important following from fellow new arrivals from northern East-Coast cities, especially those who were Irish and Catholic. Broderick, himself, was born in Washington, D.C., of Irish Catholic parents and was reared in New York City. He grew up in a highly charged political environment and learned the ways of the Tammany Hall contingent who were pioneering "Big Boss" government as a method of controlling a major metropolis. Broderick ran unsuccessfully for Congress in 1846.

Broderick's path took a dramatic turn when gold was discovered in California. Like the thousands of forty-niners who headed west in 1849, Broderick packed up and moved to San Francisco. He came to own a private mint and speculated in real estate, which made him wealthy. He also took interest in the political environment here and put his experience to work.

However, he ran smack into the other powerful body of Democratic politicians—those hailing from southern states led by Senator William Gwin. In those days, the election of senators was left up to the state legislature, in Sacramento. There, Gwin outmaneuvered Broderick, which left the former New Yorker bitter. He resolved to fight back. He shoved aside his legitimate supporters and looked to a rougher crowd to back his activities, in the way of the streets of New York. One of those pushed out remembered Broderick saying: "You respectable people, I can't depend on you. You won't go down and face the revolvers. . . . This election showed that . . . responsible people would not even face down slander and threats."[1] Many of the major characters involved in the creation of San Mateo County were among this new group of Broderick cronies. Although Broderick was never officially indicted as a player in the fixing of the county's first election, his support and encouragement of these individuals was well known. The universal recognition of him as their leader indicates his involvement—at least from a distance.

One of the most infamous players of Broderick's new group was Billy Mulligan, perhaps the principal thug in the San Mateo County election episode. Ferret-faced, just a little over five feet tall, and never more than 120 pounds, Mulligan was one of the most feared characters on either coast of the United States—and maybe Broderick's most faithful henchman. Born in Ireland, Mulligan received his education, like Broderick, in the tough Irish Catholic neighborhoods of New York City. He

became a prizefighter and gambler. Among his friends were later California companions Chris Lilly and Yankee Sullivan. A warden at the city jail later remembered him as a "professional blackleg and as desperate a character as could be found among the rowdy element of New York."[2] Despite his size, he had the reputation of being a fierce fighter, especially after having a few drinks. One of the legends about him said that armed only with a pool cue, he took on John Morrissey, a 200-pounder and one-time heavyweight champion of the world. After the battle, Mulligan chased the giant down a flight of stairs. Also like Broderick, Mulligan received training in Tammany politics.[3]

In 1847 he was jailed in New York on a burglary charge, but he escaped and fled to New Orleans. He joined up with the Louisiana Mounted Volunteers and fought in the Mexican

This photograph of San Mateo, circa 1865, shows Third Avenue looking west from the railroad tracks. The frontier-like town a few years after the county's formation shows St. Matthew's Catholic Church (at what is now Third and Ellsworth), a livery stable and hotel.

War. The Gold Rush lured him to California in 1849. Within a year in the mining districts, he became well known as a gambler, prizefight promoter, claim jumper, and dangerous ruffian. In February 1851, he shot and mortally wounded a young gambler named William Anderson during a saloon encounter at Sonora. That fall, he fought a duel near Mokelumne Hill with another hard character named Jimmy Douglass. By mid-November, he was in San Francisco, and was wounded in a shootout with a gambler at the infamous Bella Union saloon. Only six days later, he was wounded again, this time as a bystander watching a gunfight.

Once in San Francisco, Billy resumed his prizefighting and gambling. He acquired a following and involved himself in politics. He found that he could organize his friends into "parties" and then sell nominations at "conventions" for local offices to the highest bidder. It is said that he was able to obtain $28,000 for one of these nominations, with no guarantee of victory. Mulligan also learned the fine art of ballot-box stuffing, fixing many a San Francisco election for a friend.[4]

As an election worker for Broderick, Mulligan proved an invaluable asset. He loyally bullied voters and corrupted the system when convenient. He did battle with Broderick enemies with a relish. According to one story, Billy was at a saloon for a big night, dressed in his best attire. A man twice Mulligan's size was said to be berating Broderick within earshot. Billy calmly approached the poor fellow and, without saying a word, head-butted him into unconsciousness. Mulligan then left the saloon complaining that he had to change clothes since his shirt had become so bloody.

Broderick rewarded Mulligan's efforts. For two years he held the position of tax collector for the San Francisco County treasurer—a lucrative assignment. At the time of the creation of San Mateo County in 1856, he was jailkeeper under Sheriff David Scannell. Scannell was, of course, another of Broderick's men, and also from New York City.

Yet another major player from the streets of New York in the Broderick camp was James Casey. Casey had a tough reputation as well. It was said that he once took on five armed men single-handedly. Weirdly, after the fight, he was arrested instead of them. However, fearing his wrath, his combatants never pressed charges.

A sharp dresser and prematurely balding, Casey, like Mulligan, was more than an ordinary thug. By 1856, he was a newspaper publisher and a San Francisco County supervisor. In fact, his supervisoral district was part of what we would call San Mateo County today. This was quite remarkable, since Casey did not live down this way. As the story goes, in the 1854 election, he gained control of a ballot box and created a secret compartment within it. He stuffed it with write-in votes for himself and had the box used in San Francisco County's first district (the first, second, and third districts would essentially be made San Mateo County in April 1856).[5] His win was astonishing to the locals, since his was a write-in victory, and no one in the district seemed to know that he was even a candidate.

By the beginning of 1856, San Francisco was immersed in political corruption. For its ordinary citizens, who may have been too busy making money to mind their local government, trying to clean things up seemed an exercise in frustration. There simply existed more promising matters to consider. After all, in seven short years the city had become the queen of the West. Its empire, first created by the gold found in the foothills of the Sierra Nevada, now extended up and down the Pacific Coast and included lumbering, marine resources, commerce, banking, and a variety of light and heavy industries. Every other population center in the West seemed like a small town by comparison. America itself was still overwhelmingly a nation of farms and little communities. Even New York numbered only 500,000 people. Nevertheless, out in far-off California, a metropolis was growing at a rate never seen before. Some 50,000 people, or one-seventh of all the people in the state, lived in San Francisco.[6] With the rapid growth, however, came vexing problems. Despite all the wealth, the city had accumulated a $3.5 million debt (an incredible amount for those days). Moreover, services seemed lacking and crime had grown out of control.

California historian John Hittell wrote in 1878: "The political system had in 1855 reached a greater depth of corruption in San Francisco than in any other part of the United States."[7] Hittell says the worst problems of the city were caused by the inefficiencies and the crime. He laments that more than a thousand homicides were committed between 1849 and 1856, but only seven executions punished the murderers. About the police, he wrote: "Most . . . were appointed to reward partisan service, and were grossly inefficient and corrupt. They could be trusted for untiring labor in elections, but little was to be expected from them in the matter of arresting criminals who had money or influence." A San Mateo County history published in that same year blamed the political condition on the Gold Rush and the numbers and types of "heterogeneous" people arriving in the State: "San Francisco County was well-nigh overcome by the cormorants of society. There were not enough offices in existence to afford them the spoils they desired, and increased opportunities for plunder were eagerly sought."[8] (*Cormorants* refers to a greedy person and not the sea bird in this case.)

The art of ballot-box stuffing was being perfected in San Francisco. Even so, techniques of more direct impact were employed, as well. Voters had little privacy while at the polls and could be easily intimidated. Ballots were frequently handed to them with the slate of "political parties" (like Billy

Mulligan's). The entire ballot would then be accepted by election officials acting in consort with the parties. At times, gangs would seize polling stations and simply announce their winners. Routinely, the gangs would walk or ride in wagons and vote over and over again in precincts across the county.

The rural southern part of the county was easily dominated by the political powers in San Francisco. Scattered farmers and lumbermen, serviced by a few remote community centers mostly located at scarce crossroads, constituted the population base down this way. There was no newspaper catering to these people. In fact, there were few common interests between most of the residents. All

R.O. Tripp, whose Woodside Store is a museum.

Francisco Sanchez.

forms of government existed in the city to the north, including the courts. However, a small number of justices of the peace served the people of the peninsula. Because of the distance to San Francisco, they generally exceeded their powers and found themselves settling property disputes and even granting divorces on occasion.[9]

When San Francisco was first set up as a county in 1850, three districts were formed in this rural section that would constitute most of what became San Mateo County. In the 1850 election, John Treat won election for District 1, Francisco Sanchez for District 2, and R.O. Tripp for District 3. All three were legitimate representatives. John Treat, according to the 1860 census, was a local farmer born in 1822. The other two became legendary figures on the peninsula.

Francisco Sanchez was from one of the old Spanish families. His father had actually come with the Anza party of 1776 that originally settled San Francisco. As a member of an important family during the Mexican California era, he received the 9,000-acre *Rancho San Pedro* (constituting most of the city of Pacifica today). At

The Sanchez Adobe is on the site of a 1786 mission outpost. Located on Linda Mar Boulevard in Pacifica, it has been restored and may be toured by the public. The adobe is near the center of the 8,926-acre Rancho San Pedro, which was granted to Sanchez in 1839.

various times, Sanchez served as *comandante* of the Presidio and *alcalde* (mayor) of Yerba Buena. The Mexican War raged from 1846 to 1848, and while the people of the peninsula *ranchos* were inclined to peaceful relations, they were compelled to revolt after several incidents of unfair treatment. As the recognized leader in this area, in 1847 Sanchez led 100 *rancheros* and *vaqueros* against U.S. Marines and local volunteers at the Battle of Santa Clara. The skirmish and the resulting truce that Sanchez worked out with Captain Ward Marston of the Marines earned Sanchez considerable added respect

Logger's cabin in the Redwoods of San Mateo County.

Benjamin G. Lathrop of Redwood City.

among the old families and new Americans as well. Sanchez remained one of the county's most influential individuals until he died falling off a horse in 1862. Today his house is a county museum, operated by the San Mateo County Historical Association.

Also a museum for the county is Dr. R. O. Tripp's Woodside Store. Tripp, the winner of the District 3 election, was born in Newport, New York, in 1816. Orphaned, he grew up on his uncle's farm. He trained to become a dentist at Foxboro, Massachusetts, and practiced there until word of gold in California compelled him to go west. He and friend James Ryder sailed to Central America in 1849 and booked passage to California. In San Francisco, he established a dental practice, extracting teeth for $4 each and plugging them for $8. The unethical competition of other dentists in the area is said to have soured Tripp on the profession—plus, he desired to live in a more dry climate.[10] Tripp and Ryder entered into a partnership to cut logs in the Woodside area of today with William Lloyd, a blacksmith, and Alvinza Hayward, an ox driver from Amador County. Their aim was to provide lumber to build the wharves at San Francisco.

In February of 1850, the partners accidentally discovered access to the Bay at what is called Redwood City today. Tripp established a route to drag the fallen redwood logs down from the hills. He leased the right to cut timber from Luisa Soto, owner of *Rancho Canada Raymundo*. At the slough, the logs were tied together into rafts and floated up to San Francisco. Unwittingly, the partners had founded Redwood City, as others moved into the area to establish businesses made possible by the logging operations. Of course everyone was squatting on this land, which was the California way of doing things at the time. Soon the Arguello family, who owned *Rancho de las Pulgas*, brought suit on the squatters. The family's legal representative, Simon Mezes, eventually received title to the future downtown Redwood City area and forced the squatters to purchase the lands they had settled upon.

William Lloyd went on to become a farmer in the vicinity of Searsville. Alvinza Hayward eventually made a fortune in mining stocks and established a massive estate at San Mateo. In a horrific incident, James Ryder was severely mauled by a grizzly bear. He lived through the ordeal, and left the area. He forever after was known as *Grizzly Ryder*. Meanwhile, the name of the gulch where he encountered the mother bear and her two cubs took the name *Bear Gulch*. That left Tripp, now 35 years old, without partners. In 1851, he entered into a new arrangement with two shingle makers, M. A. Parkhurst and Parkhurst's partner, a man named Ellis. According to Tripp, Ellis "drank hard,"[11] and eventually moved on. However, with 22-year-old Parkhurst, Tripp established a long and productive collaboration. They finished building the Woodside Store that still stands today, a little northwest of the first (at today's Kings Mountain and Tripp Roads).

12-ox team in San Mateo County Redwoods.

As a county supervisor, Tripp rode up to San Francisco each Sunday, met with the board on Monday, and came back on Tuesday. During his time in the city, he also bought inventory for the store. Because of his political responsibilities and the fact that he resumed his dental practice at Woodside, it is surmised that Parkhurst had most of the responsibility of running the store.

In 1852 (the year that Broderick lost to Gwin in his bid for the Senate), indications are that south San Francisco County politics were changing. No longer were the representatives well-known names like Sanchez and Tripp. Instead, they were William McLane for the first district and men with, seemingly, no known first names for the second and third districts—Musgrove and Hill.

Of course, ballot-box-stuffer James P. Casey was elected in 1854. That year, newcomer Benjamin G. Lathrop of Redwood City ran against Musgrove in the second district. Lathrop sensed an easy victory. The mysterious Musgrove appeared not to be even campaigning. Lathrop was shocked when the results came back and he had lost. In fact, he was told that only three votes had been cast for him.

In Lathrop, the local voters had a substantial character (in fact, his house still stands as a county museum, too—in Redwood City). Benjamin Lathrop was born at Canaan, New Hampshire in 1815. He was a direct descendant of Walter de Lawthrope, sheriff of Yorkshire, England, in 1216. When Lathrop was a child, his family moved to South Carolina, where his father was a part owner and manager of an iron works. Benjamin worked as a store clerk and moved with his company to Montgomery, Alabama, in 1832. He traded with the Creek Indians, learned their language, and fought against them in the Creek Indian War of 1837. He became one of the first aldermen of Montgomery and was elected captain of a company of volunteers to put down a rumored slave rebellion. He established a successful business presence in Alabama, but was ruined when an employee embezzled most of his assets. He moved to Arkansas to start a new life, and then in 1849 was drawn to California.

He left business interests and resigned his position of county judge of Chicot County, Arkansas. With wife and child, Lathrop crossed the plains in company of 15 hired hands, "black and white."[12] Like most of those who came to California in 1849, he believed he would return with a fortune and adopted for himself an overly optimistic two-year plan to produce it. Once in Pawnee country, Lathrop had a scrape with the Indians after an ox went missing. Finally in California, he tried his hand at mining on the Feather River but did not strike it rich. He purchased the Southern Hotel on J Street in Sacramento. Unfortunately, the building burned down in the fire of 1852. He then moved on to San Francisco, where he worked in the auction houses. In 1854, he moved to San Mateo County, originally with the idea of establishing a country resort, the Sulfur Springs House of Purissima, on the county's coastside.

He knew very well that more than three people had voted for him in the election of 1854. In fact, after a fast canvassing of his own, he believed he had won the supervisor's race for the second district. He decided to contest the election and went to San Francisco to hire an attorney to assist him in the matter. The lawyer told him "go home and give it up . . . the roughs ruled" San Francisco County.[13]

It seems the only legitimate candidate to win office from down on the peninsula in 1854 was Andrew Teague. Teague was born in Boone County, Mississippi, in 1822. He came to California in 1850 via wagon train. He tried mining until 1852, when he returned to Mississippi to fetch his family. In 1853, he made his way back to California, settling in the Woodside area, where he became engaged in the lumber industry.

And so, by 1855, political power was hardly in good hands down the peninsula. The cliques that ran things seemed to have had two operating centers: Abbey House and Belmont. Chris Lilly's Abbey House was one of several road houses that sprung up on the road to San Jose to service the new stagecoach travel.

Chris Lilly, an old friend of Billy Mulligan, was perhaps the best-known prizefighter of the entire New York contingent now in California. During a bare-knuckle contest in 1842, he had gone 119 rounds with Thomas McCoy before an audience of 2,000 at Hastings, New York. Lilly battered McCoy until McCoy drowned in his own blood, and Lilly became the first American professional fighter to kill a man in the ring. He fled to England to avoid any legal prosecution, and then went to New Orleans, as Billy Mulligan had, and joined up with the Louisiana Mounted Volunteers, also like Billy. He served well and eventually was promoted to lieutenant. He came to California in 1850, and drifted through the mining districts with Yankee Sullivan and Mulligan, who had arrived the year before. In 1855, he was known to operate a popular cock-fighting pit in San Francisco. By 1856, he was owner of the Abbey House at the top of the hill in today's Daly City, at the intersection of Mission Street and San Jose Avenue.[14]

The other center of activity was at Belmont, where former Governor John McDougal planned an empire. He bought up a track of land that extended west along the creek from the stagecoach road. Later, this property became Carl Janke's Belmont Park, where for most of the second half of the nineteenth century huge picnics took place. The park was especially popular among ethnic communities from San Francisco, who would come down via the railroad, which was established in 1864. The crowds numbered as many as 10,000 individuals. Today, this land is occupied by the Belmont Government Center, a portion of the town's business area, and Twin Pines Park.

Nineteenth-century California historian Hubert Howe Bancroft described John McDougal as "a gentlemanly drunkard, and democratic politician of the order for which California was destined to become somewhat unpleasantly notorious."[15] McDougal was born in 1818 in Ohio. His family moved to Indiana, and he became superintendent of the state prison there in 1846. He served in the military during the Mexican War, and when word of gold in California reached him, he set out west with his brother George. Bancroft writes: "He was fine-looking, and adhered to the old style of ruffled shirt front, buff vest and pantaloons, and blue coat with brass buttons." Bancroft continues: "He used to say that there were two beings of whom he stood in awe—God almighty and Mrs. McDougal. The latter always treated him with patient kindness, although often compelled to bring him home from a midnight debauch."

After arriving in California, McDougal immediately involved himself in politics. At the state constitutional convention held in Monterey in 1849, he became chairman of the boundary-fixing committee. He favored California taking in all the territory won in the Mexican War to create one vast state that would include today's Nevada, Utah, Arizona, New Mexico, and parts of Colorado. Worries over the slavery issue and how it might play out in these new lands, plus other concerns, blocked such a plan, but McDougal made friends in the process, despite rumors that he had been on a bender during nearly the entire convention. That year, he was elected California's first lieutenant governor, although as Bancroft tells us: "He was seldom fit for the discharge of his duties." However Bancroft admits: "[S]uch was the influence of his naturally genial and generous deportment, culti-vated mind, and brilliant social talents, that only his political enemies, and not always those, could bring themselves to treat him with the contempt another man in his position would have received."

When Governor Peter Burnett tired of politics and resigned in 1851, McDougal became Califor-nia's second governor. His bid for continuing as governor in the 1852 election was hampered by two stands he made. First, he favored Chinese immigration in order to offer the new state an inexpensive labor supply. Nearly every white working person in the state objected to that. He also opposed the very popular San Francisco Vigilance Committee of 1851, which had been formed to rid the city of criminal gangs. Angered by his loss, he blamed a San Francisco newspaper editor for the defeat and fought an inconclusive duel with him near the stage road at Belmont. Perhaps this was the moment that he began plotting his resurgence, with Belmont as his center of operations.

It is doubtful that most people down the peninsula knew much about the political forces at the Abbey House or Belmont. Nor did they have much information on David Broderick, Billy Mulligan, and James Casey. However, it was the sense of at least some of the residents down this way that San Francisco was too different in its character and too far away geographically to make an adequate county seat of government. Therefore, in 1855, they petitioned the state government to create a new county, to be formed south of the Abbey House, to be called Raymundo, after lumbering areas at *Ran-cho Canada Raymundo*.

In San Francisco, the request found support among newspaper editors anxious for political reform. On April 27, 1855, a *Daily California Chronicle* editorial said San Francisco County was simply too large. Mistaking the name the Peninsula people were proposing as Romano or Romanoff "or some such Russian appellative," the *Chronicle* correctly gauged the frustrations of the people here. It rea-soned that particularly for folks "on the Pacific side—in the Miramontes portion . . . to transact any county business it costs three days—one to ride into town over the mountains, one to transact what-ever they may have to do here, and one to return." By Miramontes, the *Chronicle* was referring to the growing population on the Miramontes land grant at Pilarcitos Creek (today's Half Moon Bay). The editor also mentioned expanding communities "at the Redwoods" (Woodside) and "at the Pulgas Ranch" (Redwood City). They "would be greatly convenienced by having the few Courts they need . . . ." On matters of taxation and local government, the *Chronicle* was completely sympa-thetic. It recognized the "legislative and official swindling" in San Francisco and concluded the peninsulans "might start and conduct a county government at less cost to individuals and to property . . . ." As for representation in Sacramento, the *Chronicle* agreed that all the senators and assemblymen were from the city: "This is not a fair division of the responsibilities, the honors, the influences and the spoils of office." The *Chronicle* concluded: "If . . . the people of that section desire a new county, let them have it."

At this point in the editorial, the *Chronicle* alluded to the wishes of San Francisco reformers to simplify local government. Many felt that government in the city was too big. Every time a movement was launched and seemed to clean out city offices of corrupt influences, the rascals seemed to find jobs in county government. When a similar effort was made for county government, the rascals found their way back to city government. For the reformers, the answer seemed to lie in combining or "consolidating" city and county government to get a better handle on the situation. With one city and county of San Francisco, the good citizens could better watch their politicians and bureaucrats, and keep a more watchful eye on how tax money was spent.

The first attempt to create a consolidation act occurred in January of 1855, when State Assemblyman Robert C. Rodgers introduced such a bill. After it stalled, Senator William W. Hawks of San Francisco proposed another. It passed in the Senate on April 27, the same day the *Chronicle* editorial appeared. However it was "indefinitely postponed" in the Assembly.[16]

Predicting this outcome, the *Chronicle* asserted: "[W]e may not get the city and county consolidated during this session of the legislature," but "we must have it ere long, and the smaller the extent of the county then the better for us." The *Chronicle's* reasoning wove closely to the aspirations of the peninsulans:

The first and most effectual step . . . towards consolidating the city and county of San Francisco is to grant the petition . . . . Let us get our government and our territory as compact as possible, and our interests as homogeneous as possible, that our legislature may be as equitable as possible. Then we may be able to elect tolerably decent men, and by watching them closely and restraining them rigidly, may prevent them from stealing, as heretofore, (they have with) more then half of what they legislate upon.

For State Assemblyman Horace Hawes, the Consolidation Act was of great importance in January 1856, when he introduced his own bill. He had no interest in creating two counties. Nevertheless, he became the unwitting father of San Mateo County.

Hawes was born July 10, 1813, in Danby, New York. His family suffered from severe poverty. In 1824, his mother died and the family broke up. As a boy he was given to servitude to a nearby family. He learned carpentry, house painting, farming, and other skills. After four years of miserable and frugal life, he purchased his freedom for $50 cash and promise of another $50 as a loan. At 16, he passed examinations allowing him to become a master for a public school and also began to train to become an attorney. In 1835, at the age of 22, he received his first real taste of politics by participating in a state convention at Utica focusing on the abolition of slavery. He remained at Utica as a teacher until 1837, when he moved to Erie, Pennsylvania. He eventually held the positions of deputy attorney general, county prosecutor, and commissioner of deeds for several states while at Erie. He married there, but personal tragedy continued to follow him. His wife died after only 8-1/2 months in 1846. The next year, President James Polk gave Hawes the post of United States Council for the South Sea Islands. On June 15, 1847, he set sail from Boston and arrived in Honolulu in October. Among his adventures was a trip to Tahiti in 1848.

Along with many, the excitement of gold found in California lured him to San Francisco in 1849. By August, he was made prefect for the district of San Francisco and also assumed the position of district attorney for the city. He made it his business to pursue the "Hounds," one of the gangs terrorizing parts of the community. Bancroft judged him "an able lawyer, but with a somewhat fiery temperament that soon brought about conflict."[17]

Hawes's first great clash occurred with John Geary, postmaster and sort of the political leader of San Francisco. Geary recognized the need for money to construct public buildings, such as a jail, city hall, wharves, a hospital, and other facilities. He proposed selling underwater bay land lots to raise revenues. As an early indication of things to come, apparently city council members took this opportunity to sell the lots to themselves for reasons of speculation. Hawes recognized the situation for what it was and complained to Governor Peter Burnett. Burnett did freeze further sales, but Hawes had upset enough people that Burnett suspended Hawes's appointment as prefect. In reprisal, Hawes attempted to have Burnett impeached, but did not succeed. Hawes certainly had a chip on his shoulder when he later ran for State Assembly as a reform candidate. He won in his first attempt. Among the first causes he pushed for was the consolidation of city and county governments to help clean up San Francisco.

On January 14, 1856, Horace Hawes introduced the Consolidation Bill to the Assembly. While debate ensued, on February 27, yet another petition was presented to the Assembly requesting a new county be created out of the southern portion of San Francisco County. The Assembly passed Hawes's Consolidation Bill on March 18 and passed it on to the Senate on April 1. Somehow, after the bill reached the Senate, the two matters, consolidation and a new county, were combined.

The deal maker in the Senate appears to have been Frank Tilford. An attorney by profession, he had left Kentucky for San Francisco in 1849. He almost immediately engaged himself in local politics. In 1850, he ran successfully for city recorder, with a princely salary of $10,000 a year. Under public protest, his paycheck was reduced. Otherwise, he was known for opposing the 1851 Vigilance Committee. He lost races for mayor and California Supreme Court justice. At the time that the Consolidation Bill reached the Senate, Tilford was chairman of the Judicial Committee and Special Committee on Consolidation.

The three other members of the committee, William Shaw, Wilson Flint, and William W. Hawks, were, like Tilford, from San Francisco. All were Democrats, except Hawks, who was a Whig. The reader may remember earlier in this chapter that Hawks tried to help the people of the peninsula the year before by supporting their efforts to form a new county. In committee, Hawks opposed the combining of the two issues at first, but wanting the bill to pass, eventually went along with the others. Apparently, the committee was under great pressure from San Francisco political interests against financial restrictions within the bill—restrictions that would make it difficult for the political elite in the city to continue its wasteful ways. The new county idea was added as a sort of offering to this powerful lobby.

According to Benjamin Lathrop, this compromise resulted in the reformers having to "make terms with the thieves, by adding a clause to [this] act cutting off about nine-tenths of the county of San Francisco, establishing what is now the county of San Mateo." There was no doubt in Lathrop's mind for whom this new county was being created. "The roughs . . . agreed to accept" this arrangement, "provided it could be arranged to organize a county government" before the locals even knew what was happening.

To appease the reformers, some San Francisco officials would henceforth be bonded, and the expenditures of five key city departments would have a fixed ceiling. To appease the *roughs*, as Lathrop called them, they were given a new county—one that they could control and run their rackets in until things loosened up in the city—which they thought was bound to happen.

For those most interested in San Mateo County History, the key portion of the Consolidation Act was Section 9. Subdivision 1 states: "There shall be formed out of the southern portion of the County of San Francisco a new county, to be called San Mateo." No explanation is given for why the name is San Mateo. On the peninsula, the Spanish padre, Pedro Font, first used the name of Saint Matthew for the creek running through today's downtown San Mateo when he passed through the area in March 1776—also without giving reason why the name.

Subdivision 2 set the new county's borders. As an indication of the political forces against reform, Chris Lilly's Abbey House was kept within the boundaries of the new county. The original petition suggested a county line further south. However, recognizing Abbey House as a convenient operating station for the political leaders preparing to take-over the peninsula, the new line was placed about a quarter mile north "from the house owned and occupied by C. E. Lilly."

Subdivision 3 allowed for the people to choose the location of their county seat. Two communities vied for that honor—Redwood City and Belmont. Redwood City made sense because it had the largest population of any bayside community. Belmont, however, was the home of former Governor John McDougal, and he intended to do everything he could to make that place the seat in order to enhance the value of his own land holdings.

Subdivision 4 set the election day for organizing the new county as the second Monday in May. Many later thought this strange, since the Consolidation Act was not to go into effect until July 1. Again, the forces trying to control San Mateo County wanted early elections to grab key offices before the locals knew what was happening.

Subdivision 5 allowed for the election to name three county supervisors, a county judge, a county attorney, a county clerk, a county recorder, a county sheriff, a county surveyor, a county assessor, a county treasurer, a county coroner, and a county public administrator.

Subdivision 6 appointed three solid citizens as a board of commissioners, "to act without compensation" to organize the election. John Johnston from the coast, Dr. Tripp from the lumbering districts, and Charles Clark from the north county were named.

Subdivisions 7, 8, 9, and 10 gave the commissioners the power to create 11 voting precincts, to appoint inspectors and judges, and to declare results. The commissioners were to have their first meeting at Edward Hancock's American Hotel in Redwood City. They were required to meet two weeks previous to the election to organize for it. After the voting, the ballots were to be counted in their presence two days after the election—also at the American Hotel.

Subdivision 11 stipulated that the day after the count had been made and results announced by the commission, the new county judge could begin his duties. His first responsibility was to make sure all those elected to office actually qualified for their posts. A ten-day period was given to execute this assignment. Subdivision 14 set the county judge's salary at $1,000 per year.

Subdivision 16 allowed the new county board of supervisors the ability to create a property tax for the purpose of building a jail and a courthouse. The tax could not exceed 50 cents on $100 of assessed property.

This version of the Consolidation Act was never supported by Horace Hawes. It seems clear that the local people of the peninsula knew little about it. In the Senate there existed little interest in it after it passed through the committee and awaited a vote. The editor of the *California Chronicle* wrote "[T]hus far the Senators manifest but little interest in the details of consolidation, and though the bill has been printed, I venture the assertion that not ten Senators have read it through." On April 11, 1856, the Senate passed the act. On April 19, Governor John Neely Johnson, recently elected as the Know-Nothing Party candidate—one of the most bigoted and least capable governors in the history of California—signed the act into law. Infant San Mateo County was free-falling into the hands of a political clique, looking to take control of it for selfish gain, with little, if any, concern for the local people.

The plan of this gang was to seize three of the voting stations and stuff the ballot boxes. They took down the names of passengers on the Panama steamer that had recently arrived at San Francisco, and used these names as voters in San Mateo County. The three voting stations were Chris Lilly's Abbey House, John McDougal's house in Belmont, and the remote Crystal Springs station.

On May 6, Charles Clark and John Johnston met in Redwood City to organize the May 12 election. Dr. R. O. Tripp did not appear, refusing to participate in what he already felt was a sordid affair. The two commissioners sanctioned 13 precincts (despite the state's instructions to allow for 11). The polling places included the Abbey House, McDougal's house at Belmont, and the Crystal Springs station.

What influences the San Francisco political clique had over the two is not known. Charles Clark, like Lilly, was a roadhouse owner—the 10 Mile House, about a mile south of the Abbey House on the Mission Road. Although he was an election commissioner, he was also running for San Mateo county supervisor in the geographical area once represented by James Casey, a member of the gang, and retiring San Francisco supervisor. That Clark won in this fixed election is remarkable. John Johnston also won a seat on the board of supervisors.

Johnston was of the important family on the coastside. His older brother, James, originally came to the San Mateo Coast and convinced his three brothers to join him. James was born in Scotland in 1813, and moved with his parents to Pennsylvania, where John was born in 1833. The boys' father died in about 1834, and the family moved to Gallipolis, Ohio. James engaged himself in a series of adventures. In 1835, he went off to fight the Seminole Indians. He then spent time exploring the Rocky Mountains. In 1846, he again volunteered for military service, this time to fight in the war with Mexico. Word of gold in California had him on his way here

James Johnston. Courtesy of Smithsonian Institute.

Petra de Jara Johnston.

in 1849. Along with his brother Thomas, he made his way to San Francisco via the Isthmus of Panama. Once in California, James managed to amass some wealth. He became part owner of the infamous El Dorado Saloon in San Francisco and had other real estate holdings as well. As a prominent man of the region, James came to know some of the old *Californios* and married Petra de Jara in

April 1852. Desiring to create a more traditional life at this point, he sent Thomas back to Ohio with the idea that he and the other brothers, William and John, would round up 800 head of dairy cattle and drive them to California, where the boys could start a dairy ranch, providing milk products to San Francisco. There were a lot of longhorn beef cattle in California in those days, but not much dairy cattle. This was an inspired idea.

Among the old families James came to know were the Miramontes. While they lived at the Presidio, they owned *Rancho de San Benito* on the coastside of the peninsula. In May of 1853, James was able to purchase 1,162 acres of the rancho in order to create the dairy ranch. At about the same time, Thomas, William, and John set out for California with the

Johnston House. This classic New England salt-box style home (two stories in the front and one in the back) has been restored after many decades of neglect. The home became part of an eastern-style dairy ranch, founded when James Johnston's brothers, Thomas, John, and William brought a herd of eastern dairy cows—in a cattle-drive—across the country to Spanish Town on the coast.

herd of dairy cattle. In what must have been a difficult adventure, they crossed the plains, climbed the mountains, and endured the deserts to arrive in California. The domesticated eastern cattle were certainly the first of their kind in the San Francisco area and, in this number, perhaps in the state. They managed to get the herd to the still-wild coastside, where local tradition has it that many of the calves born in the first season were eaten by grizzly bears.[18]

While James continued to live in San Francisco, his brothers set about creating the dairy ranch and building the famous salt-box style house that still stands today a little south of Half Moon Bay. The brothers fashioned the house to look like the family home back in Gallipolis. Among the hardships was obtaining timbers for the construction in this isolated location. Coastside legend has it that a crew of a passing ship threw the lumber overboard and watched the wood drift to shore, where the brothers picked up the materials. It is probable that John Johnston was engaged in building the house in 1856, while also acting as commissioner.

The shenanigans witnessed by Gaza Haraszthy, Columbus Huffaker, and W. D. Harrington at Crystal Springs were more or less duplicated at Belmont and the Abbey House. At Belmont, Charles Fair who was running for assessor, recalled that the polling was held "in a room in the corner of McDougal's house." One of the inspectors, Benjamin Fenwick, was also running for supervisor as one of the San Francisco clique. Unlike Crystal Springs, because of the set-up in McDougal's house, it was much more difficult for locals to witness the proceedings. At the Abbey House, the polling place for the Grange or Lilly's precinct, Charles Clark, who lived in the area for three years, later swore in court that no more than 50 eligible voters lived there. Yet, 500 ballots were tabulated.

The next day (Tuesday, May 13) at Lilly's, Redwood City hotel owner Edward Hancock testified that he was invited upstairs where he witnessed the counting of the votes. Two gang members, the "younger" Theller and the "older" Theller, seemed to be in charge. Billy Mulligan was present, but not his brother Bernard, who was running for sheriff against J. W. Ackerson. At one point, Hancock remembered the Thellers calling out ten Ackerson votes, but then a voice rose up saying that Ackerson had pulled out of the race, and those votes should go to Mulligan instead. What Hancock's purpose was in being at Lilly's is unclear. Hancock admitted he knew Lilly. He also admitted to supporting Lilly candidate Robert Gray for county clerk in exchange for Lilly supporting Redwood City for county seat. He later denied offering Lilly $1,000 to double-cross McDougal by throwing in enough votes to make Redwood City county seat.[19]

That evening Lilly visited McDougal down at Belmont. There would be no double-cross, at least not on the Belmont-for-county-seat deal. A witness to the meeting, W. T. Gough (who would win in this election for district attorney), heard McDougal say: "Well, Lilly, the longest pole will knock the persimmons."[20]

The next day, Wednesday, May 14, Redwood City became a busy place. At this time the votes were to be certified and results announced by the commission at

Billy Mulligan.

Hancock's American Hotel. John McDougal, Chris Lilly, Billy and Bernard Mulligan, the Thellers, and a "large force of roughs from San Francisco"[21] were frequently seen by locals throughout the day. On the other side, J. W. Ackerson, a local running for sheriff, and Benjamin Lathrop, who had been named secretary to the commission, were on hand as well.

As the ballots began to arrive, an incident occurred that set the tone for the rest of the day. A package of ballots was rumored to favor Ackerson for sheriff. Billy Mulligan grabbed it away and was about to tear it to shreds when it was revealed that the ballots within were actually more favorable to his brother. Billy quickly returned the package.

After finally receiving the ballots, Johnston and Clark, who constituted the entire commission because Dr. Tripp had refused to be part of this smelly election from the beginning, began their canvassing with the assistance of secretary Lathrop. They attempted to do their work behind closed doors, but outside rumor spread that Ackerson looked to be beating Bernard Mulligan. Billy and a contingent of his San Franciscans burst through the door, threatened to break up the election, and began tearing up papers in the room. Lathrop grabbed what he could save and backed into a corner. The commissioners then informed Billy that his brother had enough votes to win the election, and the rumor he had heard outside was a false one. Once again Billy was relieved and said to his men: "Come, boys, get out of here." However, as an indication that all these roughs were not necessarily of the same monolithic political machine, at that moment in came Chris Lilly and his gang, demanding to know what was going on. According to Lathrop's account, no guns could be seen during the episode, but every one of the "boys" seemed to be wearing "box coats with large outside pockets, and the click of many a pistol could be heard." Hotheaded Mulligan now had to calm down the dangerous Lilly before someone was hurt. He assured Lilly everything was all right, and they all left.[22]

Now Johnston and Clark had to decide what to do. They were convinced that this was a fraudulent election. However, doing something about it at this moment could end in somebody getting killed—and that somebody could be either or both of them. They decided to go forward with the canvassing of the votes and let the courts deal with the validity of the election at a future occasion.

The results of the election were predictable—but not altogether so. In perhaps the most watched race, Bernard Mulligan received 964 votes and beat J. W. Ackerson for sheriff. Chris Lilly's bartender, Robert Gray, received 712 votes and defeated Benjamin Lathrop for county clerk. Lathrop claimed to have gotten nearly all the legitimate votes in the most populated precincts, and the few hundred votes supporting him should have been enough. However, he was beaten heavily in the three precincts seized by the gang and lost. Gang member William Rodgers tallied 1,391 votes and won the election for county treasurer over the 30-year-old farmer from New York, Curtis Baird. Another member of the clique, Benjamin Fenwick, received 647 votes and defeated James Berry for one of the three supervisoral seats. The final gang member to win was Charles Fair, who beat S. B. Gordon for county assessor. In the tightest contest, Belmont edged out Redwood City for county seat status with 872 votes. Altogether, some 1,646 ballots were counted. Not until 16 years later, when the county had twice the population, did a ballot count approach this one in number. It seems the Lilly–Mulligan–McDougal alliance had held together.

However, theirs was not a total victory. Incredibly, Charles Clark received 1,187 votes and won for supervisor. This in the territory once commanded by James Casey. The expert ballot-box stuffer had not run, and indications point to his falling from favor with the Broderick team at this time may have prevented him from entering the race. As commissioner, had Clark made a deal with the gang? Fellow commissioner John Johnston received 1,313 votes and also won, to become the third of the three county supervisors. What were the ethics that allowed election commissioners to run for office? Was this the reason that Dr. Tripp had refused to have anything to do with the election? Did he suspect his fellow commissioners of dealing with the San Francisco clique? Maybe Clark and Johnston felt that by working with this group, they might at least exercise some control over the governance of the new county for the benefit of the local people? In races not contested by the gang, A. T. McClure won for coroner, W. T. Gough became district attorney, and—perhaps most importantly, as our story develops—Benjamin Fox, was elected county judge.

Despite some victory for the locals, the San Francisco political machine had positioned itself to run the new county as planned. They could plunder the treasury of San Mateo County, wait for the right time, and take back San Francisco when the reformers had expended their energies.

Chapter 2 Footnotes

1. Arthur Quinn, *The Rivals: William Gwin, David Broderick and the Birth of California*, University of Nebraska Press, Lincoln, 1994, p. 130.

2. Herbert Asbury, *The Barbary Coast: History of the San Francisco Underworld*, Alfred A. Knopt, Inc. 1933, pp. 80–81.

3. Frank M. Stanger, "Why San Mateo County?" *La Peninsula*, vol. VI, No. 6, October, 1952. p. 3.

4. Frank M. Stanger, *South From San Francisco: San Mateo County, California, Its History and Heritage*, San Mateo County Historical Association, 1963, p. 75.

5. *Moore & DePue's Illustrated History of San Mateo County, California*: G. T. Brown & Co., Lith., San Francisco, 1878, p. 5.

6. Alan Hynding, *From Frontier to Suburb: The Story of the San Mateo Peninsula*, Star Publishing Company, Belmont, 1982, p. 57.

7. John S. Hittell, *A History of the City of San Francisco*, A. L. Bancroft Co., San Francisco, 1878, p. 241.

8. *Moore & DePue*, p. 5.

9. *History of San Mateo County*: B. F. Alley Publishers, San Francisco, 1883, p. 157.

10. Terry Fischer, "The Tripps of Woodside," *La Peninsula*, vol. XXXII, No. 2, Fall/Winter 2000, p. 18.

11. Dorothy F. Regnery, "Parkhurst's Woodside," *La Peninsula*, vol. XXXIV, No. 1 June, 1987, p. 6.

12. *History*, Alley p. 317.

13. Ibid. p. 319.

14. John Boessenecker, *Against the Vigilantes: The Recollections of Dutch Charley Duane*, University of Oklahoma, Press: Norman, 1999, pp. 202–203.

15. Hubert Howe Bancroft, *History of California*, History Company, San Francisco, 1890, vol. VI, p. 645.

16. Mark Joseph Cimino, "The Consolidation Act and the Birth of San Mateo County," January 7, 1981, student manuscript collection, San Mateo County History Museum Archives, p. 3.

17. Bancroft, *History*, vol. VI p. 213.

18. C. Malcolm Watkins, *The White House of Half Moon Bay*, Johnston House Foundation, Half Moon Bay, 1972, p. 12.

19. *County court—San Mateo County Minutes*, Hon. Ben. F. Fox, County Judge, Belmont, June 10, 1856.

20. Ibid.

21. *History*, Alley, p. 320.

22. Ibid.

Chapter 3

A New Beginning

Poor James Casey—he had not been part of the election-fixing by his friends, down in the infant San Mateo County. Being left out was a wicked blow, but not the final blow. On the same day that the San Mateo County election results were announced, Casey was goaded into an argument with a San Francisco newspaper editor, making him so angry that he shot the man down in the streets of San Francisco. The shooting had significant ramifications that led to the creation of the most famous of all the vigilante committees in western history and, as a side story, a new beginning for San Mateo County.

The man Casey shot was James King of William, editor of the *San Francisco Bulletin*. Pompous, revengeful, combative—James King of William was born James King and later added

James King of William.

on the royal sounding "of William" to distinguish himself from other James Kings living, as he did, in the District of Columbia. His father was the William of the "of William."[1]

King of William started his Gold Rush California days a lucky man, and with his newfound wealth started a bank in San Francisco. In 1851, the city was being overrun by thugs who were terrorizing residents. The residents decided to fight back. As a recognized local businessman, King of William joined with the Vigilance Committee. The committee banded together and chased two criminal gangs out of the city. The men on the committee were regarded as heroes.

King of William had success after that event. At the young age of 30, his bank was worth $250,000 by 1853. Unfortunately, an economic downturn caught him by surprise in 1854 and destroyed his bank. He was forced to work for another bank, and he became increasingly outraged by the dishonesty and corruption all around him—which he blamed for his own downfall. He decided to start a newspaper to attack those he felt were most guilty—especially David Broderick and those associated with him. His dislike of anything Irish extended to the Catholic priests and nuns in the city, whom he referred to as "agents of a foreign power"[2] (an unkind reference to the pope). By 1855, with

Assassination of James King Of William. Illustration from Frank Leslie's Illustrated Newspaper, A News-Weekly.

the possible exception of the *Alta California,* the *Bulletin* had become the most popular newspaper in the city. Many San Franciscans had suffered during the 1854 depression and, like King of William, blamed the political elite for their troubles. No one seemed so fearless in attacking Broderick and his gang as King of William. In fact, when he learned that bets had been taken on how long it would take for someone to assassinate him, King of William seemed pleased that he was irritating those he wanted to irritate.

When Charles Cora, an Italian gambler and a friend of Broderick, killed United States Marshall William Richardson over a personal argument, King of William found a hot story. Cora had enlisted the able assistance of attorney Edward Baker, once a law partner of Abraham Lincoln, and claimed self-defense. When the jury pronounced itself hung, King of William condemned the proceedings and called for a resurgence of the Vigilance Committee. Then he discovered that the new sheriff, Broderick man David Scannell, had hired Billy Mulligan to be Cora's jailkeeper. The *Bulletin* roared, "Hang Billy Mulligan" if he let Cora escape, and it added that if it were to happen, then the sheriff should be hanged, too.[3]

Sharpshooters of the San Francisco Vigilantes of 1856. Reformers or even patriots according to some historical accounts, but working in secrecy with unrestrained powers of search and seizure, often with mob mentality and impunity of law and recourse.

Broderick man James Casey now entered the fray. Using his newspaper, the *Sunday Herald*, Casey tried to turn the tables on King of William by revealing information on King of William's brother Thomas, a.k.a. Slippery Sim, a.k.a. Dead House Cove, a.k.a. the Nipper Kid, who had been a professional thief on the East Coast. Early in May 1856, just before the San Mateo elections, Casey's paper declared that King of William had attempted and failed to produce a deal to have his brother replace the recently deceased Marshall Richardson—a deal with the very political elite that King of William was so intent on destroying. Thomas King and James King of William vehemently denied this story and demanded a retraction, but none was given.

King of William decided to answer back. During San Francisco court proceedings in November 1855, Casey had admitted serving an 18-month prison sentence back at Sing Sing Penitentiary in New York. It seems that Casey had shared an apartment with a girlfriend. After they broke up, he removed the furniture from the apartment and sold it. His girlfriend had him prosecuted for larceny, and he was convicted. In Casey's mind, many had something back home better left behind, and this seemed a terribly unfair exposé.

On the West Coast, it was an unwritten convention that a person's past was to be forgotten. However, Casey's political enemies continued to bring the episode up. At first, a majority of the San Francisco newspapers wrote about it. Then the *California Chronicle* went further by linking its story to Casey's 1854 election to the board of supervisors. It revealed that Casey did not live in the precinct from which he was elected. It also accused Casey of having won the election by stuffing ballot boxes.

A few days later, King of William's *Bulletin* printed the *Chronicle*'s editorial—and continued to reprint it at intervals of every few weeks for some months. On May 14, a fresh version of King of William's editorial referred to Casey's prison sentence, the 1854 fixed election, and added emphatically that Casey deserved to have "his neck stretched."

That edition of the *Bulletin* hit the streets of San Francisco at three in the afternoon. Within an hour after seeing the article, Casey went to the offices of the *Bulletin* and confronted King of William. He complained about having his past in New York brought out again. King of William said he would not refrain from printing articles just like it in the future, and told Casey to leave.

Poor James Casey—snubbed by not being allowed to participate in the fixed San Mateo County election, embarrassed by a scathing newspaper article and, now, thrown out of his

Fort Vigilance, nicknamed Fort Gunnybags, was a sandbagged San Francisco warehouse protected by cannon and sharpshooters. Used by the San Francisco Vigilantes as its armory and headquarters, the site was on Sacramento Street near Front, Davis, and California Streets.

enemy's office with his tail between his legs—and all on the same day! This was too much. Whatever good judgment Casey possessed left him. He knew the way that King of William would start home. Shortly after five o'clock, he spotted King of William. He challenged him to draw his weapon, as if in a duel, and then shot King of William in the left breast. King of William cried out and fled a short distance, until some people on the street assisted him to medical attention. With his wits returning, Casey turned himself in to Sheriff Scannell by six o'clock. They could hear the bell of the old 1851 Vigilance Committee beginning to ring. Scannell slipped Casey a revolver for self-protection and showed him to his jail cell.

That night a contingent of San Franciscan men gathered to talk about what to do. With grim determination, they discussed their situation. There is no question that San Francisco was a wide open city, far too lenient on criminal activities of all sorts. However, there was something about this killing of a newspaper editor that felt particularly wrong. It represented the silencing of a voice of reform. It seemed un-American. Many of them remembered what they had done in 1851, when they had felt pushed to the limit. They had organized a Vigilance Committee and chased two criminal gangs out of the city who had been terrorizing residents. Since that time, the efforts of that committee had become legendary. Lionized veterans of those days, like William Tell Coleman, now stepped forward to offer leadership again. The next day, on May 15, the Vigilance Committee of 1856 began to recruit and organize itself. It ended up being huge—some 8,000 strong. Far outnumbering its 1851 secretive forefathers, this group was more open about its membership and intentions. They, the "people," as they called themselves, were going to break the hold of the political clique and their criminal allies that had too much control over San Francisco.[4]

Who were the vigilantes of 1856? They came from all walks of life and represented almost every community in the city. However, the leadership tended to be from the Protestant, Anglo-Saxon mercantile segment of the city's population. The anti-Irish feeling in San Francisco had been growing since the establishment of the Know-Nothing Party there in 1854. The Know-Nothings were actually a national phenomenon. They espoused the nativist line that America needed to be for Americans, and that foreigners—especially those Irish and Catholic, like David Broderick, Billy Mulligan, and James Casey—represented a threat to the principles and health of this country.

Certainly hatred of Irish Catholics just for who they were influenced some. But the larger issue for the vigilantes focused on the need for cleaning up local government. The merchants of the city were still feeling the effects of the economic downturn in 1854, and they resented having their precious tax dollars

A large crowd witnessed the hanging of James Casey and Charles Cora; they can be seen hanging from the building. During the height of vigilante power 8000 armed men patrolled the city. People were imprisoned, lynched, or kidnapped and deported. A fair trial with jurors deciding on the facts of a case often was not possible because Committee of Vigilance members often dominated juries. Citizens feared the vengeance of these armed vigilantes.

wasted. Nineteenth-century historian Josiah Royce perceptively determined the activities of the 1856 committee to be "a Businessman's Revolution."[5]

By Friday night, May 16, young, inexperienced, Know-Nothing Governor Neely Johnson was in town to try to quiet the situation. He, on the one hand, told William Tell Coleman and the vigilantes that they could not have Casey. On the other hand, he allowed them to become the new guards at the jail. On Sunday, the vigilantes decided they no longer wanted to work with the public officials. They pulled back their guards, and William Tell Coleman, with 2,500 to 3,000 men, surrounded the jail and demanded that Sheriff Scannell turn over Casey. Scannell gave up both Casey and another Broderick friend, the Italian gambler Charles Cora, who was still waiting for his second trial for murder.

On Tuesday, May 20, James King of William died from his gunshot wound. Two days later, as many in San Francisco were witnessing the burial, the Vigilance Committee tried Casey and Cora and found them guilty. The punishments proceeded immediately. Casey said a few words as the dreadful preparations for his execution took place. Hangman Sydney Hopkins (sometimes known as Sterling Hopkins), a well-known enemy of the Broderick contingent, gloated and whispered unkind remarks to poor Casey. Casey tried to get at Hopkins. Meanwhile, Cora stood dignified. When the lynching finally occurred, Cora died, hardly moving, while Casey flailed about. Both were then buried at the Mission's cemetery.

For William Tecumseh Sherman, major general of the California Militia (and later Civil War general), the situation in San Francisco seemed hopeless: "The government is powerless and at an end."[6] Indeed, the Vigilance Committee did not disband after the hangings. Instead, it now planned how to take back the government of the city. Many of the committee members had been encouraged when in 1854 the Know-Nothing Party had established itself in San Francisco. However, in 1855 the Democrats made a significant comeback. This, now, was the opportunity to clean things up once and for all. Recognizing that the situation was out of control, Sheriff Scannell telegraphed Governor Johnson for help. On June 2, despite his political party affiliation, Johnson ordered Sherman to rally the militia and confront the vigilantes. Sherman felt his position untenable and resigned.

The committee's next move focused on the most notorious of the Broderick ballot-box stuffers. Billy Mulligan and about 16 others were rounded up. Know-Nothing California Supreme Court Justice David Terry issued a writ of habeas corpus demanding the release of Mulligan. After all, Mulligan was still a San Francisco deputy sheriff and the keeper of the county jail. Although he was a Know-Nothing, this was too much a flagrant disregard of the law for Terry. Of course the committee ignored the writ and established a formidable enemy in Judge Terry.

Among those held by the committee was an old friend of Mulligan and Chris Lilly, prizefighter James (Yankee) Sullivan, an Irish-born convict whose last political job had been to help James Casey by stuffing ballot boxes. Sullivan was an alcoholic and was going through withdrawal while in jail. While waiting for the decision from the committee about what his fate would be, Sullivan was so sure that he would be hanged that he slit his own wrists and killed himself rather than go through the spectacle of an execution. In the end, the committee did not execute Mulligan and the rest, but they did deport them. They were put aboard ship for

Benjamin I. Fox, first San Mateo County Judge. He won the position despite ballot box stuffing and maintained his position for four years.

the East Coast and were threatened that if they ever returned, the committee would not be so lenient.

Through June the Vigilance Committee continued to hold its grip on San Francisco. When word reached the vigilantes that the federal government was sending 113 muskets to help the militia organize to oppose them, they intercepted the shipment. On June 21, one of the militiamen, J. R. Maloney, was due to testify before the newly formed Law and Order group (formed to counter the activities of the committee) about the hijacking. Sidney Hopkins, James Casey's executioner, attempted to arrest Maloney to prevent the questioning from taking place. Someone fired a shot during the resulting scuffle. Judge Terry, who was on the scene acting as an escort for Maloney, took out his bowie knife and stabbed Hopkins. The California Supreme Court Justice fled to the militia armory with vigilantes in pursuit. Committee members busted through the door, disabled the militiamen, and took Terry a prisoner.

David Terry.

Thus began a strange seven-week saga, during which the Vigilance Committee held Judge Terry, a man well-known in a variety of circles. Terry was born in Kentucky in 1823 (making him only 33 at the time of his incarceration). As a teenager, he fought in the Texas War of Independence and later served as a lieutenant in the Mexican War. He came to California in 1849 and was elected to the State Supreme Court in 1855. When it was learned that one of its war veterans had been imprisoned in San Francisco, the Texas legislature officially approached the United States Congress about doing what was necessary to get his release. Back in California, Senator William Gwin tried to intercede on Terry's behalf. As southerner politicians, Gwin and Terry had much in common. Remarkably, Gwin's opposition to the committee placed him on the same side of his arch enemy, Broderick. However, both Gwin and Broderick recognized the futility of exercising too much energy against the popular vigilantes.

Broderick's great ambition remained to become a U.S. senator. He did not want a messy fight with the committee to jeopardize that goal. Thus, when his friends were being executed and exiled, he did not come to their aid. In fact, he was hardly seen in San Francisco during the entire time that the vigilantes were in control. However, in the case of Judge Terry, Broderick decided to act. Secretly, he gave Irishman John Nugent, editor of the *San Francisco Herald*, $200 a week to run editorials defending Terry and denouncing the committee as a "mercantile junta." The *Herald*,

John McDougall, California's second Governor, and a Belmont resident that was a key figure in formation of the county.

once one of the most popular papers in the city, was ruined because of its stand. Despite the fact that editor Nugent had supported the 1851 committee, his stand on the second committee resulted in lost revenue. The merchants stopped advertising in his newspaper. Nugent held on for a few years, but in 1862, the *Herald* went out of business.

Finally, on July 19, 1856, the committee ordered Broderick himself to appear before the tribunal. Here, at last, the vigilantes had before them the man seen as representing all of the things they most opposed. However, Broderick's power was such that the committee only questioned him and then let him go.

In the meantime, Broderick was quietly giving advice and funds to the new Law and Order Party. Its members included Mayor James Van Ness, Sheriff Scannell, and former Governor John McDougal of Belmont.

In early August, it appeared that Sidney Hopkins would survive the stabbing delivered to him by Terry. On August 8, Terry was released, and the next day the Vigilance Committee decided to disband, but only after scheduling a parade of 6,000 of its members for August 18.

The work of the committee would be preserved by the new People's Party, designed to oppose the Law and Order Party. Soon the People's Party achieved its greatest victory by reducing the size of the city's budget by five-sixths, from $2,646,190 in 1855, to $856,120 in 1856, to $353,292 in 1857.

Between May 15 and August 8, the San Francisco Vigilance Committee of 1856 had executed 4 individuals, driven 1 captive to suicide, and deported about 30 others it deemed undesirable. In addition, it became apparent that many who had been part of the Broderick political clique, with their ruffian cohorts, had left on their own volition. As nineteenth-century historian John Hittell wrote: "The professional criminals, as a class, fled in terror."

What all this meant for San Mateo County was a brand new start. Not only had the major players in the San Mateo plot been removed from the scene (i.e., Billy Mulligan, Chris Lilly, and James Casey), but the lesser characters had disappeared as well (i.e., the Thellers, Bernard Mulligan, and Liverpool Jack). Only Governor McDougal remained stubbornly at Belmont.

On May 25, 1856, the San Francisco newspaper the *Wide West* recognized the situation in San Mateo County. Speaking of the "San Mateo Outrage," it demanded punishment for those committing the fraud. The losing candidates in the San Mateo election needed little prodding. Almost immediately, led by Benjamin Lathrop, they began organizing themselves to bring suit on the winners in the court of Benjamin Fox.

Fox opened his first court on June 10 in Belmont, which was still temporarily the county seat. Exactly where in Belmont this crucial court case was heard is a mystery of sorts. All the modern San Mateo County histories credit the Belmont Inn belonging to Englishman Charles Aubery Angelo as the site of the proceedings. Angelo's roadhouse is given distinction of initiating the Belmont community at the junction between the Mission road and the road through the canyon and beyond to the coast. However, within the County Court Recording book's handwritten statement of the proceedings of the day, it is states that the trial took place "in the house of J. J. Ellets."[8] Ellets was a competing hotel owner and also an early postmaster of the area.

Regardless of exactly where, the case pitted the losing candidates of the May 12 election against the five members of the gang who had won, in other words: John W. Ackerson vs. Bernard Mulligan regarding sheriff; Benjamin Lathrop vs. Robert Gray regarding county clerk; Curtis Baird (actually the court record misspelled his name as Beard) vs. William Rodgers regarding county treasurer; James Berry vs. Benjamin Fenwick regarding county supervisor; and S. B. Gordon vs. Charles Fair regarding county assessor.

Lathrop hired the firm of Peyton, Lake, and Duer to represent the complainants. Lake and Duer appeared to present the case. A Mr. Richards spoke on behalf of the defendants. Witness after witness was called upon by the complainants, including 10 Mile House owner and county supervisor Charles Clark; Redwood City hotel owner Edward Hancock; Redwood City carpenter and loser of the May 12 election for assessor Charles Fair; loser of the May 12 election for sheriff John W. Ackerson; farmer from the Crystal Springs Valley W. D. Harrington; and, also of the Valley, Columbus Huffaker. No witnesses appeared for the defense. In fact, most of the defendants were, themselves, already in jail, expelled from California, or fleeing at their own choice. Only William Rodgers, the first county treasurer, showed up. The defense asked for an adjournment on the grounds that it had witnesses, but needed time to find them. Counsel for the complainants argued that the defense had plenty of time to gather its witnesses, and Judge Fox agreed.

After the cases had been presented, it did not take long for Judge Fox to make a decision. On that very day, June 10, he found: "Frauds had been committed at Crystal Springs, and Lilly's, and Belmont; and that the judgment of the court was that the returns from those three precincts were corrupt and void and that they be excluded from the returns of the county." The complainants that had brought this to the attention of the court and had come in second in the May 12 election were pronounced the new office holders. In addition the judge found: ". . . it further appearing that Redwood City has the highest number of legal notes for the County Seat, it is further adjudged that the said Redwood City be and is hereby declared to the County Seat of San Mateo County."[9]

Thus, San Mateo County had gained a new beginning. While up in San Francisco, the Vigilance Committee still held its power, the new county's grand jury credited "the prompt and decided action of the people of San Francisco" for saving San Mateo in its August 11 report.

The first meeting of the San Mateo County Board of Supervisors took place on July 7. James Berry and Charles Clark were present. John Johnston was absent. In their first act, they appointed James McCrea and David Marvin as justices of the peace to replace the old San Francisco county justices. The board then engaged itself in the biggest issue of the day for the county—road work. The San Francisco to Santa Clara road was in terrible shape and needed repair. The supervisors agreed, authorizing expenditures up to $50 to provide some attention to the matter. Also at the meeting, County Clerk Lathrop was instructed to buy an iron safe to keep the records of the new county at a price not to go over $350. Berry and Clark considered the need for a courtroom and necessary offices. They accepted the offer of John V. Diller to rent the necessary space on the second floor of his Redwood City warehouse for $40 a month. At this rather active meeting, they additionally selected the San Francisco newspaper, the *True Californian,* as the official organ of the county, since San Mateo County would not have its own newspaper (the *San Mateo County Gazette*) until April of 1859.

At the second meeting of the supervisors, Johnston was absent again. The board had to come to grips with the fact that David Marvin had not qualified to become justice of the peace. Martin W. Lamb was selected in his place. Berry and Clark also discussed financing for a courthouse and jail.

At the August 4 meeting, all the members were present. The supervisors deliberated over taxes. They decided that Assessor S. B. Gordon could also act as superintendent of schools. Treasurer Curtis Baird made his first report, telling the board that the county had collected $638 in receipts, but had $874 in liabilities. On October 13, the board focused on health issues in the county and appointed A. T. McClure as county physician. It seemed the county had begun tackling the important work it needed to do.

However, San Mateo County's episode of political intrigue was hardly over, for John McDougal still operated out of Belmont, and he remained as combative as ever. He brought suit in the twelfth district court against John Johnston, one of the winners of the May 12 election. The case ended up in the California Supreme Court, where in October, Justice Heydenfeldt explained the findings of the court. He held the entire election illegal. He reasoned that the Consolidation Act had allowed for the county to be organized in July. The May 12 election was premature, and thus was held null and void.

This put the young county in a predicament. Courts had made judgments. Assessments had been rendered. Taxes had been collected. Benjamin Lathrop, in particular, had been busy. As county clerk, he assumed responsibility to act as recorder, auditor, and clerk for the district court, the county court, probate court, court of sessions, and for the board of supervisors. Since the county had practically no money as yet, he, at his own expense, had outfitted his offices to begin work.

The reaction of the new local leadership was basically to ignore the findings of the Supreme Court and to continue their work. Early in 1857, the state legislature straightened out the mess by issuing a temporary law allowing the current elected officials to continue until a new election could take place. The governor signed the bill on March 6, 1857. Then on April 18, only one day shy of the one-year anniversary date of the Consolidation Act, Senator Timothy Guy Phelps created an "Act to reorganize and establish the county of San Mateo."

Phelps was from San Mateo County and proved to be one of its best elected representatives of that or any age. He originally hailed from New York and came to California in 1849. In 1853, he moved to the San Carlos area, where he established a 3,200-acre stock farm and dairy ranch. Mr. Phelp's entreprenuership is further discussed in Chapter 9.

The reorganizing election took place in May. All the incumbents were reelected with the exception of Assessor S.B. Gordon, who decided not to run again. He instead made a successful bid for state assemblyman.

Progress for the new county continued through the 1850s. On February 27, 1858, the board accepted the donation of a site for a proper courthouse building and jail from S.M. Mezes, agent of the Arguello family, who had owned a major portion of Redwood City at one time. On April 3, 1858, the board let a contract with H.P. Petit for $3,000 to allow construction to begin. The county offices were moved there by December.

The first person in San Mateo County to become a citizen through its courts was Irishman Hugh Kelly. He later also served as one of the early members of the board of supervisors, elected September 1, 1869.

Chapter 3 Footnotes

1. Walton Bean, *California An Interpretive History*, McGraw Hill Books Company, New York, 1968, p. 143.
2. Quinn, *Rivals*, p. 179.
3. Ibid. 183.
4. Bancroft, *History*, vol. VI, p. 754.
5. Bean, *California*, p. 148.
6. Quinn, *Rivals*, p. 191.
7. Hittell, *History*, p. 253.
8. County Court Recording, Book 1, page 1, June 10, 1856.
9. Ibid. p. 3.

Aftermath of San Mateo County's Birth: The Characters

*T*he drama of the passage of the Consolidation Act and the formation of San Mateo County in 1856 produced a variety of characters. Some stayed on to become leaders of the new county. Others drifted on to adventures in other places.

Gaza Haraszthy and the Haraszthy family was of the latter group. By Janury of 1857, Gaza's father, Agoston, had determined to transfer his wine-grape-growing center from the Crystal Springs Valley to Sonoma County. He felt the Valley's climate to be too damp because of the fog that frequently rolled in. He noted that General Mariano Vallejo had been growing grapes in the Sonoma area since the mid-1830s. In January of 1857, he bought up some 560 acres near the town of Sonoma. Son Attila had the job of moving the grapevine cuttings from Crystal Springs. The Zinfandels and other wine grapes were the originals that Agoston had imported from Hungary. In May 1857, Agoston went to live and work at the Sonoma property. He called his new place Buena Vista and quickly built the vineyard into California's first large-scale grape-growing operation. Haraszthy is therefore regarded among historians of the state's commercial wine industry as among its most important founders. Nineteenth-century historian H. H. Bancroft refers to him as the "father of viniculture in California."[1]

But trouble was already brewing. On April 23 of that year, he resigned his position at the San Francisco Mint because of allegations that he was embezzling gold dust. Agoston welcomed an investigation. It seems that gold dust in considerable quantities had been found in the regular dust accumulating on the rooftops around the mint. Agoston explained that the shortage of charcoal in San Francisco had forced him to use methods of melting gold that caused more gold dust to fly in small particles up the mint's flues than what was the allowable wastage limit under federal law. He mortgaged his metallurgical works and other properties, including his Crystal Springs lands, and indemnified them to the treasurer of the Mint, Jacob R. Snyder, as representative of the U.S. government, to cover any losses that could be assigned to him.

In November, a federal grand jury indicted Agoston for embezzlement, suspecting that he had exceeded his legal limit of wastage by $151,550. As the case dragged on for months, Agoston was tried in the newspapers as well as the courts. Some editorials accused him of negligence as an extravagant experimenter at the expense of the taxpayers. However, people around San Francisco, and especially his former employees, defended him and his integrity. Finally, on March 2, 1861, a jury found

Agoston innocent: "[T]here is no evidence in this case to prove the slightest fraud in the defendant."[2] On June 7, his properties were given back to him.

Shortly after the conclusion of his embezzlement trial in 1861, Agoston began selling off his Crystal Springs properties. That same year, he returned to Europe as an official representative from California, sent by the state legislature to investigate methods to improve wine making back home. His subsequent report was widely read and helped California's infant wine industry in a variety of ways. By this time, Gaza and Attila had followed in their father's footsteps by establishing vineyards of their own in Sonoma County.

However, an easy life was not in the cards for this active family. Agoston found upon his return from Europe that he was once again the target of local newspapers. As he attempted to be reimbursed for his trip to Europe in 1862, his political views from before the Civil War were revealed. He had supported William

Agoston Haraszthy.

Gwin and the southern contingent of the Democrat Party in California. This group had opposed the use of federal troops to invade the South—a most unpopular stand now that California was part of the Union and trying to preserve the United States in that desperate struggle. He came under more fire for his use of Chinese labor, a disliked employment strategy among the white working classes in the state.

Locally, the Haraszthy family mended a lot of fences in 1863 when brothers Attila and Arpad married two of General Vallejo's daughters. A competitive feud over grape growing in the Sonoma Valley between the two fathers ended. The next year, Agoston scored yet another important first for California's agricultural future by introducing raisins for mass marketing.

For the ever-restless Gaza, however, the call to war again consumed him. At the outbreak of the Civil War, Gaza went to U.S. Senator Milton Latham and asked for a commission. Agoston had been a substantial contributor to Latham's campaign and a logical choice for Gaza to look to for this appointment. However, after some months, it appeared Latham would do nothing to help Gaza. So Gaza sold his Sonoma vineyard and went east to New York. He wanted to obtain the rank of colonel, but finally settled for a commission as lieutenant. He joined up with the 18th Cavalry, New York Volunteers, and participated in stopping the draft riots in New York City. Before December 1863, he had obtained the rank of captain. Using his own money, he raised his own company and raided Confederate territory in the proximity of Richmond, Virginia. He also participated in several battles as part of the Army of the Potomac. He was then assigned to duty close to New Orleans. He was captured there and was made a prisoner for 11 months at Camp Ford, Texas. With three others, he attempted an escape as the war was winding down. Pursued by bloodhounds, the trio was recaptured and accused of stealing a horse. The three were nearly lynched when news reached Texas that the war was over. In July of 1865, Gaza was made a major and served out his Army days at San Antonio until he received his honorable discharge.

Gaza was shocked to learn that while being held prisoner, the newspapers back in San Francisco had accused him of switching allegiance and siding with the secessionists. Agoston had to make an elaborate defense of his son.

After the War, the Haraszthys suffered a series of business reversals. However the resilient family now looked for opportunity and adventure in other places. By late 1867, Agoston, his wife, Gaza, and some other adventurers were off to Nicaragua. Near Corinto, Agoston was able to obtain a 100,000-acre plantation with a license for a limited monopoly from the government for the distillation of spirits for the purpose of exportation. He built a substantial distillery, cleared land for sugarcane cultivation, and constructed a sawmill for cutting hardwoods.

Sadly, Agoston's wife died of the yellow fever in July 1868. The irrepressible Agoston returned to San Francisco six months later, not to give up, but instead, to purchase machinery for his plantation. Agoston was able to convince his father, the old general, to come along on the adventure. The general did not stay long in Nicaragua. On the return trip to San Francisco, he died at sea in July 1869. Also that month, on July 6, 1869, Agoston disappeared while walking on his plantation. It is suspected that he was eaten by alligators while crossing a swamp. Eldest son Gaza sent a letter to San Francisco, dated July 22, telling of his father's demise. It was published in the newspapers beginning August 27.

In California, sons Attila, Arpad, and Bela continued in the winemaking business. Gaza, witness to the San Mateo County fraudulent election of 1856, decided to stay down in Central America. He died at Corinto after a brief bout with diphtheria on December 17, 1878. He was only 45 years old. One of the San Francisco newspapers wrote of his passing: "His frank, open, manly and easy ways won him friends wherever he went, while his decision and unflinching bravery from his early childhood marked him every inch a soldier."[3]

Although he appears in hardly any of the local histories, perhaps the most important character in the Consolidation Act—creation of San Mateo County—story is David Broderick. His unrelenting ambition to become a United States senator provided the impetus to move along the entire drama. Finally on January 9, 1857, he was elected to the post. The commission for this son of Irish immigrants was ironically signed by Know-Nothing Governor Neely Johnson. Via the Isthmus of Panama, within five weeks, Broderick was back on the East Coast. He met with a variety of friends, including Billy Mulligan. Broderick boasted of suing William Tell Coleman the next time he showed up for business in New York for having organized the vigilantes the year before.

Unfortunately for Broderick, his reign as senator did not last long. In 1859, former Know-Nothing and now Democratic Justice David Terry was preparing for being renominated to the California Supreme Court. He appeared at the state's Democratic convention that year and made a speech in which he firmly announced his support for the William Gwin, southern contingency of the party. He denounced the free section of the party as belonging "heart and soul, body and breeches to David Broderick."[4] He added that the antislavery members had more in common with black abolitionist Frederick Douglass than popular Democratic presidential hopeful Stephen Douglas.

On June 26, Broderick read a newspaper report of the speech while at breakfast at the International Hotel in San Francisco. Those who witnessed it saw the senator go wild. Ladies were present as

A unique duel—a California Chief Justice killed a U.S. Senator! It took place on September 13, 1859 just southwest of Lake Merced, in San Mateo County. Chief Justice David Terry and David Broderick were at odds over slavery and other issues—insults were exchanged which culminated in the duel.

he blasted Terry, saying at one point: "I paid and supported three newspapers to defend him during the Vigilance Committee days. . . ."[5] Broderick called Terry a "damned miserable wretch" who was as corrupt as the other members of the court.

It had been long expected that Broderick would end up in a duel with one of these southern Democrats, but everyone suspected that the duel would be fought with William Gwin. However, it turned out to be with the hotheaded David Terry instead. Terry waited for an apology until the end of his reelection campaign. When he failed to win renomination, with just a few weeks left to his term, he resigned so he could settle up with Broderick. On September 8, Terry wrote a letter to Broderick asking for an apology for his remarks. The note was delivered that same day. Broderick's friends favored a fight. The old Broderick nemesis, the *San Francisco Bulletin*, asked him to apologize and avoid bloodshed. That seemed to have the opposite effect on the senator. A day later, Terry sent his formal challenge to Broderick. Colonel John C. Hayes, former San Francisco sheriff and San Mateo County landholder, was named as Terry's second. Hayes at that time held the position of San Francisco county clerk, mostly due to Broderick's influence. However, Hayes, like Terry, had been a Texas Ranger, and that went deeper.

On the morning of September 12, the sheriff broke up an attempted duel between the two. The next day the seconds made another try at organizing this matter of honor. They crossed the county line into San Mateo County at the Davis Ranch, now a part of Daly City. With a crowd of 80 looking on, Broderick and Terry walked their ten paces away from each other and turned. Their weapons were single-shot pistols. Nervous Broderick pulled his trigger too soon, and his shot missed. Terry did better. His shot hit Broderick in the chest. The senator died three days later in what is recognized as California's most celebrated duel.

The San Mateo Hotel, at Third Avenue and B Street circa 1865.

When Terry realized that he had seriously wounded Broderick, he left in a hurry for Sacramento, and then to his farm near Stockton. A long, strange series of attempts to bring Terry to trial transpired. In November the San Mateo County grand jury indicted Terry for the killing of Broderick. The San Mateo County district attorney then issued a bench warrant to the sheriff of San Joaquin County for Terry. The courts there continued the action to March of 1860. A change in venue was arranged to Marin County. On the day of the trial, witnesses from San Francisco found themselves aboard sailing vessels on the Bay during an unusually windless day. They never made it to testify. The prosecutor moved to give up on the case, and, as a contemporary history put it, "the farce was ended."[6]

Not long after the trial, Terry went overland back to Texas in order to fight on the side of the Confederacy during the Civil War. He lived in Mexico for a while, but returned to California in 1869 to practice law. His most famous case took place in the 1880s and brought Terry back to San Mateo County. A woman named Sarah Althea Hill claimed that she was the legal wife of the senator from Nevada, William Sharon, under terms of a "contract marriage." Sharon was an immensely powerful man with holdings all over the West. Down on the San Francisco peninsula he owned the Spring Valley Water Company, which just so happened to be the sole water supplier for the city of San Francisco. He also possessed a rolling section of San Mateo County that would become a major portion of Hillsborough today. On a cottage on this property, Sharon had allegedly carried on an affair with Hill.

Hill needed a fearless protector in this fight, and found that warrior in David Terry. The case became a sensation, and with the entire nation looking on, Hill demanded part of Sharon's fortune in federal court. Sharon died in the midst of the battle in 1885, but his case was championed vigorously by his estate, most notably by Sharon's attorney and son-in-law, Francis Newlands, who among many other accomplishments, established the Burlingame Country Club on the hilly San Mateo County lands in 1893.[7]

As the episode dragged on, Terry fell in love and married his client. Their case broke apart when U.S. Supreme Court Justice Stephen Field found Hill's documentation largely fraudulent. Terry threatened Field, and the attorney general assigned a bodyguard, David Neagle, to protect the judge. When Field and Terry had a chance meeting at a restaurant near Stockton in 1890, Terry, as a 77-year-old man, struck Field and was then shot by Neagle. Neagle, who was defended by W. F. Herrin, was later acquitted of murder.

Of course the Consolidation Act had been proposed by Horace Hawes, who was not a resident down the peninsula at the time, and although he had no intention of creating a new county, the fact that San Mateo County came about as a result of the Consolidation Act has led historians to credit Hawes as the founder of the county. Because of his reform politics, his moving to

Horace Hawes.

San Mateo County, and his generous support of a variety of local causes, perhaps he is not a bad choice for the honor, although during his last days he was hardly seen as a hero to the local people.

One year after the Consolidation Act went into effect, Hawes purchased a 2,000-acre estate in San Mateo County. Today the land would include all the property in Redwood City, west of El Camino, between Whipple Avenue and Woodside Road, to the base of the hills. He bought this beautiful parcel for $20,000 as part of a foreclosure. On the site of the present Sequoia High School, he built his home.

In 1858, he married his second wife, Caroline Coombs of Kentucky. She had a boy servant, James Coombs, perhaps a slave at first. James would eventually become a well-known man in Redwood City, recognized as the Hawes's family coachman. Eventually, Horace and Caroline would have two children whom they named after themselves, Horace and Caroline. During this period of his life, nineteenth-century historian H. H. Bancroft tells us that Hawes became "a shrewd businessman" who "accumulated a large estate."[8] By 1859, San Mateo County's assessor listed him as the ninth most propertied person in the county.

From this time onward, Hawes was recognized for his charitable giving. He made major donations to the Protestant causes in San Francisco, including an entire city block bounded by Van Ness, Geary, Franklin, and Post that at another time was occupied by the Jack Tar Hotel.

As the Civil War commenced, Hawes stood loyally with the Union cause. He spoke out frequently against those sympathetic to the Confederacy. We can only wonder what this meant to his wife. His interest in national events sparked a renewed interest in politics. In 1863, he ran as the Union Party's candidate for State Senate and won, serving until 1867. As a concerned citizen, when the San Francisco–San Jose Railroad was under construction in the Redwood City area between 1863 and 1864, he gave up rights to his property so the building could continue, but only after securing the provision that all passenger trains had to stop in Redwood City. This stipulation stayed in effect until the 1890s.

In 1864, he contributed property to the people of Redwood City to create a new schoolhouse. Also that year, he gave a city lot to start a library for Redwood City. He made similar donations up in the San Mateo area. In 1866, Hawes donated property to the Catholic Church. He was eventually recognized by Pope Pius X, who gave him a medal for his generosity. In 1867, he provided land and financing to create a private school, the Laurel Institute, but it burned to the ground only days after its completion.

Thus began a series of reversals for Hawes that may have affected his sanity. In 1867, he attempted to run for reelection to the State Senate. Unfortunately, he failed to get the support of the Union-Republican Party. He ran as an independent and lost.

According to an 1883 history of San Mateo County: "From that time his health failed more and more rapidly, and his mind was proportionally weakened, so as to render him unfit for legal business for the last two or three years of his life."[9] This 1883 history published by the B. F. Alley company in San Francisco (without revealing the author or authors) was extremely unflattering to Hawes. It continued that by nature, he was "a very suspicious and eccentric man and when weakened by disease this eccentricity took the form of insanity, for without any foundation, he suspected his best friends of bad motives, and his wife even of laying plans to destroy his life by poison or assassination."

Nevertheless, his generosity toward his community continued. In 1869, he made a $2,500 gift to the Redwood City public school to build a gymnasium.

He then took a trip to Europe on his own. One can surmise that relations with Mrs. Hawes were not the best. When he returned in July of 1870, it was obvious to many that he was in failing health.

He scored some terrible local press, first in November of 1870 for being sued for $50 by a local merchant for unpaid purchases made by his wife while he was in Europe. According to the *San Mateo County Gazette,* he defended himself by saying "that he made ample provisions for the support of his wife during his absence and therefore she could not contract debts which will bind him." Other similar stories followed this one, pitting Hawes against local merchants who made sales on credit to Caroline Hawes.

On March 3, 1871, Hawes created a great sensation when he drew up a deed of trust, donating most of his Redwood City property to an entity he invented, called Mont Eagle University. He dreamed of Mont Eagle becoming a public university similar to the struggling University of California across the bay. He stipulated that the university would have a ruling body made up of five trustees. His gift would have to be matched by $6,100,000 to avoid financial problems affecting schools like the University of California. For this requirement, Hawes was heavily ridiculed, and many were convinced that he was losing his grasp on reality. Some entrepreneurs of today might call his strategy *leveraging.* H. H. Bancroft proclaimed Hawes "the first man of wealth in California to offer to give any considerable portion of it to a public institution. . . ."

He also mentioned in this trust document that his wife would receive $25,000, his son $3,600 and his daughter $3,000 a year after she turned 20 years old.

Ten days after announcing the deed of trust, at age 58, Hawes died in San Francisco. His funeral took place at the First Unitarian Church there.

Locals obviously felt sympathy for Caroline Hawes and her children. Instead of eulogizing a great man, the *Gazette* wrote:

We have no disposition to speak harshly of the dead—neither can we conscientiously praise where no praise is due. . . . He had little faith in his fellow man and many had as little in him. Redwood City is largely indebted to him for the excellent School-House and Gymnasium which our town feels proud of, and whatever may have been his personal objectives in making this donation to our school is immaterial. The Deed of Trust for Mont Eagle University . . . has been treated with derision by the press generally, and stigmatized as one of his last jokes. The whole thing will probably amount to nothing except to give his heirs some trouble in getting it annulled by the courts.

Indeed, that was exactly where the issue ended up. On November 16, 1871, Caroline brought suit upon the trustees of Mont Eagle University for assets amounting to $1,000,000. After nine days, the *Gazette* proclaimed: "The insanity is established beyond a doubt. If the truth has been half told, the widow suffered enough during the lifetime of her husband to entitle her to every dollar of his property. Hawes imagined he was the third greatest man that ever lived, the two that preceded him being Jesus Christ and Bishop Alemany." The newspaper again referred to Hawes' belief that he had been constantly surrounded by "liars and thieves."

On December 9, 1871, the testimony portion of the trial concluded. The jury then deliberated for an hour and a half. They found for Mrs. Hawes—that Horace was not of sound mind when he had created the trust. The local press applauded the verdict.

Carolyn lived for another 24 years, dying in 1895. She outlived her son. Her daughter married James A. Robinson, who became an accomplished California historian.

In 1928, while compiling his history of San Mateo County, Roy Cloud, an educator by profession, termed Horace Hawes the "Father of San Mateo County,"[10] due to his Consolidation Act. Hawes was certainly a "progressive" politician before the concept could be defined, and no matter what his many detractors in his later life might have said about him, he was a philanthropist of his local community and geographical areas beyond, long before the concept of philanthropy was in vogue among the wealthy people of America.

On the other end of this spectrum of characters is the redoubtable Billy Mulligan. Within one year after returning to New York in 1856, he was in trouble again. He shot the owner of a Manhattan gambling operation and was caught and sentenced to two years at Sing Sing Penitentiary. He was pardoned in three months, and some time between that time and 1864 returned to San Francisco. The Vigilance Committee, having disbanded, never threatened him.

For years Mulligan resumed his former activities in the city. He roamed the saloons and gaming houses, picking fights and frequently getting into trouble with the law. He became a terrible drunk, with binges ending in attacks of delirium tremens. He could become extremely dangerous at such times, with nothing to assuage him but a dose of valerian. During one of these episodes, he evaded some of his companions and barricaded himself in a room at the old St. Francis Hotel on Grant Avenue. From his window he began shooting at people passing by on the street below. He killed an innocent pedestrian. A friend tried to convince him to stop his rampage. Billy killed him for his efforts. Finally, a policeman gained access to a room across the street and shot Billy through the heart, ending the incident and the life of one of the most famous gangsters of the nineteenth century.

Mulligan's old prizefighting friend from New York, Chris Lilly, also met a violent ending. He had been seized by the vigilantes on July 8, 1856, and was then deported to Central America on August 15. He became a well-known gambler in Nicaragua, where he also established himself as a trader. His

Nicaragua days lasted only until February of 1857, however, when he was executed for aiding William Walker and his filibuster adventure.

Another of Mulligan's chief allies in the attempt to control infant San Mateo County was Governor John McDougal. After his Belmont days, the governor went back to politicking with his old friends, the southern Democrats led by William Gwin. He never quit drinking, and when the southerners fell from political grace with the onset of the Civil War, so did McDougal, for the most part. His adventurous brother, with whom he had come to California and who was known everywhere from Bent's Fort on the Arkansas River to parts of South America, committed suicide. McDougal himself attempted to take his own life several times. He finally died on March 30, 1866, in San Francisco.

Famous vigilante Sydney Hopkins, who whispered taunts to James Casey just before he was hanged and who was later stabbed by Judge Terry, stayed well known among the Broderick boys. One said of him that his greatest distinction was that "he had once been pimping simultaneously for both his wife and mother."[11] He was eventually killed at the Battle of the Wilderness during the Civil War.

Emeline Tripp.

John Johnston, one of San Mateo County's original supervisors, considered by local historians as one of the righteous politicians despite the fact that he won in the fixed election, stayed on the county's coastside. Along with his brothers he is known as one of the original dairyman in California. He and his wife, who he married in 1851, eventually had seven children. He died on January 31, 1893, at the age of 66.

The legendary figure Dr. R. O. Tripp, who was slated by the Sacramento politicians as a commissioner in the fixed election but refused to participate, continued to make history with his partner M. A. Parkhurst. On July 4, 1856, San Mateo County celebrated its first Independence Day at their Woodside Store. A flagpole was erected and a parade was organized.

Later that year, Tripp married his 32-year-old housekeeper, Emeline Skelton. Emeline, born in Lexington, Massachusetts, came to California in 1853. In February 1854, she answered a San Francisco newspaper ad for a housekeeper placed by Tripp and Parkhurst. The wedding took place on November 21, 1856.

Parkhurst became a charter member of the Woodside Library Association in 1858, the first of its kind in San Mateo County history. Tripp became the county's first public administrator in 1859. Later he continued his political career by assuming the position of postmaster in the Woodside area during Republican federal administrations.

The September 11, 1863, *Gazette* reported that Parkhurst died on September 8, "after a long illness." He was only 34 years old. Now the operation of the store became much more Tripp's responsibility.

Despite the fact that Tripp was a founding member of the Woodside Dell Temperance Society, large amounts of alcoholic beverages were sold to members of the logging and farming communities in the neighborhood. In fact, it is part of the Tripp legend that all customers to the store were offered a drink of "Continental Whiskey" on the house. Only refills needed to be paid for. Another of the legends about Dr. Tripp was his policy of "cash to the penny."[12] In other words, he did not make change. Any currency or coin over the price of an item became the store's. He continued to practice dentistry at the store, which principally consisted of teeth pulling. A liberal dose of whiskey is said to have been given to patients in order to mitigate the pain.

Robert and Emeline lived in a house across the road from the store. In 1860, Emeline gave birth to a daughter, Addie. Another child, a boy, was also born to the couple, but he died in childhood.

Emeline died in April of 1886. Dr. Tripp himself lived on until the age of 93 and operated the store until his death in 1909; by that time, he was known widely as one of the oldest pioneers of the county. Addie closed

Benjamin Lathrop.

the store after her father's death and died herself at the age of 66 in 1926. She never married nor had children.

Despite his support of the southern elements of the Democratic Party, Benjamin Lathrop continued to enjoy a successful career as a politician in San Mateo County. He was reelected as county clerk in 1859 and in 1861. Apparently, he continued his feud against his enemies from the 1856 episode. His obituary in the *Times Gazette* of March 13, 1897, states that he one day met Governor McDougal by chance up in San Francisco. McDougal accused Lathrop of trumping up charges against him and besmirching his reputation during those days. Lathrop challenged McDougal to a duel, and the former governor accepted. Seconds arranged the fight to take place on a Redwood City lot that later became the site of the P. P. Chamberlain store. However, Sheriff Ackerson arrested both men before any shooting could take place and would only release them after they promised not to resume the dueling.

Before he retired as county clerk in 1864, staunch Republican and one-time ally during the Consolidation Act days, Horace Hawes, demanded an investigation over the methods by which Lathrop ran the affairs of the county. Hawes stated publicly that "he believed Christ and some of his apostles were honest, but since their day, he did not believe an honest man had lived." However, nothing wrong was found in the way Lathrop conducted his business. Hawes then relented and made a statement commending Lathrop. Later, Hawes even made Lathrop a trustee of Mont Eagle, his failed attempt to create a university at Redwood City.

Lathrop was an early director of the San Francisco–San Jose Railroad Company, which was completed in 1864. He continued his political career by being elected to the board of supervisors. After that term, he sold property he owned in the Menlo Park area and visited Europe. He came back to California and went into the hydraulic mining industry in Shasta County. He eventually sold these holdings to San Mateo millionaire Alvinza Hayward. In 1876, he purchased a farm in Sonoma. In 1882, he moved again and took up residence in San Francisco. He died there on March 10, 1897, while in the midst of a $300,000 lawsuit against Hayward.[14]

Curtis Baird, who had lost in the fixed election to William Rodgers for Treasurer, and then was given the office by Judge Benjamin Fox, ran as a Republican for State Assembly in 1860. To demonstrate that the Republicans had not yet captured the hearts of peninsulans, on the eve of the Civil War, he lost to Stephen Douglas Democrat, James Denniston, 568 to 474. Baird was finally elected to the Assembly in 1871.[15]

Andrew Teague, who had represented the southern part of San Francisco as a supervisor before the Consolidation Act, continued to be a solid citizen as the new County came into being. Like M. A. Parkhurst, he was one of the founders of the Woodside Library Association. In fact, the library was originally housed at his place. He stayed in the lumber business for about seven years and then moved to Redwood City to practice law (for which he had been educated). After Parkhurst died, the Parkhurst family went to him for representation when they felt unfairly treated by Dr. Tripp. Teague was elected San Mateo County district attorney in 1869.

As for John Ellet's hotel in Belmont, the original base of operations for San Mateo County—where Judge Fox straightened out the fixed election and got the county off to a fresh start—County historian Al Hynding tells us: Ellet's "hotel passed thru several hands, gradually declining into a shabby speakeasy and bar before being torn down in 1949."[16]

Chapter 4 Footnotes

1. Bancroft, *History*, vol. VII, P. 44.
2. Fredericksen, "Authentic," p. 5.
3. Bancroft Library, "Haraszhy Family" manuscript.
4. Quinn, *Rivals*, p. 255.
5. Ibid. 256.
6. Franklin Tuthill, *History of California*, San Francisco, H. H. Bancroft & Company 1866, p. 568.
7. Mitchell P. Postel, *History of Burlingame Country Club*, Burlingame Country Club, San Mateo County Historical Association, 1982, p. 7.
8. Bancroft, *History*, vol. VI, p. 699.
9. *History*, Alley, pp. 267–269.
10. Roy Cloud, *History of San Mateo County*, S. J. Clarke Publishing Co., Chicago, 1928, vol. I, pp. 387–388.
11. Quinn, *Rivals*, p. 191.
12. Regnery, "Parkhurst's," p. 10.
13. *History*, Alley, p. 321.
14. *San Mateo County Times Gazette*, Saturday, March 13, 1897.
15. Rudolph M.Lapp, "San Mateo County Politics, 1860–1875," *La Peninsula*, San Mateo County Historical Association, vol. XXX, No. 1, Summer/Fall, 1996, p. 11.
16. Hynding, *From Frontier*, p. 124.

Chapter 5

Aftermath of San Mateo County's Birth: The Politics

*T*raditionally California historians' view of the events surrounding the Consolidation Act and the rise of the Vigilance Committee of 1856 focuses on the short-term gains for the city of San Francisco. Historian John S. Hittell, in his 1878 classic, *A History of the City of San Francisco*, celebrates the new efficiencies brought to the municipal government beginning in 1857, and credits the new leaders as much as the Consolidation Act itself. H. H. Bancroft, in his monumental *History of California*, published in seven volumes between 1886 and 1890, goes farther in speaking of the ten-year reign of the People's Party and its good works, boasting: "Crime never again reached dangerous proportions in the City."[1] In their view, by driving out the corrupt politicians and their criminal allies, the good citizens of San Francisco had saved their city and allowed it to prosper.

More recent California historians, such as the much-respected Walton Bean in his *California: An Interpretive History* (1968), have questioned the motives and the results of the Vigilance Committee. Likewise, modern historians focusing on San Mateo County history have examined the Consolidation Act, and all its ramifications, and have asked if the whole thing wasn't some great mistake. Frank Stanger, who studied and wrote about San Mateo County history continuously through the 1930s, 1940s, 1950s, 1960s and 1970s, questioned the wisdom of creating San Mateo County out of San Francisco. He tells about the quirky series of almost comical events that led to the political birth of San Mateo County and queries: "Why San Mateo County" at all? He points out that San Francisco County was already the smallest county in the state before the Act. Why carve it up?[2]

County historian Al Hynding, who followed Stanger in the 1980s, challenged whether the issue of independence from the city was necessary. He maintains, "[T]here is no clear evidence that the majority of inhabitants had even wanted separation from San Francisco."[3] He feels that the creation of this, the last of the nine Bay Area counties, was engineered by "San Francisco politicians and hoodlums at great future cost to the city."

He asserts that the greatest long-term effect of the Consolidation Act was to cut San Francisco off from growth. It would now have to look south, across the county line, to find a source of water and other natural resources necessary for the city to grow. It would have to dicker with San Mateo County on finding sites for an airport and a jail. As San Franciscans ran out of space, they had to come down the peninsula to Colma to create a place to bury their dead. Taxable lands in the future wealthy suburban communities were lost to the city. San Francisco, as Hittell's and Bancroft's nineteenth-century

city, might not worry about such things, but into the twentieth century, San Francisco found itself at a disadvantage, especially when comparing itself with its growing rival to the south—Los Angeles. Obviously, San Francisco could not expand to the west, north, or east because of the ocean and the bay. It could look at contiguous land in only one direction—south into San Mateo County. The great city of southern California had no problem in comparison to San Francisco when it came time to annexing territory, seemingly in all directions, in order to grow. While San Francisco was rebuilding itself after the Great Earthquake and Fire of 1906, Los Angeles overtook it as the greatest city in the West and has never looked back.

What did the Consolidation Act mean directly for peninsula people? Because of the presence of its great neighbor to the north, most economic activity and growth stayed there. Throughout the nineteenth century, San Mateo County was the slowest growing county in the Bay Area. By 1900, only 12,094 people lived here. That is about the population of Half Moon Bay and El Granada today (2006). A variety of historical consequences manifested themselves because of this slow growth, some of which were completely negative.

Hynding's comprehensive book, *From Frontier to Suburb* (1982), is replete with the struggles of thinly settled, rural San Mateo County adjacent to the sophisticated, wide-open metropolis to the north. Crime and corruption went unchecked down "in the country," as San Franciscans spoke of the peninsula, inspiring mobster Sam Termini, in the 1930s, to label San Mateo County the most corrupt in California.

Since the earliest days, if you couldn't get away with it in San Francisco (and that was saying a lot), then you could simply cross the county line, where law enforcement was weak, when available, and not present most of the time. As an example, because dueling was outlawed in the California state constitution of 1849, when San Franciscans could not settle their differences in any other way than by shooting it out, they came across the county line to so. The Broderick and Terry duel mentioned in the last chapter is an example of such illegal activity. Throughout the nineteenth century, San Mateo road houses continued to operate in the tradition of Chris Lilly's Abbey House.

At the turn of the century, with prizefighting made illegal in the city, promoters such as Sunshine Jim Coffroth moved just across the county line to organize bouts. Fights featuring Jack Johnson, the first great African American heavyweight champion, took place in what we would call Daly City today.[4] The outdoor spectacles were attended by the hundreds, and it was noted that at times there was more fighting in the stands than in the ring itself.

During the era of Prohibition (1919–1932), county law enforcement officials had a terrible time keeping up with racketeers. The San Mateo County coast became a haven for rumrunners. They would come down in their sleek, fast ships and boats from Canada, evading slower Coast Guard vessels, and land their hooch at secret rendezvous points from Mussel Rock to Ano Nuevo. Many boys from the poorer farm families on the San Mateo County coastside got their first real paying jobs loading or driving trucks for bootleggers from the city, who came down to greet their rumrunning suppliers.

Moonshiners, those that bottled their own concoctions of booze, wine or beer, were in every community down the peninsula—but especially in the north. Speakeasies, illegal clubs serving alcoholic beverages, were equally as abundant. On the coastside, at various times, nearly every prominent building served as a speakeasy—even the historic Francisco Sanchez Adobe in today's Pacifica.

After Prohibition was repealed (1933), gambling became the game of a grimy partnership of mobsters, local politicians, business personalities, and law enforcement officials. Horse-racing and dog-racing tracks, banned in San Francisco, were numerous in San Mateo County. Bookies, those in the business of brokering illicit wagering on the races, made small fortunes. The county sheriff and local police seemed powerless to control illegal gaming dens throughout the county. Daly City's John Marchbank, the brains behind the Tanforan Race track in

Daly City's John Marchbank lampooned in this editorial cartoon in the Times-Tribune.

the 1930s, was probably the strongest political boss behind the gambling interests in the county. Law enforcement officials such as County Sheriff Jim McGrath and South San Francisco Police Chief Louis Belloni turned a deaf ear to complaints about the activities of some of their best friends and supporters. In 1932, an entire city was established in the county for no other purpose than to operate a dog track and, not so secretly, gambling houses. Bayshore City, now comprising the eastern section of Daly City out by the Cow Palace, lasted two years as a legally incorporated city, complete with its own city council and chief of police.

Although law-enforcement issues were perhaps the most recognized problem of adolescent San Mateo County, its legitimate leaders saw many other problems related to economic growth and proper governance that inspired thinking about the possible reuniting of San Francisco and San Mateo County. At the same time, leaders in the city saw that to compete with Los Angeles and other emerging cities in the West, better partnerships needed to be formed with communities within the Bay Region—and especially San Mateo County.

The first major attempt to annex San Mateo County to San Francisco occurred in 1912. Six years after the Great Earthquake and Fire, San Franciscans were looking forward to their great Pacific International Exposition of 1915. With the completion of the Panama Canal, the West Coast of the United States was in position for a great new period of commerce and industry. San Francisco would need space to expand and regain its place as the queen city of the coast. City leaders felt that this was the time to show the world that San Francisco had emerged from its disaster a far better place, with great potential, including room for physical growth.

The 1912 effort called for the creation of a Greater San Francisco, which would include the entire Bay Area. The city's leaders modeled their plan after that of New York, which had established a self-governing borough system including Manhattan, Staten Island, Brooklyn, Queens, and the Bronx. San Francisco, Marin County, and San Mateo County residents voiced strong interest in the scheme. However, the East Bay cities were against it, and the Greater San Francisco plan died.

Undaunted, San Francisco tried the same plan in 1914. Peninsula opinion makers again demonstrated positive reaction to the idea. The *San Mateo Times* of November 14 editorialized that it favored the proposal that the people get the chance to vote on the possibility of annexation. East Bay opposition rose up again, and this effort failed, too.

Encouraged by San Mateo County's seemingly open-mindedness over the issue, San Francisco leaders surfaced a new concept in 1916. This time they would focus on San Mateo County only. The popular mayor of San Francisco, James "Sunny Jim" Rolph, met with leaders of San Mateo County's seven incorporated cities (Redwood City, San Mateo, Burlingame, Hillsborough, South San Francisco, San Bruno, and Daly City) and again received open-minded response. A committee of 20 individuals was created to further investigate the matter under the leadership of Reverend W. A. Brewer, mayor of Hillsborough and rector of St. Paul's Episcopal Church in Burlingame.

However, opposition developed. San Mateo County government officials viewed annexation as a direct threat to their powers—which, of course, it was. Annexation would put them out of business. City leaders in Redwood City began to calculate what loss of the county seat might mean for their community. Perhaps the biggest name to rise up against it was Arthur Redington. The Redington family had been a fixture in the mid-San Mateo County area for decades. After Burlingame incorporated in 1908, it was Arthur Redington who organized the elite families west of El Camino (and members of the Burlingame Country Club) to create Hillsborough in 1910, in order not to be gobbled up by the more middle-class Burlingame. Now as legal counsel for Hillsborough, Redington threw all his influence against annexation, believing it to be harmful to the suburban living that seemed so important to his friends.

Soon the town councils of Hillsborough and Burlingame went on record rejecting annexation. They proclaimed it a San Francisco maneuver to require San Mateo County residents to pay for bonds financing San Francisco projects. The local press possibly felt threatened by the prospect that their newspapers would lose some relevancy. With the exception of the *San Mateo County Gazette,* the county's press came out against the initiative. They continuously discussed Brooklyn and asked if some of the negative things that happened there could occur here.

Witnessing the gathering storm of opposition, San Mateo attorney Hamilton Bauer organized the Annexation League to defend the idea. Nevertheless, when in late 1916 a second meeting took place between Mayor Rolph and city leaders of San Mateo County, the spirit of cooperation had disappeared. Now the leaders from the peninsula stood against annexation.

On January 6, 1917, a group of 30 influential citizens met in Burlingame, where they formed the League to Preserve San Mateo County in order to fight off the Annexation League and the efforts of the City of San Francisco. They elected Judge Edward F. Fitzpatrick of Redwood City as their president. Among the strategies they chose was a concerted effort to bring their protests about annexation to the political leadership in Sacramento. The onset of World War I precluded discussion on the matter. It did resurface with more intensity in the 1920s.

Interestingly, in 1923, business leaders of the peninsula initiated the discussion. The Three Cities Chamber of Commerce (Burlingame, San Mateo and Hillsborough) asked for a meeting with the San Francisco Chamber of Commerce. They proposed a more modest annexation plan to include the peninsula only as far down as Belmont on the bayside and Half Moon Bay on the coast. They felt that this portion of the county was poised for significant industrial growth and only lacked enough capital in order to make things happen. They envisioned a port facility at San Mateo, a railroad to Half

Moon Bay (the coastside had a railroad, but it stopped its service in 1920) and extended streetcar service to Belmont (the streetcar service from San Francisco stopped at San Mateo in those days).

Once again the voice of conservatism arose, with Arthur Redington in the lead. He reorganized the old Preservation League. In November, a four-man debate was organized to inform the citizens of the county about the issue. Daniel C. Imboden, the director of the Three Cities Chamber of Commerce, and Colonel Charles N. Kirkbride championed the cause of annexation.

In Kirkbride, the annexation team had quite a spokesman. He had founded the *San Mateo Leader* in 1889, which eventually became the *San Mateo Times*. When San Mateo incorporated in 1894, he became city attorney, and he retained that position up to and beyond the staging of this debate, except for a leave of absence when he joined the Army during World War I. In 1902, he was a committed leader in the formation of a high school at San Mateo, and 20 years later, he was one of the principal organizers of the San Mateo Junior College (today's College of San Mateo).[5] Later, he was also a founder of the San Mateo County Historical Association (in 1935).[6]

Opposing Imboden and Kirkbride were the formidable Arthur Redington and the popular Horace Amphlett. Amphlett also enjoyed a large community following. He was a local boy, graduating from San Mateo High in 1907. He was assistant postmaster for a while and then worked for a neighborhood bank. In 1917, he joined the ranks of the *San Mateo Times*, and by 1920 was its publisher.[7]

Kirkbride proved a memorable warrior in the clash. He accused those blocking annexation with the prime motivation of protecting their tax dollars, and doing so at the expense of moving forward for the cities of the peninsula. He directly charged the opposition as standing in the way of progress. He told the audience that San Francisco's status as the leading seaport on the West Coast was at stake. He pointed to the cooperation established between Los Angeles and Long Beach as an example for securing San Francisco's and San Mateo County's economic futures.

Despite Kirkbride's stirring remarks, the annexation effort of 1923 went the way of those in 1912, 1914, and 1916. In the end, the Three City Chamber of Commerce itself, an experiment in regional cooperation, failed. With interest in its visions on the wane, it was shortly replaced by separate chambers in San Mateo and Burlingame.

In 1927, the most serious attempt to combine San Mateo County and San Francisco began. The San Francisco Chamber of Commerce commissioned the San Francisco Bureau of Government to create a comprehensive survey of the two local governments plus the economies, populations, transportation networks, law enforcement agencies, schools, water supplies, and public utilities of the two counties, with the purpose of determining the benefits and the liabilities of consolidating them. More of the piece focused on the particulars of San Mateo County and its needs for the future. The 200 page fact-filled book cost $20,000 to publish. It came out in 1928.

The *San Francisco—San Mateo Survey* stated the obvious: that with a population of 680,000, San Francisco could not grow any more geographically unless it could expand into San Mateo County. By contrast, San Mateo County, which had added 90,000 acres to its coastside (at the expense of Santa Cruz County) in 1868, possessed a land mass of 447 square miles with a population of only 65,000. In order to expand economically, the study asserted that the two counties would need to work together on adequate highways for the emerging automobile. Better port and industrial facilities needed to be built down the peninsula. The water supply of the region had to be guaranteed far into the future. Addressing these challenges in the years to come would require "some measure of governmental cooperation and joint government action."[8] The report offered that San Francisco with "ten times the assessable values of property and spending power" would be willing to assist "in financing the needs and projects deemed of common benefit to the two areas."

The *Survey* paid particular attention to the bureaucratic situation in San Mateo County. It had 71 governmental units including its central county government, 5 townships and road districts, 5 fire districts, 5 sanitary districts, 2 mosquito abatement districts, 35 school districts, 6 high school districts, 1 junior college district, 10 incorporated cities (Redwood City, San Mateo, South San Francisco, Burlingame, Hillsborough, Daly City, San Bruno, Atherton, Lawndale—later Colma—and San Carlos) and 1 public utility district. Local autonomy was possibly excessive in this system, which allowed for each township in the County to elect its own supervisor, justice of the peace and constables.

The *Survey* judged this to be expensive and inefficient. It asserted that "governmental functions" were "divided among the county, districts and cities, without uniformity and in numerous cases, overlapping." It found this "form of organization . . . too complex and decentralized for proper government operation." Among the services being duplicated in the various jurisdictions were tax assessment, tax collection, law enforcement, the courts, welfare, records storage and caring, food inspection, coroner activities, management, public health, probation (adult and juvenile) and auditing. The *Survey* was particularly hard on the disjointed purchasing practices carried out throughout San Mateo County. Each of the ten cities were taken to task for their excesses and wastefulness. In conclusion, the *Survey* showed that in San Mateo County, government costs for all purposes, including county, cities, districts, etc., came to $66.08 per capita. For San Franciscans, the cost per person was $52.21.

Despite the greater expense, the *Survey* said the actual services in San Mateo County were lacking. Law enforcement, a problem area for the county since its beginning, was heavily cited: "The sheriff and two deputies are practically the only officers with general police powers in the entire county outside the cities, and they must divide their time into 24-hour service." The total police presence in the cities was 57 officers, which seemed inadequate as well, but it was the "large sections of the county, particularly on the coast side" that seemed "without police protection of any kind, except for the limited service constables and state traffic officers," and "as these officers are employed for daytime service only, there is no night service whatever, except when the sheriff's office or constables are called in emergencies."[9]

The *Survey* also alluded to major problems to be addressed in the future, and how a regional approach would be necessary—the "disposal of untreated sewage into the San Francisco Bay," for example. It alleged that "eight cities and five sanitary districts in San Mateo County" were responsible for "a growing health menace," and "the coordination of adequate sewage treatment plants are problems requiring cooperative planning and financing."

Another issue of the future was being solved by San Francisco, and San Mateo County might benefit magnificently. The city was in the process of purchasing the Spring Valley Water Company and its watershed properties in San Mateo County. Since the 1850s, this company had been San Francisco's private supplier of fresh water. Soon the reservoirs on the peninsula would be linked up with the great water supplies being dammed up by the city at Hetch Hetchy in Yosemite Valley. This huge effort, underway since 1913, would soon be completed, giving San Francisco and its neighbors enough water to last beyond the next century. The city had financed the entire project. Now close to its end, if the people of San Mateo County helped with some of the "water debt burden" the investment for their future would far outweigh any immediate sacrifice.

Speaking of the future and future generations, the *Survey* took a hard look at the peninsula's schools. It found that some 130 school trustees had independent jurisdiction in some 42 separate districts. The *Survey* asserted: "School administration by small district is costly."[10] By contrast, San Francisco maintained a single district for its elementary, junior high, and senior high schools. The *Survey* took note of the new San Mateo Junior College District. The city still did not have a junior college. In fact, many students from San Francisco came down the peninsula to attend the San Mateo school, which was located in downtown San Mateo. Mention was made that after annexation, San Francisco should help pay for this college.

The *Survey* recognized the concerns of the citizens of San Mateo County over annexation to San Francisco. Local communities might lose their identities. Voters might lose control of their local affairs. San Francisco government might dominate the former San Mateo County government. Taxes might increase in the future to support large San Francisco projects. Finally, San Mateans might object to a certain style in which San Franciscans did their governmental business.

Indeed, the *Survey* agreed that San Francisco needed to improve "its type of government."[11] However the real answer to most of what bothered San Mateo County citizens could be dealt with by creating a borough-type government—once again like the City of New York. By using this model, the *Survey* felt that the combined efficiencies of the larger government would still allow for a proper degree of local citizens' participation.

The *Survey* reminded its readers that the San Francisco Bay Region's great competitor to the south, Los Angeles, "by a program of annexation on a large scale," had "brought about a tremendous development of its metropolitan area." To keep up, San Francisco and San Mateo counties needed to centralize and simplify their governments. Better governmental machinery would improve process that would "expedite the planning, financing and securing of projects necessary for the growth, upbuilding and orderly development of the area as a whole."[12] Therefore, the *Survey* recommended "that the two areas cooperate in a plan of consolidation as a city-county with adequate provisions for local representation of a central legislative body, a centralized administration of common governmental functions and the retention of local powers and control of local functions by local units, or boroughs."

The *Survey* also offered this advice for San Mateo County, if immediate consolidation were delayed. San Mateo County was still living with its original 1856 charter. The San Mateo County grand jury report of 1927 had suggested a new charter be adopted that would create a reformed county-manager type of system. Such a government would eradicate much of San Mateo County's wasteful practices. The *Survey* agreed with this needed upgrading and with the grand jury's suggestion that the new charter also create a single county road district and change some of the supervisoral district boundaries—both the road district system and the boundary fixing had been subject to certain questionable political practices.

Perhaps the *Survey* decided to mention this interim step because the immediate annexation of San Mateo County to San Francisco would require a complicated series of political actions. According to state law, first, each of the ten incorporated cities in San Mateo County would have to vote for it. Then the citizens of the unincorporated sections of the county would have to agree. Then the county as a whole would have to vote. Finally, San Francisco would have to have an election. A big problem would surface if any of the peninsula incorporated cities voted against the undertaking. They could not be forced to become part of the new county and could become independent or floating municipalities.

Nevertheless, when the *Survey* first appeared in 1928, the mood was positive. A meeting was organized at Burlingame High School, where W. H. Manry, the director of the *Survey*, spoke to the citizens of San Mateo County. Also on hand was M. M. O'Shaughnessy, San Francisco's legendary engineer responsible for the city's huge Hetch Hetchy water project. O'Shaughnessy spoke about the importance of two highways that San Mateo County residents had interest in seeing built— the Bayshore and Junipero Serra. The meeting did not end before a "Committee of Ten" was appointed with equal representation from the two counties—five from each—with the charge of continuing the dialogue with the hope for action in the future. One of the five on the San Mateo side was the well-known Colonel Charles N. Kirkbride, who, of course, had supported previous attempts at consolidation.

From the perspective of San Francisco School Superintendent Dr. Joseph M. Gwinn, there existed no problem with combining the San Francisco and San Mateo County school systems. However, San Mateo County's Superintendent of Schools, Miss Pansy Jewett Abbott, had a different opinion. In her estimation, the San Francisco system was hardly perfect, and she feared loss of local controls. In Abbott, the consolidation camp had a tough opponent. She was certainly the most revered educator in San Mateo County at that time.

Pansy Jewett Abbott, an experienced and accomplished educator, was appointed county superintendent of schools upon Roy Cloud's retirement in 1925. In 1926 she ran unopposed in the general election. Ms. Abbott continued to have voter support and remained in office for 25 years. She retired in 1951, and died at age 95 in 1976.

Born in Nebraska in 1881, a descendant of John Adams, her parents moved to San Jose when she was just a child. She began her teaching career at Homestead School in San Mateo in 1905, and supplemented her income by being a reporter for the *San Mateo Times* and sometimes the *Leader*. At Homestead she taught first through fifth grade and then moved on to Central School in San Mateo. In 1925, the San Mateo County Board of Supervisors unanimously appointed Abbott as superintendent of schools, a position she held for more than 25 years before retiring in 1951. She joined other conservative opinion makers in the county to force more study and debate on the matter of annexation.

Among those who kept the idea alive was the former mayor of San Francisco and, at that time, governor of California, "Sunny Jim" Rolph. Speaking in Palo Alto in March of 1931, he described the necessity of a "remarriage" of the two counties. He alluded to the "divorce" of 1854 (two years off historically speaking) and blamed the Spring Valley Water Company for the breakup (in a bit of historical interpretation that had never been heard before nor conjured up since).[13]

It was not until May of 1931 that the San Francisco–San Mateo Consolidation Committee finally announced a plan to the public. It called for a new San Francisco charter that would allow for a borough-type government with the ability to create a 16-member board of supervisors with 5 members coming from what was to be the old San Mateo County.[14]

In January of 1932, things seemed to be lined up to start the annexation process. In a first step, the San Francisco Board of Supervisors adopted a new charter, replacing the one that had been drawn up 31 years before that had allowed San Francisco to begin to plan for obtaining its own water supply.[15] D. A. "Doc" Raybould, the mastermind behind the build-up of Third Avenue in San Mateo and member of the consolidation committee, proclaimed the move a significant boost for those seeking the annexation.[16]

However, at the same time that the new San Francisco charter was being approved, a group of peninsula business leaders were pulling together to question the wisdom of proceeding. The *San Mateo Times* of January 7, 1932, described a meeting of such individuals who felt the plan still too formative, with many issues not addressed at all—in particularly the school question.

On January 9, the *San Mateo Times* came out against the annexation movement in an editorial titled "No Thank You Mr. San Francisco." The article seemed to ridicule the speech made by Governor Rolph the year before, comparing the uniting of the two counties to a wedding. The *Times* felt this would be a bad marriage. The tax advantages would all be San Francisco's, the editorial claimed. The increased bonding capacity for the city for its projects would be at the expense of former San Mateo County residents. Meanwhile, locals would lose their jurisdiction over such crucial matters as tax assessments, tax rates, and the courts. They would no longer have supervision of their police, firefighters and teachers. They would have a minority voice on the board of supervisors. The editorial liberally quoted a critical piece in the *Palo Alto Times*, which accused San Francisco of feting prominent San Mateo County personalities with its "consolidation propaganda." In conclusion, the *San Mateo Times* said that annexation would "leave this fair and independent county a helpless and disregarded suburb . . . forced to beg powerful politicians of the larger area for any improvements . . . ."

On January 14, the *Half Moon Bay Review* also came out against annexation. It editorialized: "We Can Manage Our Own Affairs." The *Review* brought up the fact that San Mateo County was at that moment finally serious about the creation of a new charter that would improve the way things were done here. With a possible charter election in the offing, shouldn't the focus of the voters be on that and not annexation? The *Review* accused San Francisco of being greedy in its quest "to gobble up San Mateo County," and asked why the city was now so much in a rush to push its "incomplete" plans.

Also on January 14, the *Menlo Park Searchlight* joined the fray, accusing the pro-consolidation camp of heavily exaggerating the support for annexation in Menlo Park. The consolidation group had listed the Menlo Park Chamber of Commerce as an early and important backer of the plan. However, the *Searchlight* asked: "Who and What is the Menlo Park Chamber of Commerce?" Answering its own question it responded: "[I]ts membership consists of but a handful of persons. It is not a charted body . . . . In fact, it is nothing but an insignificant portion of our citizenship . . ." with only ". . . half dozen or so compromising its membership." The *Searchlight*'s editor asserted: "[u]nless and until San Francisco's government develops into something cleaner, better, more business-like and more economical, than it has been during the last 12 years of which I have intimate personal knowledge, I am and shall continue to be unalterably opposed to consolidation." Apparently, something about the Hetch Hetchy project was one of "many disgraceful things" that he could "not stomach."

In fact, on the same day that the Half Moon Bay and Menlo Park newspapers came out against annexation, articles in the *San Francisco Examiner* and *San Francisco Daily News* reported that the Hetch Hetchy project would require anywhere from $9 million to $10 million more for completion. That kind of news is never welcomed, but the added pressure that the Great Depression (1929–1940) had placed on the economy and politics of the region was being felt by January of 1932. For those San

Mateo County people wanting consolidation, this Hetch Hetchy news was unwanted. It spoke to San Francisco's increasing indebtedness, which would become a burden for the newly annexed residents if the union was achieved. Such articles also implied inefficiencies in the way that San Francisco's government operated.

On January 15, the *South San Francisco Enterprise* editorialized against annexation. It picked up on the *Half Moon Bay Review*'s thinking about the charter movement. The newspaper began: "San Mateo county has been laboring along under an outgrown system of government for many years, and is now faced with the necessity of choosing between two remedies: annexation to San Francisco or a county charter form of government." The *Enterprise* lamented that it would be unfortunate if the two issues were forced on the voters at the same time. It reasoned: "The contest between the two may . . . split the ranks of the progressives. . . . Neither may be successful." Indeed, many within the old political cliques of the county were as much against the reforms in the projected charter as they were annexation. The *Enterprise* admitted that consolidation was "worthy of careful consideration," but it resented it "being rushed through to take precedence over the charter program." After all, most everyone would agree, "Local control of local affairs is a most desirable principle, and if we can devise a plan of government which will do this more effectively than in the past, there is no reason to relinquish our local control."

In the following days, the San Francisco newspapers played into the hands of the anti-consolidation forces. On January 18, the *San Francisco News* ran a story about problems with the San Francisco public school budget. On January 20, the *San Francisco Chronicle* described how the city was $213,000 short and would have to delay needed street work. The *San Francisco News* of January 20 reported how the Bureau of Governmental Research accused the San Francisco Board of Supervisors of violating the charter it had just passed by giving raises to some 800 workers without proper process. On January 21, the *San Francisco Chronicle* came out with an article about how city workers—some 153 of them—were receiving free telephone service to their homes or private offices as sort of perks. On January 28, the *San Francisco News* revealed that the Bureau of Governmental Research was readying itself to sue the San Francisco Board of Supervisors over the accumulation of a $1,200,000 debt. The new charter required a balanced budget, and the supervisors seemed incapable of delivering on that obligation. Of course, these stories were not lost on the peninsula press, which repeated them with the point of view that this was the government that might soon replace San Mateo County's.

On January 29, the *Redwood City Tribune* ran a story about how San Francisco Sheriff E. J. Fitzgerald had given some 2,000 deputy sheriffs badges to friends that vested them with "certain special privileges." The *Tribune* concluded that "political revelations of that sort are among the factors" causing "non-receptivity" to the San Francisco overtures.

During the end of January and beginning of February, public meetings took place throughout the county focusing on annexation. On January 22, the *San Mateo Times* reported that two Hillsborough attorneys had addressed 75 members of two organizations—the Burlingame Women's Club and the Peninsula League of Women Voters—in a debate at Burlingame. Edward Treadwell, the first mayor of Burlingame back in 1908, represented the pro-annexation side. Conservative Arthur Redington was, of course, against consolidation. On January 27, the *Times* ran a story describing how South San Francisco City Attorney J. W. Coleberd had addressed the San Carlos Community Club at City Hall. He branded the annexation movement as a "surrender of liberty." In early February, Coleberd faced off against Edward Treadwell at a meeting of residents in East Palo Alto. The debate took place at

Ravenswood School. At the end of the meeting, the East Palo Alto Chamber of Commerce announced that it would go on record against annexation.

In Half Moon Bay, on February 3, the Chamber of Commerce organized a meeting during which its leaders spoke of incorporating the entire coastside from Pescadero to Salada Beach (part of today's Pacifica). In this way the residents of the coast would be able to vote in the first election on the matter of annexation. If they remained unincorporated, they would have to wait for a second election, specially designed for the county's combined unincorporated areas. Included with those supportive of the Chamber at this meeting were some of the oldest family names of the coastside—Cunha, Hatch, and Dutra among them. County Supervisor Manuel Francis and publisher of the *Half Moon Bay Review*, George Dunn, also supported the Chamber.

That same night, at the Benjamin Franklin Hotel in San Mateo, the group trying to create a new charter for the county came out against plans to have the consolidation issue placed before the voters in April. According to the *San Mateo Times,* the charter study committee "declared war on the San Francisco plan of rushing this county into an annexation vote before it has a chance to decide on adoption of a county charter." Leaders of the charter group included Frank McVeigh, Heim Goldman, and Burlingame City Councilman Frederick Peterson, indicating a cross-section of county representation. They also included some names familiar to those against annexation, including Arthur Redington and Half Moon Bay Chamber of Commerce members N. L. Rizzo and Alvin Hatch.

Secretly, the annexation proposal was the best thing that ever happened to those in San Mateo County wanting political reform through a new charter. The bootlegger and gambler never had more power on the peninsula than in 1932, and local politicians and officials many times were their helpers. A charter reform movement could hardly have inched ahead if not for the specter of something conceivably bringing yet more change—annexation to San Francisco. The old power elite knew something had to happen on the reform side to prevent consolidation. Progressive peninsulans wanting a new charter owed much to the annexationists—even as they condemned them.

In fact, the first interest in adopting a new charter began with the electoral victory of the Progressive Party in California in 1911. The state legislature authorized the counties to create charters allowing for their better management on a businesslike basis, while allowing for greater autonomy from the state. Alas, by 1930, only 5 of the 58 counties in California had moved forward. In 1930, the state again asked the counties to review their charters. Some in the county felt that if something was not done, the state might move ahead and consolidate San Mateo and San Francisco counties on its own.

In San Mateo County there were plenty of abuses that a strong county-manager style government might better control. Well-known scandalous conditions involved the Road Department. Each year the state granted San Mateo County monies to improve its roads from a gas tax. In 1930, this amounted to about $200,000, which was divided among the county's board of supervisors to spend at their own discretion in their districts. This was too tempting for some of the board members, and they abused their authority. Supervisor Rosalie Brown hired two of her sons as foremen on work programs in her district. Colma dairyman Albert Witt, elected in 1932 with the aid of the Marchbank gambling organization, had a road built to his property, while other more worthy jobs went on hold.

In 1931, 28 citizens from all around the county came to form a charter study committee. Burlingame City Councilman Fred Peterson and *San Mateo Times* publisher Horace Amphlett led the group. They desired to create a new charter giving considerable powers to a manager in the like manner of a city manager. It is interesting to note that in the county, only Redwood City, San Mateo, and Hillsborough had city managers at the time. In Burlingame, Fred Peterson's town, voters had rejected having a manager by a margin of three to one, in 1926.

The charter study committee proposed that the board of supervisors would appoint the manager for a four-year contract. The appointee could not already be an elected official. The county assessor and county clerk would continue to be elected, but most other county government assignments would be made by the manager on the basis of merit and not political influence. The new charter would also mandate that the county supervisors be elected at large, instead of by district, hopefully enabling better leaders with countywide following to assume office. Also, the road districts would be consolidated, discontinuing the abusive practice of allowing the supervisors to decide how state funds would be employed for highway work.

Despite the fact that the annexationists were taking most of the heat from those wanting no change, powerful individuals lined up against the charter study committee as well. Among them were Supervisors Witt and Francis. They argued that a strong county executive would undercut the work of elected officials, who had actually been given

Horace Amphlett visits the dog track at Belmont. (Horace Amphlett is second from right.)

their powers by the people. However, as the weeks rolled by in 1932, it was becoming more and more apparent that the unpopularity of the annexation camp was benefiting the charter study committee.

Perhaps recognizing their own role in the downfall of the annexation movement, the San Francisco newspapers began a defense of sorts. On February 9, the *San Francisco Examiner* attempted to reason with the people to the south: "Intelligent and progressive San Mateo County people are well aware of this fact . . ." that the two counties must ". . . grow together." The *Examiner* explained that the recent bad press smeared on the city was actually a healthy thing: "There is much talk about the inefficiency of city government. But that is just the point—there IS much talk about it." In cities, the *Examiner* enlightened its country neighbors, government was discussed fairly thoroughly: "Every little misdeed of an official gets dragged out into the limelight." The *Examiner* offered: "The result is that in a city government the officials don't 'get away with' half that they often do in county government." Continuing with its amazing stream of consciousness, the *Examiner* gave an example to the simple people of the peninsula: "People who live in Jacksonville, Fla. doubtless think that life is unsafe in Chicago, because the papers are always full of Chicago crimes. Yet there are more murders to the thousand of population in Jacksonville than there are in Chicago!"

Experts from state offices also spoke in favor of annexation. The February 12 edition of the *South San Francisco Enterprise* announced that State Director of Finance Rolland A. Vandergrift supported the consolidation of San Francisco and San Mateo counties as a cost-savings move. In order to balance budgets, he recommended the overall reduction of counties in California from 58 to 45. Vandergrift lamented that California had the second highest tax burden in the nation. Reducing the number of counties could be part of the answer. However, when pressed, even Vandergrift admitted that San Mateo County's adoption of a county-manager system would help reduce expenses as well—at least locally.

Despite the sharp reasoning of San Francisco newspapers and endorsement from state officials, the San Mateo County press kept up its assault on annexation. The *Redwood City Tribune's* editorial headline of February 12 read: "Glory of Residing Under S.F. Flag Would Be Empty." It supported the coastside communities and the county charter study committee position that an April vote on annexation, one month before an election to appoint 15 freeholders whose responsibility it would be to create a new charter, was premature. The *Tribune* predicted: "[T]he people will select a board . . . to draft a document that will replace the horse-and-buggy day charter."

The February 17 edition of the *San Mateo Times* and the February 19 edition of the *South San Francisco Enterprise* reported a rather uneven confrontation between the pro- and anti-annexation leadership at Lomita Park (part of today's Millbrae). About 150 members of the Associated Volunteer Firemen of San Mateo County gathered to hear Colonel Kirkbride speak in favor of annexation. *Times* publisher Horace Amphlett surprised Kirkbride by showing up and making what the *Times* labeled "an editors' debate" out of the meeting. Amphlett scored heavily when he informed the volunteers that with annexation they would lose any preference for being hired as professional firefighters. Amphlett roared at them: "What would you volunteer firemen get . . . Nothing. You aren't even mentioned."

Meanwhile, the charter movement continued to gain momentum. On February 16, Stanford University Professor Edwin A. Cottrell spoke before some 200 people at a meeting of the San Mateo Park Improvement Club at Park School. Cottrell told the crowd that they needed to pass the new charter, with a county-manager type of system, to defeat "old fogyism" in the county. He also warned against annexation.[18] Cottrell's appearance was fashioned as heroic by the *San Mateo Times* since it had run a headline the day before the meeting saying that Cottrell had had a threatening telephone call telling him to be reserved in his comments, otherwise "watch out." Four days after his appearance, the *Redwood City Tribune* reported that the professor denied that a threat had been made. Instead, he said: "A man called me up to say, 'You are all wet and had better look up the facts.'"

On February 22, the *Redwood City Tribune* allowed Frank McVeigh, executive secretary of the San Mateo County Charter Study Committee, to write an editorial. In it he pleaded that the charter needed the attention of voters in the county over the annexation issue. At this point the charter supporters really had to go to work. The February 25 edition of the *San Mateo Times* spelled out a rather daunting set of tasks if the charter advocates were to succeed. In order for the election of 15 freeholders to occur on May 3, the study committee, now composed of 70 members, needed to nominate candidates between March 7 and March 29. Each had to be a voter in the county for five years and had to own property here as well. Each had to gather 1,200 endorsement signatures of legitimate county voters. Once the freeholders were elected, they would have to do fast work in order that the new charter get on the November ballot—the same ballot, nationally, that pitted Republican President Herbert Hoover against Democrat Franklin Roosevelt.

At the same time, the San Francisco newspapers continued to print the kind of stories that inspired the charter reformers to move ahead. On the same day that the *San Mateo Times* reported the complicated job in front of the study committee, the *San Francisco Chronicle* revealed that a $23,363 deficit in the City's Lighting Fund would require it to darken some streets in San Francisco. The next day the *Chronicle* printed a story telling how the Municipal Railway had run up a $494,170 deficit.

Again, the peninsula papers ate up this kind of news. The *South San Francisco Enterprise* of February 26 alleged that: "San Francisco people as a whole have paid entirely too little attention to their own affairs." The newspaper, in fact, saw a pattern: "Looking back through San Francisco's municipal history, we discover that this laxity is more of a fixed habit than a temporary lack of interest."

As the *San Francisco News* of March 1, reported that the city's wasteful practices had cost it $154,000 that should have been used to help build a new cancer institute, the *Burlingame Advance* reported (the next day, anyway) that the nominating committee of the new San Mateo County Charter General Committee was close to ready to submitting 15 candidates for the freeholders election. Nominating Committee Chairman Frank Barrows made his announcement from the Benjamin Franklin Hotel.

As April approached, the month that had been slated for the consolidation issue to come before the voters in the incorporated cities of the county, pressure was kept up by the forces against annexation, especially out on the coast. On March 3, the *Half Moon Bay Review* announced that there would be a "mass meeting" March 12, at the Half Moon Bay Theater, during which time the "Evils of Annexation Will be the Feature of the Meeting." The Half Moon Bay Chamber of Commerce, the Montara Chamber of Commerce, and the Coastside Civic Union sponsored the evening, which showcased speakers Horace Amphlett, Arthur Redington, and J. W. Coleberd. Redington and Coleberd railed on about annexation and reminded the audience that those living on the unincorporated coastside would not be able to vote in the first election on the subject.[19] Redington encouraged the coastsiders to incorporate on their own. Amphlett accused San Francisco of acting selfishly.[20] Hugh Pomeroy, of the San Mateo County Planning Commission was also on hand to discuss the workings of the potential new charter and how it would specifically help the coastside.

Almost symbolically, as the rhetoric was reaching its full strength among San Mateo County leaders dead-set against consolidation, San Francisco was finding itself in need of expanding itself into San Mateo County. Its waterworks, its cemeteries, its airport, and now the city needed a new county jail. On March 8, the *San Francisco Examiner* reported that the San Francisco Board of Supervisors had authorized the expenditure of $47,500 to buy a site west of San Bruno from the Jersey Farm Company for a county prison. Sheriff E. J. Fitzgerald recommended this Sneath Ranch location and a plan to create a work farm on the land so that the inmates could help pay for their keep by laboring in the fields. Some $850,000 in bonds would need to be passed in order that the jail and farm be established.

Not about to let up, the peninsula press kept up its onslaught. On March 11, the *San Mateo Times* reported that there would be a debate among college students over the annexation issue on March 15, at the San Mateo City Hall. James Byrne and James Hickey of San Mateo Junior College would take the anti-annexation side. R. A. Wood (resident of San Mateo) and Leonard B. Schmidt of Golden Gate Law School would take the pro position. The March 16 *Times* proclaimed the annexationists clear losers in the contest. Meanwhile, the news from San Francisco continued its controversial tone. On March 22, the *San Francisco News* announced that the city's board of supervisors had authorized yet another bond issue election—this one for $6.5 million—to support the increasingly criticized Hetch Hetchy project. The supervisors set the election date at May 3. At this point, it was more than obvious that the political leadership in San Francisco had much too much to contend with, and the annexation bid was lost.

Of course it did not help a bit that yet another battle was about to embroil the two counties. On April 1, the *South San Francisco Enterprise* printed an editorial, warning north San Mateo County residents that San Francisco had just passed new laws requiring the hog farms in its Butchertown district to move out. Some of the hog ranchers had already established themselves in San Mateo County, and many more would come if something were not done. The smell and filth of hog farms left much to be desired, as described by the *Enterprise*.

Unfortunately, that April (the month during which the first annexation election in the peninsula cities should have taken place, but was now postponed), the news out of San Francisco kept getting worse. On the 27th, the *San Francisco Chronicle* revealed that the City was in need of $2.5 million for its rail lines. That same day the *San Francisco Examiner* described how the San Francisco superintendent of schools intended to balance a $200,000 deficit in his budget. He proposed laying off 91 teachers and closing four night schools. In May, it was trouble out at the San Francisco Municipal Airport that grabbed headlines. Airport Superintendent Roy N. Francis was called into the office of his boss, Edward G. Cahill. Francis fainted during the meeting, and afterward it was announced he had "resigned," his place being taken by World War I flying ace Bernard "Mike" Doolin.[21]

In June, the *Belmont Courier* weighed into the consolidation fight, kicking the proverbial dead horse. Its June 3 edition quoted San Carlos author and attorney Frank V. Kingston, who warned peninsula residents that they would lose their state senator in the process of annexation.

June was also the month that the hog fight reached its nadir. In a sympathetic article, the *San Francisco Call* of June 9 reported on San Mateo County residents voicing "vigorous objections" surrounding the "hog exodus" from the city. The *Call* agreed with the protesters that the new sites in San Mateo County were already unsanitary. Of course, the "raisers just naturally moved to San Mateo County as the closest place." The *Call* remarked over the frustrations of peninsulans: "First came the cemeteries. . . . Then the sanitariums, later the jail and now come the hogs." E. E. Bramble, publisher of the *South San Francisco Enterprise*, wrote a scathing editorial asking San Mateo County to not allow the intrusion of these ranches in the unincorporated portions of north county. "We will not shoulder this burden, this ignominy of becoming San Francisco's dumping ground," he wrote in the June 10 edition of his newspaper. Similarly, the *San Mateo Times* of June 16 blasted away at this latest insult delivered by San Francisco. Hog pens had already been built southeast of San Mateo. The *Times* supported the work of the San Mateo Chamber of Commerce to keep the "hog influx" out of San Mateo and its surrounding neighborhoods.

In August, as San Mateo County and peninsula city officials wrestled with the hog controversy, the *San Francisco Examiner* attempted to revive the annexation issue. In its August 26 edition, it editorialized that San Mateo County residents needed to see the potential tax savings involved with consolidation. It explained that the county represented "a vivid example of redundant government." Over the issue of losing local character and values, the *Examiner* ridiculed the notion: "Burlingame, San Mateo city and Hillsborough are so knitted that a postman can't tell where he is."

By the time of this editorial, the annexation issue was dead anyway. Local leaders, fiercely independent, had certainly done their part to stop the effort. However, it was the Great Depression that killed the consolidation effort begun in 1927. When the combining of the two counties had first been mentioned and the California economy was strong, people in San Mateo County could see a vigorous partner to the north, with great financial resources and an international reputation as great city. Sadly, the Depression exposed San Francisco's weaknesses. It had always struggled with corruption and waste. It was easier to hide such things in good times. In bad times, as cash became short for financing big projects such as the Hetch Hetchy water project, money became much more a problem. As the bad times got worse, just repairing streets, keeping them lit, and operating schools became challenges. The San Francisco newspapers, widely read among peninsulans, kept everyone aware of the city's shortcomings. The peninsula's leadership and press recognized that this proposed marriage would be with a less-than healthy suitor and rejected his advances.

However, the stepchild of the annexation attempt, the charter movement, had another ending. The various charter committees did their jobs well. When the freeholders revealed their plans for the new charter, every newspaper except one supported their work. Only the *San Mateo Times* rejected it, citing its opposition to the section of the new document requiring county supervisors be elected at large, instead of simply by district. The *Times* felt that this took too much power away from local people. In November, during the election in which Americans decided to accept the leadership of "New Deal" candidate Franklin Roosevelt, the people of San Mateo County adopted the new charter by an almost two-to-one landslide. It went into effect in January of 1933.

This would make a nice ending to the charter story, except the old guard, represented by the political establishment of the county and its secretively supportive gambling allies, still held great power. On the board of supervisors in 1933 was Marchbank ally Albert Witt of north county. Manuel Francis, who had been against the charter from the beginning, was still on the board. His family had long been a force in coastside politics. His father, Joseph, a Portuguese immigrant, had been elected as a supervisor in 1908. Manuel, elected in 1920, held the position as almost a family birthright. Representing the San Mateo area was Rosalie Brown, of road scandal fame, and the county's first women supervisor. She had been appointed to the post in 1920, succeeding her husband, who had just previously passed away. Representing the south county was "Honest John" Poole, an appointed representative from Redwood City, who also ran a freight business. The senior member of the board was Dr. Clarence Thompson of Pescadero. The physician had been elected in 1908, and was known for owning the old Swanton House and other properties on the south coast.

This group of supervisors was hardly supportive of the spirit of reform brought with the new charter. They correctly judged the strong county-manager segments of the document to be threats to their powers as elected officials. And so, when it came time to appoint a manager, they hired someone that would not be likely to change things too much. They chose Walter Kellogg, whose only political experience was a stint as school board trustee. Kellogg was fairly well known in the county. His father-in-law, John Britton, was vice president and general manager of the Pacific Gas and Electric Company. Kellogg, himself, was the district manager for Pacific Gas and Electric at Redwood City for the 13 years previous to this appointment.

Kellogg proved to be largely ineffectual as the first San Mateo county manager. Historian Alan Hynding tells us that in his first 18 months, he made only three appointments, and of these two had to be dismissed—one for drinking on the job and the other for mental illness.[22] After four years of futility, Kellogg and the supervisors found themselves the object of public scrutiny and the subject of ridicule among the Bay Region's press corps.

The November 1936 election served as a resounding defeat for the old guard. In contests that forced the candidates to run for supervisor on a countywide basis, instead of by district, Daly City Mayor Hugh Smith was able to defeat Albert Witt. Reform-minded James James won the race for the seat in mid-county. He had been fired the year before as county engineer for not cooperating with the political powers wanting to continue to do business as usual. On the coast, former allies during the annexation fight squared off. Alvin Hatch, representing change, beat long-time incumbent Manuel Francis. Two days after assuming office, the new board fired Kellogg. Two months after that, they hired Ernest Rolinson, a college-trained civil engineer who had served as city manager of Santa Barbara and had most recently been city manager of Redwood City since 1929. Rolinson proved a good choice for the position. In his first year (1937), he managed to cut the cost of the county's budget by $126,000.

Once more one might hope that the tale of San Mateo County's era of political intrigue would end. Unfortunately, all this reform came too quickly for some. After all, the county was still in the grip of gambling interests. However, reform-minded residents must have been surprised when in 1937, Fred Peterson rose up against them. Peterson had chaired the important charter study committee back in 1931, which made possible the adoption of the county-manager government. Now, however, Peterson felt that the pendulum had swung too far. He asserted that the county had fallen into the hands of civil service administrators with dictatorial powers. He denounced the board of supervisors for relinquishing too much of their authorities and advocated that the manager's position become elective rather than appointive.

Alvin Hatch.

Of course that ran completely contrary to the spirit of the charter movement, which sought to remove politics from the operation of the county government. Nevertheless, with backing from the entrenched gambling interests and the *San Mateo Times*, Peterson prevailed. In June of 1937, only 25 percent of the county's voters showed up to the polls. They agreed with Peterson that the people would choose the next manager. The popular Peterson then filed to run against Rolinson and beat him by 3,000 votes in an election that drew 65 percent of the electorate.

Fred Peterson.

This represented a significant setback for the reform minded. During the 1940s, Peterson won reelection twice. Finally in 1948, the county's voters decided to return the manager's position to appointive. The county's population was burgeoning, from 77,000 in 1930 to more than 200,000 in 1950. The new residents refused to have anything to do with the business-as-usual practices of the past. The gambling interests were forced out, and so was Fred Peterson. In 1950, he was replaced by Robert Stallings, a young administrator who initiated a tradition of highly competent managers, lasting through to today.

However, the same growing population of the county, also affecting the Bay Area and California as a whole, would now require cooperation harkening back to the thoughts of the consolidationists at the beginning of the century. The difference was that by the 1950s, regional government was no longer a wish for the future where certain governmental savings could be achieved and development projects launched. Instead, it had become a vital necessity for the economy and environment of San Mateo County and its neighbors.

The San Francisco Bay, itself, became the most significant early joint concern for Bay Area jurisdictions. By 1925, the nine Bay Area counties and their 50 cities had a combined population of 1.5 million people. Little, if any cooperation was present in matters of environmental awareness, such as sewage treatment. No better example can be found than in the sad story of San Mateo County's Pacific City.

On June 28, 1921, the Three Cities Chamber of Commerce endorsed the idea of creating a grand amusement park at Coyote Point. A group of investors formed the Pacific City Corporation and raised $100,000 to purchase 90 acres on the northwest side of the Point and 250 acres of submerged land. According to the *San Mateo Times* of September 10, they intended to create a park that would rival New York's Coney Island. By late spring 1922, $10,000 worth of lawns, shrubs, and trees had been planted. Streets were laid out, water hookups were installed, and a $60,000 dance pavilion was completed. Also present were a Ferris wheel and smaller rides, a railway, restaurants, concession stands, and game booths. The waterfront was being improved into a comfortable beach, complete with bathhouse, bandstand, a 30-foot pier, and a playground. On July 1, 1922, opening day, some 27,000 visited Pacific City, and another 51,000 came the next day. On July 4, the amusement park claimed 100,000 in attendance. By the time it closed for the winter in November, the operating company said that 1,000,000 people had experienced Pacific City.

When the park reopened on May 19, 1923, the great roller coaster, "The Comet," billed as the second largest roller coaster in the United States, was ready to thrill the public. However, in the second season, the crowds diminished. Competition from Playland in San Francisco and Neptune Beach across the Bay hurt, but the most cited reason for the failure of Pacific City was contamination from sewage. The growing bayside cities of Burlingame and San Mateo allowed their raw sewage to run into the Bay close to Coyote Point and the bathing beaches. For health reasons, swimming in the Bay waters had to be restricted. When Pacific City closed for the winter in 1923, it did so for good. For years, huge remnants of Pacific City stood to remind San Mateo County people of this failed venture. "The Comet" was finally torn down in 1933; the dance hall stood until 1946.

The county's economy was dealt another blow during the 1930s when its shellfish industry was wiped out. At the turn of the century, the oysters coming from the waters just off the San Mateo County Bay lands supplied the entire West Coast market and fueled a million-dollar-a-year industry. However, the polluted condition of the Bay began making it harder and harder to cultivate the oysters as the twentieth century rolled on. Then in 1932, the industry was devastated by a report by J. C. Geiger, M.D., and J. P. Gray, M.D., in *California and Western Medicine*, which confirmed suspicions linking typhoid epidemics in San Francisco to contaminated shellfish harvested from the San Mateo County Bay line. By 1939, all commercial shellfish operations had ceased, never to return.[23]

As conditions worsened during the 1930s, a new sensitivity to the region's Bay line began to develop. With the completion of the San Francisco–Oakland Bay Bridge in the middle of that decade, Oakland's waterfront area, which before had been little more than the back door to the city, suddenly became the front door, and the stench and general environmental decay from organic pollution became readily visible to the entire population of the Bay Area as they traveled from west to east Bay shores. Talk began of regional associations necessary to clean up the Bay, but World War II interrupted progress on the matter.

By 1947, the pollution problem has spun out of control throughout the state. That year, the State Board of Public Health refused to issue permits for disposal of untreated waste in California. This step forced action in the Bay Area. A San Francisco Bay Regional Water Quality Control Board was set up

Pacific City, San Mateo circa 1923.

to ensure organic sewage would get at least some treatment before flowing into the Bay. By 1959, some $130 million were spent on plants. Still San Mateo County jurisdictions were counted among the worst offenders of breaking rules and not coming up to standards. In 1963, the Quality Control Board found San Mateo County seven times over the legal limit regarding pollutants in its bay line waters. The board threatened to enact legal action, which led the county to join a South Bay Tri-County Sewage Committee to deal with the abuse.

By the early 1960s, Bay Area residents were not just concerned with the polluted condition of the Bay, but also with the fact that the Bay was shrinking. In 1964, it was estimated that 60 percent, or 188 square miles, of the Bay's marshlands had disappeared, and 53 square miles of the Bay itself were gone. Nineteenth- and early-twentieth-century agricultural projects had drained and filled such places as Brewer's Island (today's Foster City). The development of San Francisco's airport, beginning in 1927, and the creation of the Port of Redwood City in the 1930s added public projects to the list of encroachments on the Bay. As developers in the postwar era looked to build housing for the expanding population of the county, bay land projects such as that at Redwood Shores, north of the Port of Redwood City, became the concern of a strengthening environmental movement that demanded a regional approach for better dealing with not just the Bay, but air pollution, coastal preservation, open space along the central hill country of the county and other issues.

The Bay Area had a population of 3,216,700 taking up some 1,286 square miles by 1960, but those that cared about the environment of the Bay Area found little political framework to help them. The most recognized regional body that existed, the Association of Bay Area Governments (ABAG), seemed ineffectual. The member governmental bodies voiced support of such issues as stopping bay fill, but continued to lobby for the projects in their own jurisdictions. The growing environmental movement demanded action outside of the powers of the existing authorities.

San Francisco Chronicle newspaper columnist Harold Gilliam declared the region to be in an "environmental crisis." He warned his readers that they should "cherish memories" of the San Francisco Bay, because soon the filling projects around the great estuary would change the region into another Los Angeles—overbuilt, overpopulated and polluted.

Grassroots organizations rose to put a stop to the land filling of the Bay, most notably the Save San Francisco Bay Association in Berkeley. Another influential group that had great influence was Citizens for Regional Recreation and Parks, later known as People for Open Space. Its president, Mel Scott, wrote an important study in 1963, titled *The Future of San Francisco Bay*, in which an elaborate argument is laid out describing why the disappearance of the Bay would hurt the region environmentally, recreationally, and, perhaps most importantly, economically. Scott placed monetary value on the Bay's value as a port, a source of food fish, industries such as salt, cement and mineral products. He stated how the Bay's importance to tourism and recreation businesses was becoming increasingly significant to the Bay Area's economy. He argued that from the point of view of local government, the various revenue streams supported by the existence of the Bay contributed more to the tax base than if the entire Bay was filled as a gigantic housing tract.

The Mel Scott approach proved effective in convincing the local press to support the save the Bay movement. Scott suggested that it was time to end the "Balkanized" control of the natural resources of the Bay Area. Regional government, he asserted, must be created to safeguard the future.

Land-fill projects all around the Bay Region came under close scrutiny. In San Mateo County, perhaps the most heated fight took place at Brisbane. Here the Sunset Scavenger Corporation had bought 250 acres of marshlands from the Crocker Land Company for use as a garbage dump. For the next 25 years, San Francisco's daily 1,600 tons of solid waste were to be disposed only blocks away from a residential portion of town. San Francisco Mayor John Shelley answered the protests: "You can't let the garbage lie in the streets."[24] Brisbane City Council Chairman Dr. Paul Goerche repeatedly blasted back at San Francisco and its "filler barons." In a move reminiscent of the 1960s, he formed a committee, "Garbage A-Go-Go" to help publicize the local save the Bay campaign.

The combined efforts of the environmental groups of the Bay Area forced Governor Pat Brown to call a special session of the legislature together in 1964. San Mateo County representatives of ABAG were notable in defending the fill projects on the books to more fully develop the peninsula. They condemned the Save the Bay Association as a group of "drumbeating ladies and bird watchers" and asked, "Are all planned projects to be delayed because some citizens like to look at water?"[25] Nevertheless, momentum was on the other side. Legislators with 20 years and more experience witnessed an unparalleled barrage of telephone calls and letters. One group of protestors sent thousands of small sacks of sand. Their message rhymed with the Pepsident Toothpaste television commercial of the day: "You will wonder where the water went if you fill the bay with sediment."[26]

The result of all this activity was the formation of the San Francisco Bay Conservation and Development Commission (BCDC) in 1965, which imposed a moratorium on most fill projects. Harold Gilliam wrote that a Magna Carta type of achievement had been accomplished by the environmental groups. Indeed, the BCDC was the first state organization in the country to govern an estuary in a regional manner.

The BCDC was given a four-year license to protect the Bay. In 1969, its continuation was evaluated. The political climate was most favorable for its renewal. By the end of the 1960s, opinion polls ranked pollution and other environmental concerns as tied with the economy for the secondmost pressing problem facing Californians (the Vietnam War being number one). This time, approval would make the BCDC a permanent body of state government. Governor Ronald Reagan signed the bill institutionalizing the BCDC and commented: "This bill will save the Bay."[27]

The BCDC is one of many regional bodies that today govern the lives of San Mateo County residents. The fierce spirit of independence, born out of the Consolidation Act of 1856, and fought for politically during the early part of the twentieth century, will continuously be encroached upon as the twenty-first century moves forward. Regional government may be the answer for many of the most pressing issues of the future, including those involving the environment, economy, and transportation. At some point in the future, the debate about the relevance of having a San Mateo County government may surface again.

Chapter 5 Footnotes

1. Bancroft, *History,* vol. VI, p. 754.
2. Stanger, "Why", p. 3.
3. Hynding, *From Frontier,* p. 61.
4. Samuel C. Chandler, *Gateway to the Peninsula: A History of the City of Daly City,* City of Daly City, 1973, p. 57.
5. Mitchell P. Postel, "The Junior Community College Movement of San Mateo County: 1922–1987," *La Peninsula,* vol. XXIV, No. 2, October 1987, p. 3.
6. Mitchell P. Postel, "San Mateo County Historical Association: 1935–1985," *La Peninsula,* vol. XXII, No. 3, May 1985, p. 4.
7. Mitchell P. Postel, *San Mateo: A Centennial History,* Scottwell Associates, Publishers, San Francisco, 1994, p. 181–182.
8. San Francisco Bureau of Government Research, *The San Francisco–San Mateo Survey,* San Francisco Chamber of Commerce, 1928, p. 2.
9. Ibid. pp. 26–27.
10. Ibid. p. 5.
11. Ibid. p. 6.
12. Ibid. p. 175.
13. "Rolph Visions S. F. Peninsula's Consolidation," *Redwood City Tribune,* March 23, 1931.
14. "S. F.–San Mateo Merger Plan Formulated," *San Francisco Examiner,* June 6, 1931.
15. "We Try Something New," *San Francisco Chronicle,* January 8, 1932.
16. "Charter Called Big Aid to County Merger," *San Francisco Examiner,* January 8, 1932.
17. "Coast Moves to Thwart S. F. Union," *San Mateo Times,* February 4, 1932.
18. "Cottrell says New S. F. Charter Full of Holes; S. M. System Scorned Too," *San Mateo Times,* February 17, 1932.
19. "Coast Hears Charter Aids," *Burlingame Advance,* March 14, 1932.
20. "S. F. Selfish In Annexation Move," *Redwood City Tribune,* March 14, 1932.
21. "Francis 'Resigns' as Airport Chief: As Airport Chief Faints at News," *San Francisco Examine,* May 28, 1932.
22. Hynding, *From Frontier,* pp. 233–234.
23. Mitchell P. Postel, "A Lost Resource: Shellfish in San Francisco Bay," *California History,* California Historical Society, San Francisco, vol. LXVII, No. l, March, 1988, p. 41.
24. Mitchell P. Postel, "Vigil on the Golden Gate: The Environmental History of the San Francisco Bay Since 1850," Master of Arts thesis, University of California at Santa Barbara, April, 1977, p. 43.
25. Ibid. p. 57.
26. Ibid. p. 44.
27. Ibid. p. 64.

Part *Two*

Historic Themes

Introduction

Part II of this sesquicentennial history of San Mateo County is a series of essays based on research and development of the current exhibits existing or being installed by the San Mateo County History Museum in Redwood City. Back in 1994, when the Museum Board and staff began to think about a new museum and what the exhibits should be, the parent organization of the Museum, the San Mateo County Historical Association, organized a number of meetings with community leaders, historians, Historical Association volunteers and our staff to develop the themes. Albert Acena, PhD, and Mark Still, PhD, both of the College of San Mateo, led the effort. We received terrific input from over 200 interested individuals who represented the various geographical parts of the county (North, Central, South and Coast), ethnic and racial groups, the business community, political leaders, historical societies, preservationists, arts organizations and other interested parties. The guidance of Historian Kenneth Jackson, PhD, was sought out. Dr. Jackson, author of the definitive book on the history of the American suburb (*The Crabgrass Frontier*)[1], was flown out from Columbia University by the Association in order to review the emerging themes of the museum planners and offer advice on how to best tell our story.

In the end, we decided to establish six permanent exhibit galleries along with a variety of interactive galleries, theaters, and restored rooms within our 1910 courthouse building. We knew we would have to develop this museum in phases due the high cost of creating quality displays. Our purpose in creating all of the six permanent galleries was to place San Mateo County History in context to larger themes of California, western and American History—that is—why our local history is important to the world outside the peninsula, and how outside developments have had an impact on our peninsula. We felt this the proper approach for a local history museum entering the twenty-first century. Diverse audiences of residents and visitors could hardly be expected to fully appreciate a presentation dedicated, to the memory of a few founding families, a trap many small history museums fall into. We also wanted to avoid the traditional chronological approach to California History—the Indians, the Missions and then came the freeways approach. Placing San Mateo County History in context allowed us to explore the peninsula's uniqueness, while letting us see the changing world's influences on our county.

The first gallery we completed was *Nature's Bounty* in 2000. It tells the story of how the early people of the peninsula successfully used the natural resources here and how those resources were used to help build and sustain San Francisco, the most important city in the West during the latter part of the nineteenth century and early part of the twentieth.

Three of the exhibit galleries will explore suburban topics (as of July of 2006, two of the three should be completed). Transportation, architecture, lifestyle and infrastructure and other significant facets of suburban development will be featured. San Mateo County having the first commuter rail road on the West Coast stretch through it in 1864, and having the first portion of state highway built through it in 1912, claims formulation of many nuances in the way westerners looked at suburban living. This is reflected by the presence of the great estates of the original wealthy California families after the completion of the San Francisco-San Jose Railroad. In later years, the county's automotive history allow, for a variety of architectural and lifestyle nuances that have had impact far beyond the county's borders.

Mission outpost building at San Mateo Creek drawn by William H. Dougal in 1850.

Another gallery will explore the peninsula's rich history of diversity. Today San Mateo County is noted as being one of the most ethnically and racially mixed places in the world. This is not a new story. The peninsula has been a place of great diversity since Gold Rush times.

Finally San Mateo County's legacy of great entrepreneurs who have lived here and/or have established their industries here is of importance. Particularly since the beginning of World War II have great innovations in the fields of electronics, high tech and bio tech made international headlines.

In formulating the themes for these galleries, I have had the privilege of working with a terrific team of curators, archivists, and educators on our staff. Early on in the work our curator was Amy Heath and our museum educator was Lisa Dolehide. Later Karen Bry and Matt Woodside served as curators and Carmen Blair became our education director. Most recently we employed a team of curators to help create the last three galleries. They are Everett Thomas, Sheila Braufman, Gentle Wagner and Stephen Sutley. Of course, our museum archivists played significant roles. Marion Holmes, who passed away, was a terrific team player. Carol Peterson has assumed the responsibility and is a great asset for the Historical Association. Volunteer Archivist, Joan Levy, provided much help for this project. I would like to give added thanks to Carmen Blair for helping select the photographs for this book.

Part II: Introduction Footnotes

1. Kenneth Jackson, *The Crabgrass Frontier*, Oxford University Press, New York 1985.

Chapter

Nature's Bounty

One of the dominant themes of San Mateo County history focuses on its rich natural resources. The peninsula's earliest people recognized the wealth represented within their plentiful environment. Later the Spanish realized that without the resources here, the Mission San Francisco de Asis would not succeed. The area's rolling lands made good pasturage for the rancho families of the California-Mexican period, and once San Francisco was established, the peninsula's natural bounties enabled it to become the West's greatest city during the nineteenth century.

The Peninsula's Original Environmentalists

The oldest artifact ever recovered in San Mateo County is a 5,500- to 8,000-year-old crescent-shaped scraper found in 1994 at Seal Cove within San Mateo County's Fitzgerald Marine Reserve on the coastside.[1] Radio carbon dating was employed to estimate the tool's age. Other scrapers like this one have been found in California, and have been estimated to be at least 10,000 years old. It is made of Franciscan chert found in areas east of the San Andreas Fault. The person(s) who used the scraper were here before the Ohlones, who are believed to have established themselves on the peninsula about 5,000 years ago. These first people distinguished themselves from the Ohlone by not living in villages. Instead, they were nomadic. That is, they moved as the seasons changed to areas of natural abundance. The Ohlones brought change in that they gathered their acorns and stored them in granaries within villages that they lived in at least part of the year.

Mission records tell us that present San Mateo County was site of 10 to 12 major tribelets with between 100 to 200 inhabitants. The total population of this area was therefore 1,000 to 2,400 people when the Spanish first arrived. They were part of a linguistic group that we call the *Ohlone* today. These people lived from Contra Costa County to Monterey County and actually spoke a variety of different dialects. It is estimated that at the time the Spanish arrived, there were about 10,000 Ohlone. In fact, the Ohlone and other Indian people of Central California represented the densest population of Native Americans, north of Mexico.

Gaspar de Portola's Spanish expedition of 1769 was first to encounter Ohlone on the San Mateo County part of the coast at Pescadero Creek. His party reported the people as sporting wreaths of

leaves in their hair and toting red-painted staffs. Farther up the coast, at San Gregorio, the explorers noted that some of the men wore capes of leather or plant fiber. Women also used the fiber for their skirts. It seems no other garments were worn. Five years later, Father Francisco Palou observed that the men of the bayside wore beards. They carried throwing spears or darts, as well as bows and arrows. Near today's Belmont, Father Palou encountered a boy who declared *me apam*[2] or "you are my father," and accompanied him on his expedition.

The most populated portion of San Mateo County is now underwater. Just behind today's Crystal Springs Dam lived a group of people who called themselves the Shalshon or Salson. To the east of them were rolling hills that dropped off to the Bay. Acorn-bearing oaks, seed grasses, and buckeyes were everywhere. To the west were the coastal mountains, less forested than today, with wild-cherry bushes, as well as deer and other game animals. They called their largest village Uturpe; it was situated on San Mateo Creek. North of it was Alahmu, later named Sawyer Camp. In 1776, as Spanish Explorer Juan Bautista de Anza was passing through, the Salson were at war with a group of Indians to the north.

Ohlone Indian woman.

South of the Salson were the Lhamshin with small villages at today's Belmont and a larger village at San Carlos. Farther south, near present North Fair Oaks, de Anza encountered a village. His soldiers dubbed the people there "The Shouters."[3] They called themselves the Putshon. A large village also existed in the vicinity of downtown Redwood City. Other triblets existed at Pacifica, Half Moon Bay, San Gregorio, and Pescadero.

It was plain to the Spanish and other early observers that the Ohlone had lived in a stable environment for a long time. The evidence was everywhere. Shellmounds, the Indian refuse piles, were 30 feet deep and a quarter of a mile across in some places. Well-worn trails were pressed as much as a foot and a half below the surrounding land. It appears that the Ohlone had been free of major floods, wars, famine, and communicable diseases for 5,000 years.

The Europeans gushed at the richness of the environment. Animal life abounded. There were large herds of elk, pronghorn antelope, and deer. Predators included wolves, coyote, mountain lions, bobcats, bald eagles, condors, and grizzly bears. Flocks of geese, ducks, and sea birds could darken the sky. On the bayline there was plentiful shellfish. On the coast existed sea lions and seals. An occasional whale washed ashore and presented opportunity for a feast. French observer Jean F. G. de la

Perouse remarked: "There is not any country in the world which more abounds in fish and game of every description."[4]

This incredible environment did not evolve by accident. The Ohlone were excellent caretakers of their land. They managed their healthy world by never taking from it more than they needed, and they curbed their needs by controlling their populations. They limited their sexual contact by ritual—that is, two years after giving birth for women and before the hunt for men. They accepted homosexuality and practiced abortion.

They also periodically purposefully burned the land. Fire kept brush from taking over meadowland, which was so important to the large grazing animals. It helped perpetuate the digger pines, an important source of nuts, by encouraging the germination process. Fires fostered certain grasses for seed gathering, and burning at certain times also prevented the buildup of fuel for truly disastrous fires. And so when the Europeans remarked about the park-like setting of the Ohlone, they were speaking about a place that was largely created and managed by these native people.

Not only did they live well with their natural environment, but they also lived well with one another. Wars did occur, but they were limited affairs, usually ending when one person was killed or wounded.

Government was based on the generosity of the family community. A chieftain's responsibility was to maintain the status quo, which in general was thought to be perfect. He (and sometimes she) needed to keep peace within the triblet, and with the other triblets. The leader cared for the old, orphans, widows, and the crippled. A chieftain set dates for ceremonies, entertained visitors, and did what was necessary to assure that the triblet's linage continued. The Ohlone ranked one another not by their material possessions, but by how generous a person was.

As were all the coastal people of California, the Ohlone were Stone Age—that is, they did not know of metals. They were prehistoric—that is, they had no written language. They were hunter-gatherers—that is, they had not mastered agriculture. However negative these three anthropological terms may be, they overlook the successful way in which the Ohlone lived.

Typically, their villages were located close to freshwater creeks. Shellmounds surrounded these sites. Houses, granaries, ramadas, and smokehouses were constructed out of willow branches and tule reeds. The tule was a remarkable building material because of its ability to successfully insulate the houses. The reeds were cut with saws made from the scapulas of deer. The houses ranged between 6 to 20 feet in diameter. Sweathouses were common. They were dug into the earth and plastered with mud. They were for men only, who would use these places for spiritual inspiration before the hunt.

As hunter-gatherers, the Ohlone ate most anything, including insects and lizards. Only a few animals were not consumed for religious reasons. Acorns of several species were the great staple of their diet. The women gathered them and stored them for year-round use. With stone mortars and pestals, the women would pound the acorns into a meal, leach out the bitter tannin, and cook the mush in expertly woven baskets. The mush was heated by placing hot stones into the baskets and then stirring them with a wooden utensil.

Many times what the people ate depended on seasonal preferences. During the cooler months, when they might be inclined to live near the Bay, they would catch geese and ducks using nets and cleverly crafted tule decoys. The men would fish using harpoons, nets, and cage traps. Shellfish were in abundance, as the ancient mounds showed the early explorers. Shells were also utilized for jewelry, money, and basket ornamentation. On the coast, seaweed was gathered and pressed into cakes. Sometimes the women sun-dried the vegetable matter and scraped it for salt. The men caught marine mammals, sharks, and sturgeon.

During the warmer months, the men would hunt deer, tule elk, rabbit, quail, skunk, raccoon, and even coyote, bobcat, and mountain lion in the woodlands. They used bows and arrows. The arrowheads were made of chert or obsidian, indicating that trade was taking place between the Ohlone and people of the interior. The men expertly flint-knapped or stone-worked flakes into sharp arrowheads. While the meat was important, so were the hides. Bone awls were employed to poke holes in the hides for sewing. Even the animal's sinew was used to create binding material. Also in the woodlands, women would find grass seed and herbs. Soap root was harvested for a variety of uses, including as a food, soap, material for making brushes, and as a poison for use in catching fish.

Along creeks, willows could be found for construction of houses. Willow fibers were used in basket making. Berries were found near the creeks as well. Ohlone women used special cone-shaped mortars for grinding the berries. Men used harpoons, weirs, and baskets to catch salmon and steelhead trout.

In short, at first look, the Ohlone people of the peninsula were a simple people in a variety of ways. Granted they were Stone Age, prehistoric, and a hunting-gathering people. However, these measures of human advancement may be overlooking some things. The Ohlone lived a subtle lifestyle that makes us think that they were more sophisticated than the first look reveals. Before the coming of the Spanish, the people here felt they had a utopian existence. They had all they needed from nature to live a comfortable life. Some scholars have estimated the average life span of an Ohlone was about 40 years. This compares favorably to European life span during the eighteenth century. In fact, when considering infant mortality, this compares favorably with many civilizations today. Such were the natural advantages of his environment that the average Ohlone man may have had to spend only about 15 hours a week doing the things necessary to provide for the triblet. The women, of course— with the heavy gathering responsibilities, acorn preparation, and basket making—worked harder. Their leisure time was largely taken up by gambling.

The favorable nature of the Ohlone's world on the peninsula before contact with the Spanish (1769) was due in large part to the life ways of these people. They treated their environment as they treated one another—with understanding and respect.

The Spanish Period on the Peninsula

The Spanish first arrived in what we would call San Mateo County in 1769, with the expedition of Captain Gaspar de Portola. Portola was following the orders of Visitor General of New Spain, Jose de Galvez. Galvez was politically ambitious and interested in giving his sphere of influence the look of expansion. He therefore devised a scheme to colonize Alta or Upper California as a way to protect Spanish holdings in North America from Russian and possible British aggression.

Back in the 1540s, Spain had largely given up on lands north of Mexico. The region seemed to contain little in the way of riches, and the people resisted Spanish civilization. Galvez's plan for *defensive expansionism* relied on the extension of the Franciscan chain of missions from the Baja north. In 1602, the explorer Sebastian Vizcaino had mapped the California coast and indicated that there were two excellent natural harbors, one at San Diego and the other at Monterey. The San Francisco Bay had yet to be discovered. Portola, with the father president of the Baja and future Alta California missions, Junipero Serra, was to found the first mission and presidio at San Diego and then push on to Monterey and establish the second settlement. A string of missions, all a day's walk apart, would then be built to link California with Mexico. In Galvez's mind, the lack of actual pioneers ready to create a Spanish California would be offset by Christianizing the California Indians and making them full subjects of the king of Spain. The missions were to exist for ten years only and then be secularized—that is, the lands would be returned to the Indians, who would run California as a Christian agricultural colony, loyal to the king of Spain. The mission buildings would be converted into parish churches staffed by Indian priests.

Gaspar de Portola and his 60-man expedition were the first European overland explorers of Northern California. Misled by inaccurate maps, they endured months of physical hardship.

With about 300 in his party, Portola started from the Baja on January 9, 1769. This overland expedition was to be supported by three ships along the way, the *San Antonio*, the *San Carlos*, and the *San Jose*. He arrived at San Diego with only about half of his original party. Here he rendezvoused with the *San Antonio* and *San Carlos*. Dozens were sick, and the expedition's doctor had lost his mind. Serra stayed at San Diego to establish the first mission as planned. Portola took the healthy soldiers and Father Juan Crespi with him to find Monterey. The *San Antonio* was sent back to Mexico for supplies.

The route taken was referred to as *El Camino Real*, the King's Highway. The plan called for linking up with the *San Jose* at Monterey. Sadly, the *San Jose* was never heard from again, and when Portola arrived in Monterey, he could not believe it was what he was looking for. The bay did not appear to be the natural harbor that Vizcaino had shown on his map of 1602. They continued up the coast, past today's Santa Cruz County, and into present-day San Mateo County. At the end of October, they found themselves at Point San Pedro, now Pacifica. The party understood from some Indians that a ship had been seen anchored to the north. Hoping that this could be the *San Jose,* Portola sent his lead scout, Sergeant Ortega, up the hillside to the east. Once on top of the hill, Ortega accidentally discovered the San Francisco Bay. He returned to camp with the disappointing news that a ship was not sighted, but some arm of the sea had been seen. The whole party then climbed the hill. Unfortunately, from that vantage point (today's Sweeny Ridge) the Bay could be seen but not the opening to the Bay—what we refer to as the Golden Gate. And so, instead of continuing north, the expedition descended the hill on its east side and proceeded south down the San Andreas Valley. Their attempt to round the Bay ended on November 11. While Portola's scouts advanced into the East Bay, they did not explore north enough to see the Golden Gate. Portola felt his mission a failure and decided to return to San Diego, following the route they had blazed coming up.

They made it back to San Diego on January 24, 1770, after subsisting on 12 of their mules. Portola, in his report to Galvez, proclaimed the Russians should be allowed to have California. The worthless nature of the country would serve as punishment for their aggressive ambitions. Obviously, he saw little potential in the lands he had seen or the people he had met. It must be remembered that as a gentleman and career soldier from Spain, Portola probably looked down on this far-off frontier and desired mostly to be able to return to Europe.[5] However, the Franciscan Juan Crespi saw much more in this exploration, especially the great estuary they had seen. He felt it a "prodigy of nature" and asserted that further investigation was warranted.

That year Portola set out by land and Father Serra by sea, in the *San Antonio,* to found Monterey. Portola soon after retired and left the military affairs of California to his second in command, Lieutenant Pedro Fages. In November, Fages led a small party into the East Bay. From the hills they finally discovered the Golden Gate. Two years later, Fages, with Father Crespi, further explored the East Bay, the Suisun Bay, and Delta.[6] Now the Spanish were beginning to get an idea of just how important Portola's accidental discovery had been. This great bay was the key to California. If Spain could control it from the Golden Gate, it could control the delta, and if it could control the delta, it could control the two great navigable rivers of the Central Valley, the Sacramento and San Joaquin.

In 1774, Captain Fernando Rivera y Moncada, the military governor of California following Fages, set out from Monterey with Father Francisco Palou. Their mission was to explore the peninsula and locate the Golden Gate from the south. At today's Palo Alto, Palou noted that this site would make a great place for a mission. The party climbed Mount San Bruno and Mount Davidson and found the Golden Gate, finally realizing how close Portola had been.

Pedro Evanico, the last Indian survivor of the San Mateo Mission Outpost, lived near the San Mateo bayshore.

The next year, the new Spanish administrator of New Spain, Viceroy Antonio Maria de Bucareli, decided that a presidio and mission must be established at the tip of the San Francisco Peninsula. However, it still needed to be proved that the Golden Gate was navigable. In August of 1775, Lieutenant Juan Ayala sailed the *San Carlos* through. He then spent six weeks surveying the Bay. Pilot Juan Aguirre surveyed the San Mateo bayline for the first time.

Meanwhile, Captain Juan Bautista de Anza opened a land route from the central part of Mexico to California. In 1776, he brought a contingent of more than 200 settlers to help establish the settlement at San Francisco. Although he had the opportunity to select the sites for the presidio and mission, Anza was recalled to Mexico before the settlers could actually found San Francisco. His second in command, Lieutenant Jose Moraga, and two Franciscans were given that task. In June, the settlers arrived, and in October they had finished building a temporary wooden structure near Dolores Creek, officially named Mission San Francisco de Asis. The territory of the mission was determined to include all of present-day San Francisco and most of San Mateo County, except the tail portion of the county on its southern coastside.

For the Franciscans the primary goal continued to be Christianization of the native people. Early on the fathers made progress with a group of Indians from a nearby village. However, the Salson

people, from down on the peninsula, attacked this group and forced
them to flee across the Bay. Relations were renewed, but then a fight
broke out between some of the soldiers and the Indians over one of
the soldiers' wives. Finally in March
of 1777, contact was established
again, and in June, the first baptism
took place.

As the months went by, the
padres began to realize the sorry
potential of having created the mission at the tip of the peninsula.
Most of the prospective Indian neo-

Ohlone Indians in a tule boat.

phytes lived south of the mission. Good fresh water and wood were scarce. There was not enough
grazing land for the important herds of cattle the Spanish had brought with them. The soil and climate were not adequate for the types of agricultural pursuits the missionaries envisioned. Father Palou
had recommended Palo Alto as the site for a mission on the Rivera expedition of 1774, and Father
Pedro Font had thought that a mission at San Mateo Creek would be an excellent choice when he
accompanied Anza in 1776. Incidentally, Font gave the creek its name (for reasons unexplained),
which eventually became the county's name.

Nevertheless, the fathers had to establish the mission close to the presidio in order to adequately
supply the soldiers, and the presidio had to be close to the Golden Gate in order to protect it and the
rest of California from any foreign interloper. By 1785, the padres had reached the decision that an
agricultural outpost needed to be established down the peninsula. They selected the San Pedro Valley
on the coast (the current site of the county's Sanchez Adobe Historic Park), and close to where Portola had camped before his famous discovery. Here was the first place south of the mission that a creek
produced fresh water all year around. The Indians proved friendly, and the soil was fertile.

The first year, roving grizzly bears ruined a harvest, but within a few years some 300 neophytes
with their overseeing priests were providing important food and other supplies to the mission. Mission
records reveal that some 2,760 yards of fencing was built, and 36 acres of wheat were planted, along
with 9 acres of corn, plus pear and peach trees and grape-vines. Unfortunately, in 1792, this very successful outpost was hit by disease. California Indians had been free of communicable diseases before
the coming of the Spanish, but now they were exposed, and with little immunity to these sicknesses
they died off in large numbers. While some operations continued at San Pedro after 1792, it ceased to
be the place of great activity that it had been.

The padres had no choice but to find a new location for an outpost. The next year, in 1793, they
established a hospice, as local historians call it, at San Mateo Creek, roughly Baywood Avenue and El
Camino today. Here, under the supervision of two lone priests, a substantial success was achieved.
Although epidemics did bother the San Mateo outpost, they did not have the devastating effect that
they did at San Pedro. For one thing, the population of people kept at San Mateo was only about a
tenth of what it had been on the coast. By 1810, its herd of cattle numbered more than 10,000. Its
herd of sheep was a similar number. There were also hundreds of horses and mules attached to the

San Mateo settlement. Meanwhile, 11,098 bushels of wheat were harvested in 1812—its highest production year.

The story of the San Pedro Valley and San Mateo outposts is not unusual in that many of the Spanish missions had agricultural assistance farms. However, the degree to which the Mission San Francisco de Asis depended on its outposts is unique. The mission at Delores Creek could not possibly have survived without the pasture lands and farming locations down the peninsula.

That the Spanish struggled for adequate pasture land on the San Francisco Peninsula is reflected in the relations between the soldiers at the presidio and the missionaries. Originally, the soldiers and the padres were allowed to have their own herds of cattle. Each spring the calves belonging to the soldiers were branded with an "R" for *rey*, or king. The priests branded theirs with an "F" for Franciscan. Few, if any, cattle were owned by individuals, since nearly everyone was attached to either the presidio or the mission. The problem developed as the two herds grew—there simply wasn't enough pasturage to feed all the animals. The fathers convinced the Spanish authorities that only one herd was necessary in 1791. The Army then was forced to buy its cattle from the padres. Friction resulted when the soldiers complained of being overcharged. Finally, in 1796, Diego de Borcia, the Spanish governor of California, allowed the soldiers to have their own ranch, called Buri Buri. It included the south side of San Bruno Mountain, all of today's South San Francisco, San Bruno, Millbrae, and the northern portion of Burlingame.

Mexican Rancho Times

Beginning in 1810, revolution spread among the Spanish colonies in the Americas. Support for the California missions, which had not been much before, was drastically cut. In 1821, Mexico achieved its independence. Part of the promise of the Mexican Revolution was the long-promised secularization of the mission lands. Franciscan control over the neophytes was abolished. In theory, the Indians were to be organized into self-governing pueblos under the direction of their own alcaldes and other officers. Under the new laws of the Mexican constitution, the Indians were to receive land on which to make themselves self-supporting. This never happened.

Secularization did occur, but the Mexican governors of California granted the land as favors to former soldiers of the Spanish regime and other political friends. By the end of the Mexican period, about 500 of these land grants would be issued in California, 17 of them in what we call San Mateo County today. The poor Indians sort of went with the land as permanent laborers. On the San Francisco peninsula, many stayed at the mission at San Francisco, but more came to live at the old outpost at San Mateo.

Mission San Francisco de Asis was secularized in 1831, and prominent individuals of the area began preparing petitions for their land grants. Land grants in California amounted to nearly 100,000 acres in places. However, on the peninsula, they were much smaller, the largest being the 35,250-acre Rancho de las Pulgas, given to the Arguello family in 1835. It consisted of today's south San Mateo, Belmont, San Carlos, Redwood City, East Palo Alto, Atherton, and Menlo Park. The peninsula's grants were smaller because of the good quality of the land. More cattle could be raised here than on the land grants in the arid southern part of California, for example. There was also more competition, with numerous interested people living at the San Francisco, Santa Clara, and Santa Cruz mission communities.

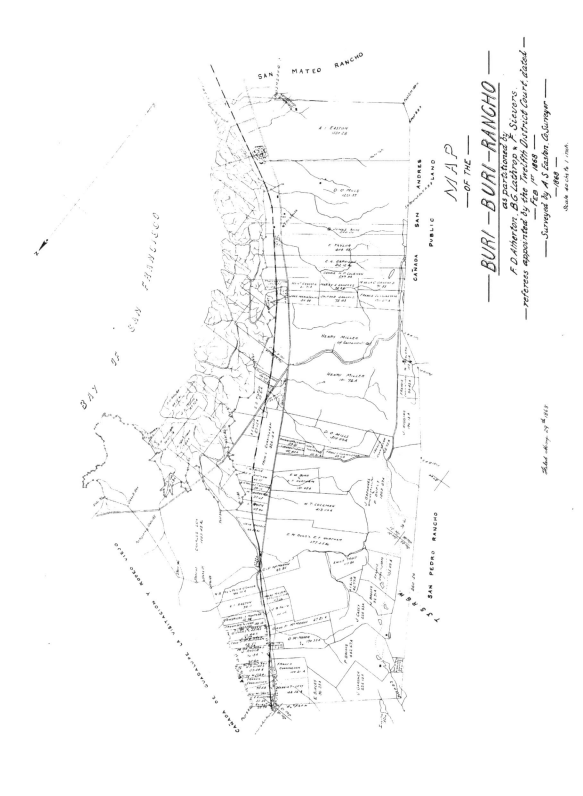

Buri-Buri Rancho. Map made in 1860, as the Buri-Buri Rancho which extended from the bay to the San Andreas Valley, covering Colma, South San Francisco, Millbrae and more, was partitioned.

The culture of the Mexican period of San Mateo County history, as it was for all of California history, was based on land. The California herds of long-horn cattle were the first great ones of American western history. Like most of coastal California, the peninsula was divided up among great families to become ranchos, with the primary mission of raising cattle. Jose Sanchez came to occupy the former soldier's rancho in 1825. Four years after secularization, in 1835, he received title to his Rancho Buri Buri. Sanchez was an exception in that he tilled the soil. Most of the rancho owners did not. They thought that farming was beneath their dignity as gentlemanly cattle ranchers.

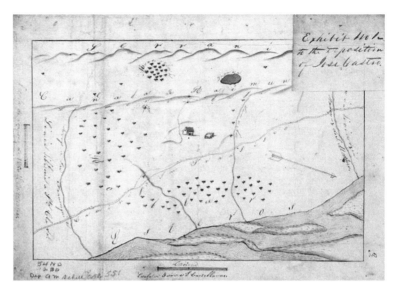

Map Diseño for Rancho de las Pulgas. These hand-drawn maps were presented in court as evidence of land ownership by rights of land grants.

Among the changes brought on by the Mexican Revolution was the concept of free trade. The rancheros had a definite taste for the manufactured goods of the United States and other places. During Spanish times it had been illegal to trade with the representatives of any nations except Spain. Now, the restrictions had been lifted. However, what was there to trade for the manufactured items? Certainly there was enough beef, but without refrigeration, meat could not be offered. The rancheros were rich in land and cattle, but cash poor. That is, there was not much currency or coin in California. The padres had the answer, though. They discovered the applicable commodities long before. The hides and the tallow from the cattle could be bartered. The hides back east were tanned into leather for all sorts of products. The tallow, or fat rendered from the animals, could be used as fuel, or for creation of soap, candles, and other things.

On the Mexican ranchos of the peninsula, and throughout California, one could witness the beginnings of the American western cattle-raising tradition.[7] California *vaqueros*, as the first cowboys of the Old West, organized rodeos or roundups decades before their Texas counterparts. The roundup was the time when calves identified their mothers and then were branded. Branding was important because the cattle were allowed to roam over the *open range*—that is, there was no fencing separating the great ranchos. Some of these original cowboys were full-blooded California Indians, but most were of mixed blood. They were peerless horsemen. At *matanza*, or the slaughtering time, vaqueros might, for the sheer sport of it, despite the sharp long horns of the beef, cut an animal's throat from the saddle while on a dead run. Carcasses were left where they fell for crews of mostly Indians, who skinned off the hides and cut of the fatty portions to be cooked as tallow. These crews made bags from the hides to contain the tallow.

For the rancho owners, life was simple, generous, and wealthy. They had frequent dances and picnics. Sporting activities included bear and bull fights. A ring for that purpose was built at Yerba Buena, as San Francisco was called in those days. Grizzly bears were plentiful. They loved the practice

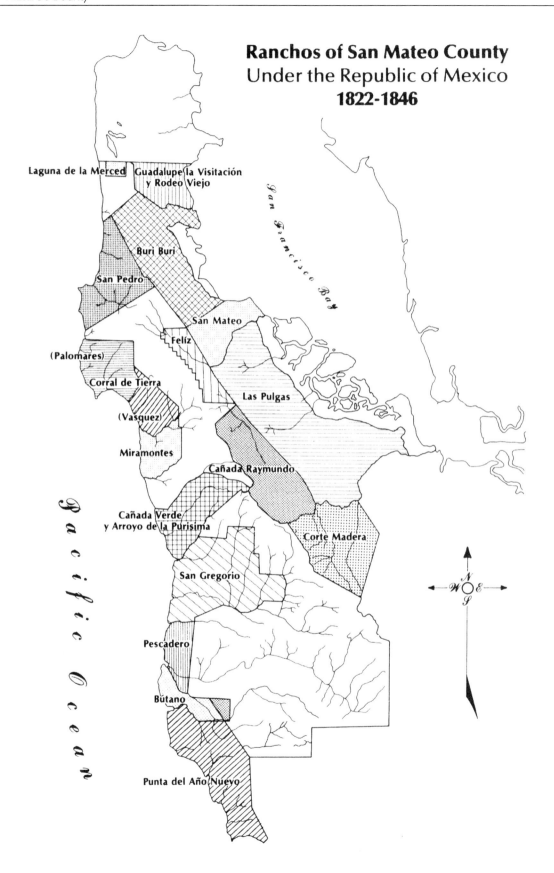

Ranchos of San Mateo County
Under the Republic of Mexico
1822-1846

San Francisco Bay

Pacific Ocean

Laguna de la Merced
Guadalupe la Visitación y Rodeo Viejo
Buri Buri
San Pedro
San Mateo
Felíz
(Palomares)
Corral de Tierra
(Vasquez)
Las Pulgas
Miramontes
Cañada Raymundo
Cañada Verde y Arroyo de la Purisima
Corte Madera
San Gregorio
Pescadero
Bútano
Punta del Año Nuevo

N
W E
S

of the *matanza*, when the carcasses of the cattle were left on the open range. It has been estimated that the grizzly bear population in California increased dramatically during the Mexican California era.[8] Therefore, there were plenty of these animals for bored vaqueros to play with.

California was not any more a focus of attention during Mexican times than during the Spanish era. Instead, this place remained a thinly settled territory vulnerable to foreign aggression. By 1845, there were probably not more than 7,000 Mexican citizens in California (excluding the Indians). In what would become San Mateo County, the local population did not exceed 500 (and that *included* the Indians, representing a significant depopulation since the time of Ohlone contact with the Spanish).

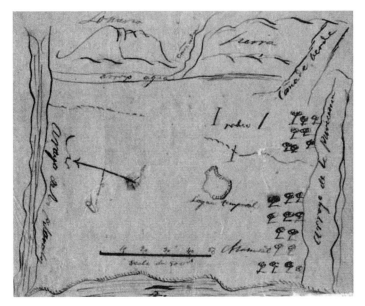

Rancho Miramontes, 1841. This land grant of 1 square league, 4,424 acres, including most of today's Half Moon Bay.

The leading family of the peninsula was the Sanchezes. Jose had come to California as a child with the Anza party of 1776. As a soldier he settled in San Francisco in 1791. He rose in rank to sergeant during Spanish times, and became a lieutenant in 1827, under the Mexican regime. Sanchez took part in more than 20 campaigns in central California, skirmishing against Indians and on missions of exploration. In 1836, he retired to his Rancho Buri Buri, formerly the land reserved for the soldiers during the Spanish era.

His 15,000-acre land grant was measured out by his son-in-law, Francisco de Haro, with the help of some vaqueros and friends. Using lengths of ropes as units of measure, Sanchez's entire rancho, 25 miles around, was surveyed in one day. It is said that when it came time to measure out the portion of the land grant on San Bruno Mountain, de Haro agreed with his father-in-law that climbing it seemed a waste of time; so the distance was approximated.

Sanchez was quite energetic. As mentioned previously, he grew crops on his land (mostly wheat, but also corn and vegetables). He built an *embarcadero*, or boat landing, for shipping his hides and tallow. His cattle herd, initially about 2,000 head, multiplied significantly. He died in 1843 at the age of 67. However his family continued to be the most important on the peninsula.

His son Francisco, previously mentioned in this book for his political activity during the early American period, received title to Rancho San Pedro in 1839. This 9,000-acre land grant would cover most of today's Pacifica. At the age of 32 he became captain of the militia at the Presidio of San Francisco, and two years later, in 1842, he became *alcalde*, or mayor, of Yerba Buena. When war came, it was Francisco who led his fellow Californians against American troops and volunteers at the Battle of Santa Clara in 1847.

Other members of the family also held land grants down the peninsula. In 1837, Jose's son-in-law, Francisco de Haro, acquired Rancho Laguna de la Merced in the Daly City area of today. Grandson

Domingo Feliz was awarded Rancho Feliz, a large portion of the present northern watershed area, in 1844.

Through the years the Sanchez family desired a piece of the peninsula that was known as Rancho San Mateo. Rancho Buri Buri was to its immediate north and Rancho Feliz was to the west. It made sense that the Sanchezs would want this land as an extension to their holdings. However, over those years, the various governors of California resisted the Sanchezes because of the existence of the Indian community still living at the former Spanish agricultural outpost. Finally in 1845, Governor Pio Pico issued the land grant—not to any of the Sanchezes, but to his own clerk, Cayetano Arenas. Pico lived down in the Los Angeles area and probably had never even seen Rancho San Mateo. He made the grant because California was in fiscal crisis, and he had no way to pay his young assistant; he instead issued him a land grant. With the Bear Flag Revolt and the threat of violent actions in the north, Cayetano's father, Luis, encouraged his son to sell off the property to the American mercantile firm of Henry Mellus and W. D. M. Howard. After the Gold Rush enriched the partners, Howard bought out Mellus and created the first of the great estates on the peninsula. One of the "improvements" he made was to throw the last inhabitants of the mission Indian community off his property. Where the majority of those people went is lost in history.

Out on the San Mateo coastside, there were several land grants issued. Among them was that of the Vasquez family, who received lands north of Pilarcitos Creek. Another family, the Miramontes', owned the land grant south of the creek. Both families held their land grants as absentee owners until the Mexican American War. At that time the Vasquez's and Miramontes desired to avoid violence and moved to their remote ranchos. At that time there was not even a road that led out to the isolated coast. At Pilarcitos Creek near the ocean, the Vasquez's built some adobe houses on the north side and the Miramontes (with 13 children) built some on the south side. Soon friends and relatives joined them here, and as the years rolled by other Spanish-speaking people came to this place, which the locals called San Benito. Over the hill it was referred to as Spanishtown. It is now known as Half Moon Bay. Thus, the first town in what we call San Mateo County today was born.

One did not necessarily have to be Hispanic to receive title to one of these land grants. A person had to be a Mexican citizen and Catholic. Some foreigners did obtain grants on the peninsula, however, by acquiring Mexican citizenship. Irishman John Copinger acquired Rancho Canada Raymundo in 1840. This property included a major part of today's southern watershed area. American Jacob Leese switched his citizenship and was awarded Rancho Guadalupe la Visitacion y Rodeo Viejo in 1841. This property included the northern portion of San Bruno Mountain and today's Brisbane and the eastern districts of Daly City.

The Treaty of Guadalupe Hidalgo ended the Mexican American War in 1848, and protected the land grants of the Mexican Californians. Nevertheless, within 15 years most of the grantees were rendered landless. After the Gold Rush began, the land in California took on more value. Squatters created legal problems for the rancho owners. A land commission, organized in 1851, made it mandatory that the land grant recipients of the Mexican era legally prove their ownership. While most in California prevailed, the land rich, cash poor rancho owners had to pay fees for attorneys. They also had to provide for various property taxes. Many mortgaged their places and lost their land to the banks. Others sold off their property to meet expenses. For example, on our Peninsula, the Sanchez family's Rancho Buri Buri was broken up with the family owning only 5% of it. The Arguello family of Rancho de las Pulgas defended its holdings by giving about 25% of its land to their attorney S. M. Mezes (this included the embarcadero area in Redwood City and a major portion of today's Belmont).

Among the few exceptions was Francisco Sanchez, who managed to hold on to his rancho until the day he died, after falling off a horse in 1862.

A New Era Begins: The Logging Industry

Gold was discovered in California in 1848, and by 1849, the "world was rushing in."[9] In that one astonishing year California was transformed from the little known to the subject of conversation nearly everywhere. Some 90,000 Argonauts arrived just in that first year. Some found fortune, many more did not. As the miners gave up, large numbers of them came to San Francisco where there existed significant opportunities to make money in a plethora of ways. San Francisco was instantly becoming the Queen City of the West. Everybody and everything destined for the mining districts stopped in San Francisco first. Just between August and November, the city grew from 6,000 to 15,000 people. Building materials, water, and food were in demand. As the months and years rolled by, to a great extent, resources down the peninsula provided for these needs.

Lumber for building the wharves, the warehouses, the hotels, the saloons, business offices, stores, and other important structures became necessary. The Spanish had first cut timber down the peninsula in the Woodside area back in 1777. During Mexican times, a stream of American and European sailors jumped ship at Yerba Buena and came to work as woodchoppers in the forests of the *Sierra Morena* (or Dark Mountains, as the Spanish named our Kings Mountain area—from Highway 92, south along Skyline Boulevard). Among the first Americans in the area was Bill "the Sawyer" Smith. Smith and this rather rough group of men were continuously at odds with Mexican officials for tax dodging and running illegal stills. However, these early residents of the hill country feared the pesky grizzly bears more than any human. Indeed, conditions in this mountainous region remained quite primitive before the Gold Rush. The lack of power equipment to carve up the huge trees meant that the great stands of Redwoods were largely left alone.

The first saw mill was constructed by Charles Brown, owner of the 2,800 acre Mountain Home Ranch, in 1849. As the months went by and San Francisco grew, the need for lumber increased. Between 1850 and 1852, San Francisco burned down six times. After each catastrophe, to a certain extent, lumber from down the peninsula was used to rebuild. In 1852, the firm of Baker and Burnham established the first truly large mill. Gang Mill, as they called it, was in Bear Gulch. It possessed 26 upright saws, two edgers, and a planer powered by two steam engines run off of three boilers. By 1853, Kings Mountain had 14 mills carving up its Redwood trees.

The extent of the activity can be somewhat understood by looking at school records. In 1859, Redwood City, the county's largest town at the time, had 89 children registered in its schools. The two districts in the Woodside lumbering area had nearly 200. As the years went by, the logging region, which began in the Woodside area, advanced up Kings Mountain to the Skyline and then extended over to the coast side of the Mountain.

One of the most successful of the lumber entrepreneurs was Frenchman Eugene Froment. He built his mill between the headwaters of the Tunitas and Purissima canyons. Around his mill sprang up a small village called Grabtown. There are a variety of theories about how Grabtown got its name. The most plausible suggests that the company never built enough shacks to house all it lumberjacks. When one became vacant, the loggers would scramble for the right to move in—grabbing some sheltered living space.[10] Although still shown on some topographical maps, nothing remains of Grabtown. It burned to the ground before the beginning of the twentieth century.

San Francisco in 1849.

Because it took two days to travel between his mill and Redwood City, Froment built the Summit Springs Hotel at a mid-way point in 1868. Eventually, eight families came to live there and operated a shop, saloon, store, blacksmith shop, school, and stable. It was at the Summit Springs House, in 1871, that old Nosey Tom lost his nose in a fight. Like Grabtown, nothing remains of Summit Springs. Its site is about 500 yards east of Skyline Boulevard off Kings Mountain Road.[11]

Nearby, and about the same time that Summit Springs began offering services, Frank and Honora King opened a saloon, and later built a boardinghouse as well. The two became legendary characters of the mountain country, and, of course, Kings Mountain is named for them. Mr. King kept the saloon and cut hair. Mrs. King ran the boardinghouse and prepared wonderful meals for their guests. Local historians report that Mr. King, of German origin, was the favorite fan of his wife's cooking, for he was "very stout," and this was to blame for his "inactivity." The Kings situated their "Kings Mountain Brow House" on land partly belonging to the Borden and Hatch lumber company and the Greer family. When, in 1888, the Greers finally got around to suing the Kings for squatting on their lands for 20 years or so, the judge found in the Greers favor, but gave the Kings 30 acres anyway.

Two ports developed simultaneously on the bayside to serve the lumber industry. At today's East Palo Alto, Isaiah C. Woods established Ravenswood in 1849. Here was the best place on the south bayshore for a port. Solid land came close to deep water at this point. Nearby was good acreage for farming. Woods, himself, established his own Woodside Dairy. Of course, the logging districts were also close.

Woods was born at Saco, Maine, in 1825 to a well-established family. Unfortunately, his father died at sea when Woods was only 14, and he was forced to help support his family—his mother and two younger brothers. He became a successful storekeeper, and married Eliza Fitch in 1845. He left New England in 1847, to seek fortune. As owner of a schooner, Woods left New Bedford and reached Honolulu in October of 1848. He learned of the discovery of gold in California and arrived at San Francisco in November. Here he sold his cargo and rented out his ship. He dabbled in various financial dealings—banking, commodities, and passenger ships. As an early leading businessman, he helped the city in various civic and cultural matters. He assisted in establishing the first public school and the Chamber of Commerce. He sponsored the performance of Stephen Massett, a popular singer

Redwood City in 1878.

and actor. Besides his Ravenswood investment, Woods also became president of the Pacific and Atlantic Railroad Company in 1855.[12] It is likely that Woods's interest in Ravenswood was related to his dreams of a transcontinental railroad. He planned for Ravenswood to be the western terminus of the railroad. He foresaw a railroad bridge across the bay that would not be completed until 1911 with the construction of a low-level trestle from Dumbarton Point.

Unfortunately for Woods, his hopes for Ravenswood were dashed. Local historians blame competition from the other bayside port, Redwood City, for his failure. There are also reports of questionable business dealings that forced Woods out of the country. However, these stories seem exaggerated. Woods was a victim of the San Francisco business depression of 1855. During that downturn, he was forced to abandon his dreams of a railroad and sell his San Francisco home. Much of his Ravenswood property was disposed during a sheriff's sale. He left the county with his wife and son for Australia, but he returned to California in 1857 to become involved with the organization of southwestern stagecoach companies. In fact, he was appointed the superintendent of the San Antonio and San Diego Stage Line, the first to provide passenger and mail service to The Pacific Coast.

During the Civil War, he served under John C. Fremont as a captain in the Commissary Department. He became the transportation overseer for Missouri and rose in rank to colonel. After Fremont was relieved, Woods went to Nicaragua, where he helped create a stagecoach line and railroad. The effort failed in 1868, and he returned to California that year. The idea that he was chased out of the country in 1855 can be further doubted because Woods's mother remained in the Menlo Park area during all these years. She finally died there in 1869. In San Francisco, Woods resumed his business career. He managed a wood preservative company. He later helped to establish a winery in San Jose. He died in the home of his brother on Mare Island in 1880.

Redwood City, the second of the two bayside ports, had a successful history. As discussed previously, this is the story of Dr. Robert O. Tripp and company. They established an embarcadero here in 1849. Lumber cut from the Woodside and Kings Mountain vicinity was dragged to the port by teams of oxen. At high tide the lumber was piloted out the winding slough to the Bay. Around the embarcadero clustered a variety of merchants and other businesses—and thus, Redwood City was born.

Of course, many people were squatting on the Arguello family's Rancho de las Pulgas. The Arguellos called on the services of Simon M. Mezes to protect their properties in court. Mezes came to California in February of 1850. Evidence suggests that he had been president of a bank in Puerto Rico. Upon arriving here, he recognized that his legal and financial background, plus his ability to read and write in Spanish and English, would enable him to start a legal practice defending the claims of the old Mexican land grantees. Mezes successfully piloted the Rancho de las Pulgas title through the United States Land Commission and various court challenges. For his services he received about a quarter of the rancho, including the embarcadero area.

Saloon at the summit of La Honda Road.

He surveyed the property, divided it up into lots, and sold the parcels to the folks already present. His map laid out the streets in downtown Redwood City as they are known today. Of course the former squatters were not thrilled with all this. They had hoped that Mezes would fail with his defense of the Arguello family claim and thus they would be able to acquire the land without having to pay for it—invoking squatters' rights claims. Mezes irritated the locals still more by naming the place on his map Mezesville. The lots sold for about $75 each, and most people did buy the property they were sitting on. However, when the post office was established in 1856, they chose the name Redwood City for their community and not Mezesville.

Logging was the first great industry for San Mateo County as the American period began. After a couple of decades, the great stands of Redwoods were mostly taken; those that remained became less and less accessible. Lumber

Cutting down an old growth Redwood.

from other parts of California and the West Coast became easier to harvest.

During the 1860s, agriculture rose above the lumber industry in importance to the county's economy. By the 1880s lumbering was in decline, although forms of logging activities lasted deep into the twentieth century and are even revived from time to time to this day.

Water

Hermann Schussler, designer of the Crystal Springs Dam. Completed in 1889, it is the largest concrete block dam in the world.

Of all the peninsula resources utilized by San Franciscans to make their city great, water was most important. Lumber, agricultural products and additional food items could be imported from other locations. Water, however, could not. The padres of the Spanish era had recognized the lack of adequate fresh water as a substantial limitation at Mission San Francisco de Asis. Their decision in 1785 to create an agricultural outpost down the peninsula was greatly influenced by this realization. By 1860, the population of San Francisco was approaching 78,000. Lack of fresh water was universally recognized as the city's greatest resource problem. Staggering financial losses were sustained throughout the 1850s because of fires. Absence of water for fire fighting was a condition that had to be remedied. Even drinking water was difficult to obtain. Water had to be barged in from Marin County and then was sold by the barrel. Water peddlers had regular routes throughout the city. Some strapped barrels to the backs of donkeys and sold the precious liquid by the bucket. One source notes that during certain times of the year, buckets of water were sold for a gold dollar each.[13]

Recognizing a business opportunity, private companies were organized to answer the demand. The Mountain Lake Water Company became the first to deliver water into the city from the Presidio. In 1856, the Bensley Company was formed and successfully dammed the mouth of Lobos Creek under the direction of Engineer Alexei Waldemar von Schmidt. Now two million gallons a day could be brought in by flume and tunnel. In 1858, George H. Ensign organized yet another company, the Spring Valley Water Company. Originally it drew water from a single spring near Portsmouth Square, never producing more than 5,000 gallons a day.

The Bensley Company was certainly the most important water company servicing San Francisco. However, in 1860 its chief engineer, von Schmidt, left the company after a bitter dispute. He then offered himself to Bensley's smaller competitor, the Spring Valley Water Company. As Spring Valley's new chief engineer, and a major stockholder to boot, von Schmidt began to plan bringing more substantial water supplies in from newly formed San Mateo County.

He decided to place a dam on Pilarcitos Creek, due east of today's coastside community of Montara. Although the watershed site was only half a square mile in size, it had many things going for it. It had the highest annual rainfall, at 49 inches, on the peninsula. It had a good high elevation at 1,875 feet, giving it rapid flow into the city. Von Schmidt finished construction of a preliminary system in 1862, and began delivering peninsula water to the city that summer. A grand celebration on the Fourth of July marked the occasion.

In 1864, von Schmidt left the Spring Valley Company, and Calvin Brown became chief engineer. On October 8 of that year, Brown hired Hermann Schussler as his assistant. The 21-year-old immigrant from Zurich could hardly speak English. He arrived in San Francisco riding a horse with little more than a carpetbag of personal belongings. However, he was well schooled in Switzerland and already had engineering experience. Schussler's salary began at $50 a month. His first assignment was to assist in completing the Pilarcitos Dam project.

Meanwhile, Spring Valley's greatest rival, the Bensley Company, was encountering difficulties with its water supply. Soil was eroding into its Lobos Creek reservoir, and its customers began complaining about muddy water. Not long after that, Bensley was caught tapping into a Spring Valley main. Bensley failed soon after, and Spring Valley became the sole supplier of water for San Francisco.

Construction of the Crystal Springs Dam.

In May 1866, Schussler became chief engineer for Spring Valley. His first accomplishment was the completion of the Pilarcitos Dam to a height of 70 feet in 1867. At the time, it was one of the world's tallest earthen dams, containing some 600 million gallons of water. Taking a lesson from the Bensley fiasco, Schussler made it a policy for the Spring Valley Water Company to purchase not just the reservoir site for future projects, but to acquire the surrounding watershed area as well to guarantee the purity of Spring Valley's product.

In 1868, Schussler built an earthen dam at San Andreas Creek, just west of present-day Millbrae. San Andreas Lake, like Pilarcitos, had a gravity-feed system delivering its water into the city. During his long career, Schussler developed a great reputation in the fields of pressure piping and tunnel engineering. His first major work in these fields involved setting pipe through a tunnel from Pilarcitos Lake to San Andreas Lake. The project was begun in 1868 and went 3,400 feet. Few projects like it had ever been accomplished before.

Next, Schussler began to plan for the creation of Upper and Lower Crystal Springs Lakes. In order to build dams for these, the Spring Valley Water Company would need to enlist the aid of the courts. Within the Crystal Springs Valley, many farms had been established along with a small town. The courts condemned these properties, at times reimbursing the owners at only 10 percent of the actual real estate values.

In 1877, Schussler completed Upper Crystal Springs Lake, just west of today's Belmont. Two years later, the town of Searsville in the southern part of the county was condemned as part of a project to create Searsville Lake. Schussler's greatest project was the building of Crystal Springs Dam in 1890, which allowed for the creation of Lower Crystal Springs Lake, just west of today's Hillsborough. Schussler built this dam with interlocking concrete blocks. At 150 feet high, it is the largest of its kind ever built.

By 1900, the Spring Valley Water Company owned 20,000 acres of peninsula watershed, from the San Francisco County line to the southern reaches of San Mateo County. As a monopoly, the company made great profits, although the public did not always appreciate its business maneuverings. It was also the source of continued speculation. Many wondered when San Francisco would purchase its water supply, as other great cities across the United States had done already.

In 1875, the great California capitalist William Ralston felt the time was fast approaching. He and Charles Felton bought Spring Valley, hoping to sell the holdings of the company to the city at a huge profit in order to recoup on losses sustained at Ralston's Bank of California. Ralston had guessed wrong. The city was not ready to buy Spring Valley. Because of his error, he was fired from his position as president of the Bank of California. The next day, his body was found floating in San Francisco Bay. Perhaps he died as a result of a swimming accident; perhaps it was suicide.

Finally in 1900, the citizens of San Francisco voted to adopt a new charter that would allow the city to own its water supply. San Francisco leaders began planning for a system that would last throughout the new twentieth century and into the twenty-first. They targeted Hetch Hetchy Valley in Yosemite National Park, a beautiful spot about 20 miles north of Yosemite Valley. It is about half the size of Yosemite Valley. The city would build a dam here, and pipe the sierra water across the Central Valley, through the Coastal Mountains, over the San Francisco Bay and up to the San Mateo County watershed lakes, all by gravity feed. From the start, conservationists led by John Muir opposed the project.

The Great Earthquake and Fire of 1906 gave further impetus to those wanting the change. Motivated primarily by profits, the Spring Valley Water Company was accused of not properly maintaining its water delivery systems. A great tribute to Hermann Schussler can be made in that his dams held. The massive Crystal Springs Dam had not a crack. If it had failed, the little hamlet of San Mateo would have been washed away. However, pipes and other portions of the infrastructure did buckle. Spring Valley was widely blamed for the absence of water when it came time to fight the fires, which did a great amount of damage to San Francisco.

After a 13-year fight, the City of San Francisco prevailed. Because this project was to be initiated on federal lands, it took an act of Congress to go forward. In 1913, President Woodrow Wilson signed the Raker Act allowing the Hetch Hetchy project to begin. John Muir died a few months later, some say of a broken heart.

The next step was the passing of a $45.6 million bond issue to get the construction going. Eventually the citizens of San Francisco would have to tax themselves for $120 million to accomplish the ambitious project. For most of the project's life, Michael Maurice O'Shaughnessy was the lead engineer. Mayor "Sunny Jim" Rolf hired O'Shaughnessy. Rolf gave the Dublin, Ireland educated engineer considerable freedom in order to get the job done.

This was a daunting task. Considerable construction difficulties would need to be overcome, to say nothing of a World War, inflation and then the Great Depression. One of the first things that had to be done was the creation of a 68 mile railroad to supply the construction site at Hetch Hetchy. Completed in 1917, it hauled cement, personnel and everything else necessary around the clock. Meanwhile, City sawmills carved up some 27 million board feet of wood for construction purposes.

Counting all the dam building, powerhouses, and other improvements, perhaps the most amazing engineering and construction achievement involved the creation of a 28.5 mile-long tunnel through the Coastal Mountain Range. The tunnel would cost nearly a million dollars a mile and 12 lives. Altogether 89 men lost their lives during the building of the great project.

Meanwhile, two years after the earthquake and during a financial crisis, William B. Bourn stepped in and purchased the land, the delivery systems, buildings and power plants of the Spring Valley Water Company, and immediately commenced the job of selling it to the City. Bourn was born in San

Francisco in 1857. He inherited the failing Empire Gold Mine, and was able to revive its profitability. During the 1890s, he invested in several local gas companies, selling them off at great profit to the emerging Pacific Gas and Electric Company. He used this capital to buy the Spring Valley Water Company.

Now that he had it, he would have to deal with San Francisco politicians, bureaucrats, attorneys, engineers, and the people of the city in general in order to sell it. Recognizing this as a long-term negotiation, Bourn decided to buy up 700 acres of land for $90,000 to build a lavish estate at the southern end of Upper Crystal Springs Lake, which he called *Filoli* (short for his motto—Fight, Love, Live). He hired famous architect Willis Polk to design the home. Polk modeled the mansion after an Irish country house with adaptation for expanded space and classical embellishments.[14] In September 1917, the Bourns moved into their new estate. They were going to have to spend some time there. The sale to the city was not finally achieved until March 1930. The citizens of San Francisco bonded themselves again—this time for $41 million to buy the company.

Cost overruns, political problems, and general bad temper because of the Depression of the 1930s resulted in the removal of O'Shaughnessy in 1932. A new city charter created the Public Utilities Commission, and O'Shaughnessy was made a mere consultant. William Bourn died in 1934, and so did O'Shaughnessy—on October 12. Only 12 days later, on October 24, the first Hetch Hetchy water flowed through to the San Mateo watershed at a water temple on the east side of Upper Crystal Springs Lake, especially built for the celebration (this was a temporary structure; today's Pulgas Water Temple was built two years later).

The completion of the Hetch Hetchy project certainly proved beneficial for the citizens of San Francisco, San Mateo, and other counties in central California. At a capacity of 400 million gallons a day, Hetch Hetchy could produce ten times that of the old Spring Valley Water Company.[15] Water now traveled 150 miles across California to the watershed lakes in San Mateo County.

The 20,000 acres once owned by a private company now belonged to a public body, the San Francisco Public Utilities Commission's Water Department, whose responsibility it became to keep those 20,000 acres clean and pristine in order to protect the water supply. Thus, the peninsula's first significant acreage to be set aside as open space came into being. One wonders, if John Muir could have known that the peninsula would now have this forested watershed, with its wild life habitat, protected from the waves of development in the twentieth and twenty-first centuries, whether he might not have been so disappointed with the passage of the Raker Act and the creation of the Hetch Hetchy water project.

Agriculture

For many forty-niners, the true opportunity of California laid in returning to occupations they had been most familiar with back home. For the majority, this meant farming. The expansion of San Francisco during the nineteenth century gave those who knew the land a new start. Rowdy San Franciscans of the Gold Rush era may have preferred to drink, but they had to eat, too. No better place to provide agricultural products to the city existed than its closest neighbor—San Mateo County.

The first crops to come up to the city were potatoes and cabbage grown by American and Irish pioneers in what is now the northern part of San Mateo County. J. G. Knowles and James Johnston established the first dairies about 1853. As discussed earlier, Johnston's place was out on the coast, and he probably concentrated on cheese and butter production because of the distance and transportation problems associated with getting commodities up to the city. Knowles, however, established his dairy in today's Daly City area, and was the first from down on the peninsula to bring milk to San Francisco.[16]

Knowles came to California from Ohio during the excitement of 1849. He tried his hand at mining for two years on the Feather and Yuba Rivers, and then gave up to enter into the dairy business. He started in the Sacramento area, and then, at the age of 25, created his 140-acre peninsula dairy. He became an established part of the community in the North County. He married here and had seven children, five of them sons.

Brothers Isaac and E. W. Steele, former carpenters from New York, also arrived during the Gold Rush. By 1857, they were engaged in the dairy business at Point Reyes in Marin County. In 1862, they expanded their operations to the south coast of today's San Mateo County (the south coast from San Gregorio Creek to Point Ano Nuevo was not originally part of San Mateo County). They leased some 17,000 acres in the Pescadero vicinity from Loren Coburn, who had consolidated a couple of the old Mexican land grants and had become the greatest landowner in the area. The Steele ranches became substantial providers of cheese and butter for the San Francisco market.

The Steele family had strong abolitionist beliefs. One of Isaac's and E. W.'s brothers served in the Civil War as a general for the Union. In 1864, to show their patriotic spirit, the Steeles made a huge cheese as part of a benefit for the Sanitary Commission, an early progeny of the Red Cross. This wheel of cheese weighed in at about two tons. It was exhibited at San Francisco and then auctioned off for $2,820.

By 1867, the Steeles had expanded their land holdings into 11 ranches ranging from Pescadero to Ano Nuevo. From their headquarters at Green Oaks Ranch, they managed more than 1,000 dairy cows, which supplied San Francisco with thousands of tons of dairy products on a weekly basis. When the south coast became part of San Mateo County in 1868, the Steeles easily became the most important dairymen in the county.

From its former status as open range during Mexican times, San Mateo County was completely changed by 1860 as a land of farms. Travelogue writer Baylard Taylor noticed the difference. On his first trip to California in 1849, he walked from San Francisco to Monterey to witness the Constitutional Convention. Once on the peninsula, he recorded that during a 20-mile stretch, he could not even find a spot to have some fresh drinking water. The only things of note that represented human occupation were the buildings belonging to the Sanchez family at Rancho Buri Buri and the old mission outpost building at San Mateo.[17]

Ten years later, Taylor was amazed at the change. He saw farm after farm on El Camino Real—likewise down the center of the county's Crystal Springs Valley, and over on the coast, there were 150 farms. It was obvious that agriculture had become the main occupation of the county's residents. Besides the tons of butter and cheese produced by the dairies, farmers in 1860 harvested 165,000 bushels of wheat, 100,000 bushels of oats, 2,900 barrels of beans, and additional crops such as corn and rice. They also produced wool, mutton, and pork. The state census that year credited the total value of agricultural lands and the personal property of farmers of San Mateo County at $1,490,407.

During the late 1860s and early 1870s, American and Irish farmers in the North County experienced a series of growing seasons that were particularly cold and foggy. Their barley, oats, and other crops did not fare well. A potato blight at the end of the decade made things worse, and many of the settlers had to give up.

Cascade Cheese Factory and residence of R. E. Steele, Pescadero in 1878.

However, for farmers in other parts of the county, particularly out on the coast, the 1870s were good years. In 1873, a visitor to Half Moon Bay noted that crops of grain were being grown "from the ocean to the mountains."[18] In the Purisima Valley southeast of Half Moon Bay, Henry Dobbel had planted 900 acres of potatoes by 1878. Meanwhile, Irish immigrants had established themselves in the Valley near the village of Purisima at a place that became known as Irish Ridge. Here they also planted potatoes. During the 1870s, at Purisima, Portuguese farmers planted hay, grains, and horse beans.[19]

Serving this part of the coast was a wharf built by Josiah Ames, near Half Moon Bay. It was noted that, on average, a thousand sacks of grain were shipped from here each day during the California grain boom of the 1870s.

Without doubt, the success of farmers on the coast in the 1870s was assisted by one of their neighbors—farmer, blacksmith, newspaper publisher, politician, and inventor R. I. Knapp. Knapp hailed from Sullivan County, New York. He came to California by sailing to the Isthmus of Panama, crossing it via covered wagon, and then boarding a ship for San Francisco, arriving here in 1863. He first settled at Bloomfield, near Petaluma in Sonoma County, but by 1871 had found his way to the Half Moon Bay area.

On this isolated part of the coast, he dabbled in farming, but was better known for his blacksmith business. He repaired farmers' tools, shoed their horses, made wagons, and began inventing things like a two-wheel cart and, more importantly, a side hill plow. In 1967, his granddaughter remembered her grandfather as "a staunch Yankee with strong principles."[20] She recalled that he was most considerate of others: "There was a watering trough in front of his shop where large lumber and grain teams could water, and also a separate weather-sheltered faucet, and a tin cup hanging on a chain." In fact, she told how Knapp created Half Moon Bay's early water supply by building a reservoir and then used flumes to act as a delivery system, complete with filters and gravel traps.

It was probably because of his consideration of others that he invented his innovative plow. Knapp watched as his neighbors struggled to till the fertile but difficult to work hillsides on the coast. They were mostly using the Killgore Plow, which had a beveled blade, but was heavy and clumsy to use. After repairing Killgore after Killgore, he decided to create his own plow in 1873. It quickly became so successful and unique that he had three different patents on the implement by 1875. Initially, Knapp made every plow by hand, hammering out each share with a sledge and anvil. By using a carbon steel bottom, hard wood beams and handles plus a cast iron standard, he invented a lighter, but sturdier, plow. In addition, he attached a simple locking device that kept the plow in place when adjusting the blade. With hillside farming, reversing the blade was necessary after completing each furrow. A farmer could now, for the first time, reverse the blade without having to let go of the plow and thus the animal harnessed to it.

A reporter from the *San Mateo County Gazette* made a trip to Knapp's Half Moon Bay plant in 1878. The writer described each plow as weighing 75 to 80 pounds when fully equipped—light compared to anything before—and yet the plow was said to be "strong and durable and ought to last a lifetime."[21] The reporter mentioned that Knapp was busy "making a hundred and has an order to send the lot to a firm in San Francisco for shipment to Oregon. . . ." The reporter also noted that Knapp had invented a special machine for cutting and grinding his shares into shape. The instrument, some would call a drop hammer, could cut "steel plates a quarter of an inch thick like a piece of paper while a change in the appliances of the same machine fixes it for punching the same plates, with a single motion."

Eventually, the plow became popular in other places. Knapp's plows were sold throughout California and also were very much in demand in the Hawaiian Islands. When the patents expired, two midwest companies, the John Deere Plow Company of Moline, Illinois, and the South Bend Chilled Plow Company of Indiana, produced exact copies of the Knapp Plow.

Knapp was sort of a Renaissance man of the San Mateo County coastside. Among his many interests was the buying and running of a newspaper, the *Coast Advocate*.

The Millbrae Dairy and the San Mateo Dairy were just two of numerous dairies.

Granddaughter Ethel remembers how the press was set up on one side of the shop: "My aunt and uncle sat on high stools setting type, sometimes one of us on their knee."

The *Coast Advocate* became a Prohibitionist newspaper under Knapp's ownership. In fact, Knapp became a state leader within the Prohibitionist Party. He twice won its nomination for governor. Sadly, he had little following, even in his own county. In the election of 1900, he ran for state senate and received only 50 votes out of some 2,500 ballots cast. He moved away from the coast after that defeat and lived in San Francisco. He died in 1904.[22]

While the farmers on the coast were succeeding with their endeavors, over on the bayside, during the 1870s, dairy ranchers continued to expand their operations. In fact by the end of the Civil War, dairy ranching had replaced logging as the county's most important industry. The 2,500-acre R. G. Sneath Dairy at today's San Bruno was an excellent example of this blossoming activity. Its huge barn, 248 feet by 48 feet, was three stories tall. Also on the property was a fully equipped blacksmith shop, a cooling house where the milk was cooled after its straining, and a milk-can washing and sterilizing center. Teams of six mules per wagon hauled Sneath Dairy milk to a plant on Howard Street in San Francisco. It is said that California's first registered purebred animal, a calf named "Cloudy," came from the Sneath Dairy.

Other bayside dairies of note included the Millbrae Dairy, known for its Holstein cattle, and the Baden Dairy in today's South San Francisco area, owned by Robert Asbury. Among the laborers at the early dairies was a boy named John D. Daly.

Of English-Irish origins, John Daly was born in Boston, Massachusetts, in 1842. As a boy, he gathered cranberries and worked at other odd jobs in order to earn money to help pay his family's passage from Boston to California. The Dalys made it to the Isthmus of Panama, but here the mother died of the Yellow Fever. Somehow, Daly became separated from the rest of his family, who returned to the East. John pressed on to California on his own, arriving in San Francisco at the age of nine without any family or friends.

He went to work on the dairy ranches in the northern part of San Mateo County. As a laborer, he met Lillie Carrick, who was visiting the proprieties of the ranch he was working. He courted the

John Daly's San Mateo Dairy.

sixteen-year-old girl and married her. Unfortunately, she died a short time later. Daly eventually met and married another—Florence Smart.

By 1870, Daly established his own dairy in the very northernmost section of San Mateo County. He distributed milk and eggs from a plant on Valencia Street in San Francisco, under the name of the San Mateo Dairy. On his 250-acre ranch, he built a ranch house and barns that became among the largest structures in the North County. He employed about a dozen laborers, who later indicated they had great respect for the man. One noted: "Mr. Daly had very little schooling but possessed a great intellect. He could estimate the size and condition of land—good or bad—while engineers were still figuring. He had a general knowledge of most every subject, especially business and science."[23]

When the April 18, 1906, Great Earthquake hit, Daly and other ranchers joined local farmers in providing food for refugees leaving San Francisco via the Mission Road. Like other residents of North County, everything would change for Daly after the Earthquake. In May of 1906, he and seven other dairymen who had been distributing milk in San Francisco found their customers so badly scattered that they consolidated their routes and founded the Dairy Delivery Company—the forerunner of the Borden Company.

Only one year later, Daly joined other North County landowners by selling much of his property to the San Francisco refugees so they could begin building their suburban homes near the streetcar line. Daly did retain between three and four acres between San Jose Avenue and Mission Road. He moved his old horse barn to this place and built a small house. Here he devoted his time to flower growing.

Already a power in county politics, Daly also successfully dabbled in real estate and banking. When Daly City incorporated in 1911, his name was taken for the town out of respect for this self-made man on whose land the original city was situated. He died in 1923, at the age of 81.

By the end of the 1870s, out of a total population of 8,700 people, 960 said they owned or leased their own farms, and 40 said they were dairymen. Thus, agricultural activities continued to be easily the most important occupation in San Mateo County, especially when including the many laborers who worked these farms and ranches. Ten years later, in 1890, San Mateo County ranked second in the state of California in cheese production, at 522,000 pounds, and fifth in milk output. In 1880, its largest crop was potatoes at 200,000 bushels, but by 1890 this had decreased to 70,000. This did not mean that San Mateo County farmers had become less productive—instead it pointed to the fact that the farmers were being attracted to new kinds of crops and that the farming population itself was starting to change.

By the 1890s, Italian and Japanese growers began to influence San Mateo County agricultural history. These hard-working new immigrants found great success in farming, especially in crops that had not been emphasized before.

Perhaps the best example is the local history of the artichoke. Initially introduced to the United States in 1806, the first planting of artichokes for commercial purposes in California is said to have taken place in the 1890s at today's El Granada by Italian farmer Dante Dianda.[24] Further down the coast, at Half Moon Bay, John L. Debenedetti, the son of Joseph Debenedetti, an early merchant of Pescadero and Half Moon Bay, became known as the "Artichoke King"[25] for his work in encouraging Italian immigrants to come to the area and engage in artichoke growing. The Italian government later recognized Debenedetti's services to the Italian American community by conferring on him the prestigious Chevelier Cross.

During the 1890s, the *Coast Advocate* recognized the increased agricultural activity on the coastside and spoke of the steamer *Gypsy* that sailed every Friday from San Francisco with freight to trade with the farmers of Half Moon Bay at an outlet at Pillar Point. A little south from there, J. P. Ames's wharf, now referred to as Amesport, also saw steamer traffic. One account tells of the ship *Santa Cruz* stopping at Amesport for 6,000 sacks of grain on a Saturday night and continuing its voyage at Pigeon Point by taking several hundred barrels of oil from the whaling station there.[26]

By 1906, Italian farmers had 1,500 acres of artichokes under cultivation just around Half Moon Bay. In 1909, they began growing Brussels sprouts in the San Pedro Valley.

In North County the Italians had significant influence as well. In 1894, it was noted that farmers in the North County had shipped almost two million pounds of cabbage to markets as far east as Chicago. After 1900, North County Italian farmers were also specializing in artichokes, sprouts, cauliflower, turnips, carrots, beets, and strawberries. They helped revive potato growing by introducing a variety of the Oregon potato—hardier and more blight-resistant than the potatoes formerly planted here.

Japanese growers in San Mateo County became involved with vegetable farming in the late nineteenth century. They also helped launch the flower business. Already skilled in growing flowers back in their native land, Italians joined the Japanese in flower growing by the end of the nineteenth century. From their farms in North County, they exported a variety of blooms, including violets.

Just after 1900, professor of horticulture at the University of Tokyo, I. Takahashi, opened a nursery at Montara and started the strawflower industry in San Mateo County. Recognizing this success once more, Italian farmers just down the road at Half Moon Bay began to realize that growing flowers could net more cash than food crops and began growing flowers there as well.

Expanding their markets, of course, assisted the flower growers to make their industry succeed. In 1904, Italian growers in North County were able to export their violets to the World's Fair and Olympic Games in Saint Louis. Also that year, H. L. Goertzhain of Redwood City figured out that by using cheesecloth to filter the rays of the sun, chrysanthemum growing could be significantly increased. By 1907, the Enomoto family had begun extensive utilization of this method with great success. In 1915, Sadakusu Enomoto shipped a carload of chrysanthemums to New Orleans for the All Saints Day celebration and proved that mums could be exported long distances with substantial profits.

By 1900, the face of agriculture had changed quite a bit. The number of farms had actually decreased from 669 in 1880, to 574. However, land dedicated to agriculture had doubled between 1870 and 1890. Farm size during those 20 years had grown from 200 to 320 acres. By 1900, there existed 39 large farms of 1,000 acres or more and many small farms of 50 acres or less. The trend of smaller farms was especially prevalent in North County. After the 1906 Earthquake, suburban communities at Daly City, San Bruno, and South San Francisco saw their farmlands begin to give way to housing. Dairies disappeared and were replaced by hog, poultry, and vegetable farms. Flower growing continued to be important. Even as late as 1920, 20 percent of the land in North County was given over to flower growing.

Out on the coast, farming activities were much enhanced by better transportation. By 1908, the Ocean Shore Railroad was serving the farmers of the coastside as far down as Tunitas Creek. In 1920, the Ocean Shore went out of business, but four years before, an auto road had been built to San Francisco, and trucks could now bring crops to market in San Francisco.

Chrysanthemum growing, the main type of flower grown in Redwood City, was first dominated by Eikichi and Sadakusu Enomoto in the early 1900s.

Coastside farming, March 1971. Credit: Robert Toren.

In the years before World War II, agriculture continued to represent an important part of San Mateo County's coastside and bayside economies. In 1930, the number of livestock of all kinds was 17,533, up 5,000 from 1920. This included nearly 10,000 head of dairy cattle. In 1940, the number of dairy cattle increased still further to more than 13,500. San Mateo County dairy products that year were valued at $911,168. Field crops that year were valued at $439,000. Fruits and nuts brought in $181,000. Vegetables brought in $2,454,000. Some 5,361 acres, valued at $401,000, were devoted to the growing of peas. Artichokes were on 2,356 acres, valued at $309,000. Brussels sprouts were on

2,071 acres, valued at $260,000. Lettuce was grown on 1,430 acres, valued at $352,000, and cabbage was farmed on 1,038 acres, valued at $196,000.

Besides dairy cattle, there still was a significant amount of other kinds of livestock in the county. In 1920, the value of pork was $253,000. By 1940, the 58,000 swine had a value of $696,000. As related in Chapter 5, San Francisco had made it illegal to raise pigs in the City during the 1930s, and many of the swine farms from there had taken up land in San Mateo County—particularly in the north. The 207,000 poultry population in 1940 was valued at $242,000, the 2,000 sheep at $16,000, and the 48,000 rabbits at $17,000.

Even the number of farms was up to 829, far surpassing nineteenth-century figures. However, by 1940 only 4 percent of the population of the county counted themselves as working in agriculture. Then the onset of World War II and the housing boom of the postwar period pushed agriculture almost completely off the bayside and made intrusions on the coastside as well, minimalizing most agricultural endeavors, with the exception of flower growing.

In 1940, flowers brought in more money, at $2,712,000, than all the vegetable crops combined. As late as 1970, San Mateo County ranked second in the state in the production of flowers, with a crop valued at $23,511,000.

Bayland Resources

The maritime industries of San Mateo County have had considerable impact. They supplied San Francisco and other markets with a variety of foods and other products. Interestingly, with the exception of coastal whaling, nearly all of this activity has been on the bayside and not on the coast. Because of the lack of a good harbor, fishing on the coastside was inconsiderable during the nineteenth century. The good harbor at Half Moon Bay was not constructed until midway through the twentieth century.

To prove this assertion, we can look at the report of David Starr Jordan of the U.S. Commission of Fish and Fisheries in 1880. He was making a survey of the maritime industries on the West Coast and found the San Mateo Coast fishing activities "very inconsiderable."[27] He commented: "The towns along the ocean—Pescadero, San Gregorio, Purisima, and Half Moon Bay—are all too small to offer any local market, and their means of communication with the interior are so imperfect that they cannot compete with Monterey and Santa Cruz in supplying the San Francisco markets. He could find only one Portuguese immigrant and ten others "who fish when they can find nothing else to do" on the entire coast. Another report, this one from 1904, reports the entire catch on the coastside as a 75,000-pound harvest of abalone by two men at Pigeon Point, which earned them $2,500.

On the bayside it is a different story. The rich environment of the San Francisco Bay allowed for a variety of fish and shellfish industries, the most lucrative being the oyster industry.

During Gold Rush days, oysters were the most sought-after seafood in the world. Up in the diggings, a plate of them cost $20. Because of this great demand, oysters from the San Francisco Bay were tried on the market. Unfortunately, they proved too small and gritty in taste for the forty-niners. During the 1850s, a group of businessmen attempted to bring larger Washington State oysters to San Francisco. Among these businessmen was John Stillwell Morgan, an oysterman from New York who California Historian H. H. Bancroft credits with retrieving a cargo of the bivalves from Washington in 1853. Until 1867, Morgan's and three other companies provided California with its oysters. He owned underwater acres off Washington to harvest the oysters and 30 acres off Sausalito to hold the catch until market conditions were right. A disease killed off significant populations of the Washington oysters in 1867, and oysters were nowhere to be found in California until two years later.

The year 1869 brought the transcontinental railroad, and A. Booth and Company shipped three carloads of live eastern oysters to San Francisco. The three carloads flooded the market, and so A. Booth took a page from Morgan's book and stored the oysters off Sausalito. Oystermen in California took note that not only did these much-desired eastern oysters survive in the Bay, but they grew considerably.

San Mateo County oyster beds located in San Mateo in 1890's. Besides a commercial opportunity, oysters have a natural filtering benefit to bay water. In 2006, research in oyster farming in the bay expanded with government funding for studies in South San Francisco and Redwood City.

In 1872, Samuel J. Purseglove acquired underwater lands surrounding an old wreck known as Corville's Hulk, just north of a slough off today's Millbrae. He became the first to bring eastern oysters to the mudflats off San Mateo County. Meanwhile, in 1871, John S. Morgan bought out the holdings of A. Booth and Company. In 1874, he built his first establishment off San Mateo County, near Millbrae as well. Morgan set out to methodically buy out all his competition along the San Francisco

Oyster industry floats and packing boxes, San Francisco Bay, 1891.

Bay. He found that his oyster beds off San Mateo County were particularly valuable. He knew that during times of floods, silty water created oyster kills off Marin and Alameda Counties. With the added problem of siltation derived from the hydraulic mining operations in the Sierra and its foothills, the more remote bayline of San Mateo County became the best bet for continuing the eastern oyster business. At a point in the 1870s, the San Mateo bayline became the only place where commercial oyster operations existed, and until its final demise in the 1930s, this was the only place that oysters were harvested.

The increasing value of the industry can be determined in part by the mounting value of the underwater lots reserved for Morgan's operations. Lots valued at one dollar an acre in 1870 could bring one hundred dollars in 1890. This had everything to do with the continued desirability of the oyster during the latter part of the nineteenth century. In the United States it was still the most popular form of seafood. French observer P. de Broca wrote in 1876: "This delicious article of food has become so necessary with every class of population that scarcely a town in the whole country can be found without its regular supply . . . It is considered one of the most common and cheap means of subsistence."[28]

By the 1880s, the United States was the world's greatest producer of oysters for market. The gross value of the catch was more than $15 million in 1891—more than five times that of salmon, which was second. In California, the oyster was likewise the most valuable fish food delivered to the market. By the last decade of the nineteenth century, California was the sixth in the nation in oyster production, and virtually all of the marketable oysters came from the beds off the San Mateo County bayline. In 1897, the catch was valued at $1 million. The peninsula's oysters were not only sold in California, but the San Mateo County oyster industry was the sole supplier for the entire Pacific slope of North America and the islands of the Pacific as well.

While the marketing of eastern oysters in the West was successful, the industry faced vexing problems. For one, although easterns were noted for growing some three times faster in the San Francisco Bay than on their native beds, they could not reproduce here. Some oystermen felt the Bay waters' summer temperature did not get high enough to allow for reproduction. Therefore, each year, boxcars full of "seed" oysters were sent west. The seeds were placed in barrels—about 5,000 in each—and then packed in ice for the trip across country. Between 1887 and 1899, an average of more than 100 box carloads were sent annually.

Once the seeds arrived off the San Mateo County bayline, the Morgan Company would prepare beds as carefully as a farmer cultivates his fields. The beds had to be leveled. Clean shell was then laid down, upon which the young oysters could attach themselves. Seeds, which were about the size of a dime, were first brought to the beds off Belmont and East Palo Alto, where the water was calmer, allowing for the seed to "set" more easily. After they grew to about the size of a quarter, the oysters were plucked out of the Bay and moved to the beds off San Mateo and Millbrae, where the tidal action was greater, and hence there was more food. After the oysters grew to about six inches, they were harvested. This harvesting took place once a year. The workforce was almost entirely made up of Scandinavian seamen. Among oystermen, this process was universally known as the *California Method*.

The reproductive limitation of eastern oysters was not the only obstacle facing Bay oystermen. Natural enemies of the bivalve included the local stingray. The predator proved destructive enough that scantling fences had to be built out in the Bay to protect the beds. A two-legged enemy was known as the oyster pirate. Gangs of men from the East Bay would cross the Bay in the middle of the night and raid the beds. Famed novelist Jack London, as a teenager, became an oyster pirate. In order to mitigate the depredations of these desperados, houses on piles were constructed in the Bay, from which the hired guns of the oyster company could guard the beds.

John Stillwell Morgan's company dominated the oyster industry in the San Francisco Bay by absorbing nearly all its competitors by 1886. Only the M. B. Morgahan Company contested Morgan after that date. Morgahan owned beds off Millbrae. However, Morgan finally absorbed Morgahan in 1912. By 1923, the Morgan Oyster Company owned 16,583 acres of San Mateo County underwater lands. Its six houses and miles of scantling fences stretched out from Point San Bruno to Dumbarton Point. Sadly, as discussed in the previous chapter, the pollution of the San Francisco Bay did in this industry in the 1930s.

Another flourishing maritime industry of the bayside was shrimp fishing. Its origins also begin with the completion of the transcontinental railroad in 1869. However, this time the reason has to do with the release of a significant labor force. Thousands of Chinese helped the Central Pacific Company build the rails from west to east. When the job was done, they were released to find employment in other places. Many wished to engage in occupations they knew best back in China—and many had

Chinese Camp, San Francisco Bay.

been skillful fishermen. Unfortunately, discriminatory laws kept the Chinese from being able to fish for most catches. Because there was limited white competition with it, many turned to shrimp fishing, with which they had considerable experience back home.

Along the bayline off Marin, San Francisco, and San Mateo counties, "China Camps" material-ized as bases of operation for the shrimp fishermen. The first formed in San Mateo County was at Redwood City in 1869. By 1880, the most important camp existed at San Bruno point. Here, dozens of men sailed 12 junks and snagged hundreds of tons of shrimp with 100 nets. The Chinese estab-lished other significant camps at Burlingame and San Mateo. The census of 1880 tells us that 177 Chinese shrimp fishermen were in the county. However, the tally was taken in the off-season, when fewer were present. In addition, the Chinese were suspicious of government researchers, and not all may have wished to reveal their presence. Thus, it can be surmised that far more than 177 Chinese were engaged in fishing for shrimp in San Mateo County.

As with the oyster industry, the Chinese shrimp fishing operations of the Bay were unique and colorful. The fishermen built their junks out of local redwood. They ran from 12 to 50 feet in length. They had flat bottoms, to avoid getting stuck in the mud at low tide. Their lateen sails gave them a distinctive look as they plied the Bay. A federal observer wrote of them: ". . . they sail well, remain-ing free, and are light and buoyant."[29] Each boat was operated by a three- to five-man crew. Part of the success of the Chinese fishermen was their employment of their traditional bag nets. These conical devices had a 42-foot opening. The circumference decreased and ended up at 4 feet. The mesh also became progressively smaller toward the 4-foot end. The large end of the net was opened toward the current and easily trapped the planktonic (nonswimming) shrimp at the small end. Typi-cally, each boat would drop about 30 nets. During the peak years of the industry, in the 1890s, it was noted that a single boat could capture 7,000 pounds of shrimp in a single day.

About half the catch was boiled at the camps and then sold fresh in San Francisco. The other half was boiled, salted, dried until hard, and then crushed. The meat was then removed from the shell. Merchants in Chinatown, who owned most of the camps, then exported these dried materials to China. The meat was used for consumption, and the shell sold as fertilizer.

In 1892, the peak year for the shrimp industry, about 1.5 million pounds of shrimp were fished out of the Bay. This catch satisfied the demand for shrimp for the entire Pacific slope of the United States. The San Mateo County camps accounted for approximately 25 percent of this yield. As will be discussed in Chapter 8, the repressive policies of California officials gradually diminished Chinese shrimp fishing yields. In 1910, the bag net was outlawed, and this pushed the camps in San Mateo County out of business forever.

A smaller offshoot of the oyster and shrimp endeavors was the soft-shell clam industry. The soft-shell clam is not indigenous to the San Francisco Bay; however, it made its way west, probably with the eastern oysters, by mistake. Unlike the easterns, the clams could reproduce in the Bay and were dug and sold in the off-season by Chinese shrimp fishermen. Through the late nineteenth century and early twentieth, the San Mateo County clam market represented a majority of the entire catch in California. As restriction after restriction was leveled on the shrimpers, they turned increasingly to clam digging. In 1904, the peak year for San Mateo County clam production, 216,000 pounds of clams were marketed, with a value of $6,000. As with oysters, as the twentieth century progressed, pollution limited production. The Chinese largely abandoned the pursuit before 1920. By 1930, San Mateo County's output came mostly from tidal lands owned by John Connell near South San Francisco. Like the oyster industry, the clam business did not survive San Francisco typhoid linkages in the 1930s.

Two other industries of the bayline do not involve harvesting living creatures for consumption, but have great importance. Retrieval of salt for industrial use and tabletop consumption, plus the dredging of ancient shell deposits for cement, are unique and significant stories.

The Leslie Salt Company has its roots here in San Mateo County. Its importance goes far beyond its employment for use at home to satisfy taste. Salt in the Bay Area has historically been utilized in the production of chlorine, ammonia, soap, detergents, bleaches, sanitization compounds, soil stabilizers, weed eradicators, water softeners, vegetable oil, pulp and paper products, petroleum products, paper products and processing for fruits, vegetables, meat, fish and hides. The Leslie (or Cargill) properties even today are one of the few places in the United States where salt is recovered by means of solar evaporation.

Salt from the Bay was simply scraped off baylands as far back as Spanish times. With the early American period, demand, as with everything else, went up. In the East Bay, various concerns used salt ponds to create a very crude product that most consumers felt unsuitable for human consumption. About 1900, several companies began operations at Redwood City. Around that same time just south of San Mateo, C. E. Whitney, a former employee of the East Bay salt king himself, August Schilling, started up a plant. All the early companies on the West Bay used Japanese immigrants for their labor pool. The workers received 90 cents for their 12-hour day, and they toiled six days a week.

For a brief time the San Mateo firm was called the C. E. Whitney Co. However, Whitney decided to change the name in honor of an uncle to the Leslie Salt Refining Company. The original plant was built in 1903, and stood just west of the railroad tracks on the other side of today's San Mateo Main Post Office on Delaware. It is indeed hard for San Mateans today to imagine that everything east of the tracks at that time was salt ponds. C. E. died that same year, but his family kept the business going. By 1907, they had consolidated with the Redwood City companies, and became known after the mergers as the Leslie Salt Company.

For the West Bay salt industry, and particularly the Whitneys and their San Mateo plant, the next 15 years was a golden time.[30] In 1910, the San Mateo refinery achieved the status of being the first on the West Coast to install the vacuum refining method, essential in the production of finer table salts. Finally, Leslie's innovation elevated the use of Bay salt for use with foods. In order to distinguish its product, Leslie developed its famous cylinder shaped container. Red with a tin top and cork, the company asserted that the cylinder was stronger than its boxed competitors and thus better protected the product. In 1913, the San Mateo plant won first place for salt production at the California Land Show and Home Industry Exhibition in San Francisco. By 1919, production at San Mateo had reached 25,000 tons, some five times the first yield in 1904.

The history of the salt industry of the San Francisco Bay Area is replete with consolidation and merger. In 1924, Leslie merged with some of its East Bay rivals. In 1931, this new corporation decided to centralize some of its activities. The age of the 1903 plant, coupled with the City of San Mateo's decision to annex the land holdings of the company (implying higher taxes), inspired it to close the San Mateo plant.

Leslie Salt Works, located west of the railroad tracks, north of what is now Highway 92 at Delaware Avenue. Photo by AGC Hahn for the Panama Pacific International Exposition, held in San Francisco 1915.

Cement dredge, the *Texas*, working out of the plant at Redwood City.

The Schilling family eventually gained control of the entire Bay Area salt industry. Nevertheless, because of the well-known Leslie name, attributed to the Whitneys' hard work in advertising, packaging, and refinement methodology—the new company retained the Leslie name in the next large consolidation in 1936. Into the 1970s, Leslie was the largest private owner of land in the Bay Area. The current salt works at the Port of Redwood City were built in the 1950s. Today, the Cargill organization owns the Leslie facilities.

The unusual character of the peninsula's salt industry is matched by its cement story. It begins with Redwood City educator, mayor, and businessman, George A. Merrill. As organizer for the Redwood City Harbor Company, he had his firm dredging off of Redwood City in 1913. By accident, he discovered vast quantities of fossilized oyster shell (not Morgan Company oyster shell, but native shell many thousands of years old). A series of studies revealed that this material was perfect for the manufacture of cement. Interest in the discovery led to the creation of a plant at Redwood City by Pacific Portland Cement. Its original annual capacity totaled 1.1 million barrels a year. This process of making cement is totally unique. The Redwood City plant was known as the only one of its kind to use ancient shell in the creation of cement.[31] Perhaps the greatest claim to fame for the plant was the fact that its cement was used to create the original San Mateo Hayward Bridge in 1929.

Chapter 6 Footnotes

1. Mark G. Hylkema, *Seal Cove Prehistory: Archaeological Investigations at CA-SMA-134, Fitzgerald Marine Reserve, San Mateo County, California,* 1998.

2. Alan K. Brown, "Indians of San Mateo County," *La Peninsula,* vol. XVII, No. 4, Winter 1973–74, p. 6.

3. Ibid. p. 18.

4. Malcolm Margolin, *The Ohlone Way,* Hayday Books, Berkeley, 1978, p. 7.

5. F. Boneu Companies, *Gaspar de Portola: Explorer and Founder of California,* Instituto de Estudios Ilerdenges, Lerida Spain, 1983, p. 105.

6. Frank M. Stanger, Alan K. Brown, *Who Discovered the Golden Gate?* San Mateo County Historical Association, 1969, p. 20.

7. Joe Mora, *Californios,* Doubleday & Company, Inc, Garden City, New York, 1949, pp. 18–19.

8. Tracy I. Storer and Lloyd P. Tevis, Jr., *California Grizzly,* University of Nebraska Press, Lincoln, 1978, p. 128.

9. J. S. Holliday, *The World Rushed In,* Simon and Schuster, New York, 1981, p. 300.

10. Frank M. Stanger, *Sawmills in the Redwoods,* San Mateo County Historical Association, 1967, p. 65.

11. Kenneth L. Fisher, "Kings Mountain's Colorful History", *La Peninsula,* vol. XXVI, No. 3, November, 1990, p. 16.

12. Albert Shumate, *The Notorious I. C. Woods,* The Arthur H. Clark Company, Glendale, California, 1986, p. 36.

13. Mitchell P. Postel, "San Mateo County and San Francisco's Search for Water", *California Vignettes,* San Francisco Corral of the Westerners, p. 51.

14. Donald P. Ringler and George Rossi, *Filoli,* Private Printing, Hillsborough, California, 1978, pp. 4–24.

15. Hynding, *From Frontier,* p. 265.

16. Williams H. Moebus, " Agricultural Development in San Mateo County," manuscript within the Archives of the San Mateo County History Museum, June 1942, p. 8.

17. Bayard Taylor, *Eldorado,* University of Nebraska Press, Lincoln, 1988, p. 93.

18. Clint Miller, "Introduced Plants of the Coastside", *La Peninsula,* June 1972, vol. XVI, No. 5, p. 18.

19. Blair Hyde, "Purisima", *La Peninsula,* Feb, 1956, vol. III, No. 4, p. 4.

20. Ethel Knapp Neate, "The Knapps", manuscript collections, San Mateo County History Museum, 1967.

21. "An Important Enterprise," *San Mateo County Gazette,* Nov. 2, 1878.

22. Horace G. Knapp, oral history transcription, San Mateo County History Museum, by F. Hal, 1937.

23. Samuel C. Chandler, *Gateway to the Peninsula,* City of Daly City, 1978, p. 24.

24. Moebus, "Agricultural," p. 13.

25. Betty Lochrie Hoag, "Mrs. Giannini's Family," *La Peninsula*, Spring, 1973, vol. XIII, No. 2, p. 21.

26. Stanger, *South*, p. 140.

27. Mitchell P. Postel, "The Legacy of a Lost Resource: The History of the Fishing Industry off the San Mateo County Bayline," manuscript collection, San Mateo County History Museum, Oct. 1985, p. 1.

28. Mitchell P. Postel, "A Lost Resource", p. 29.

29. Ibid. p. 32.

30. Mitchell P. Postel, "More than a Grain: "The History of the Salt Industry in San Mateo County", *La Peninsula*, vol. XX, No. 3, Summer 1980, p. 16.

31. Tim Orazen, "The Ideal Cement Plant at Redwood City," 1979, manuscript collection of the San Mateo County History Museum.

Chapter 7

Suburban San Mateo County

The built environment of San Mateo County is largely the product of suburban development in the era after World War II. In 1940, the county's population stood at 112,000. Within 30 years, it grew nearly fivefold to 555,000 (the 2000 census puts the number at 707,000). During the 30 years that included World War II and the postwar boom, the mass construction of housing and the infrastructure necessary to support all the new people coalesced into the peninsula familiar to us today. Anybody who knew San Mateo County before 1940 testifies to how different a place this is today. By contrast, anybody who has lived here since 1970, in the 36 years since the postwar building boom, will say that there has been change, but the peninsula is still mostly recognizable. The roads and highways are mostly the same. Institutions like hospitals, government centers, libraries, and schools are largely in their same places and recognizable. Most of the single-family homes had been built, and the majority of them look very much the way they did in 1970.

Thus, the war and postwar years are crucial to our understanding of San Mateo County's past. The developers of this 30-year period had the most dramatic impact on the built environment of the peninsula in our history. However, the *California Dream* they sold was based on the creation of this area as a suburban retreat a century before, with the estate builders of the railroad era. At the beginning of the twentieth century, new middle-class commuters, emulating the lifestyles of the rich and famous, added their nuances to the dream, creating significant desire for suburban *California Living* in the modern age.

To understand this story, one must realize that the history of the peninsula as a suburb starts with the possibility of a commute. Beginning with the San Francisco–San Jose Railroad, convenient transportation made the commute possible. Another thing to remember about this story is that suburban living was not always possible for everyone. At first only the elite could manage it. As transportation improved with streetcars, the automobile, and public conveyances, more people could look to San Mateo County as a place to live while working in San Francisco or another Bay Area urban center.

The Railroad Era

The railroad made possible the idea that the suburb could be a desirable place to live. Throughout history, up until the building of railroads in the nineteenth century, areas outside the cities were for

the lower classes. Because of the lack of transportation, the wealthiest citizens of a major city in Europe or the United States desired to live as close as possible to the urban core, where business, government, culture, and entertainment were centered. In places a little less convenient, but still close to the activities of the cities, the middle class dwelled. The further from the center, the less expensive the real estate, until one reached the suburbs, where the poorest people eked out their existence.

The railroad changed all that, especially for Americans. As the tracks were extended from the industrializing cities of the northeast—such as New York, Boston, and Philadelphia—the American upper classes, who in many cases were *creating* the festering terrible urban conditions, wanted to lift their families out of the increasing squalor of such cities and deliver them to the healthier confines of rural life in a new suburban way. The railroad made a comfortable and rapid commute possible. The elite of America's industrializing society made first use of it and established their estates and exclusive communities in the country.

Out in the West, such a life must have seemed impossible at the time of the Gold Rush. In the famous year of 1849, as San Francisco grew at a rate of 2,000 people a month and as San Jose was expected to become the state capital, the status of land transportation between the two towns was not much different than when the trail was originally blazed by Anza back in 1776. For most of 1849, if a traveler decided against going from San Francisco to San Jose by boat, he was on his own to walk or find a donkey, mule, or horse to help him get there.

Finally, that autumn, only a few months after the first stagecoach service in California was established at Sacramento, John W. Whistman started up a stage line to connect San Francisco with San Jose. The starting point for his stagecoaches was Portsmouth Square (today's Chinatown). Since he started business as the rainy season was beginning, Whistman made no promises about when stages would arrive or leave. Nevertheless, the ride was expensive—two ounces of gold, or $24 to $32, depending on the fluctuating price of gold at the moment.

The journey was slow and uncomfortable, too. Whistman's equipment was primitive. The great Concord stages were not available in California as yet. Instead, he employed an old French omnibus—really, just a wagon with benches installed—pulled by some mules and half-wild mustangs. It took nine hours to get to San Jose when conditions were right and longer if the weather was bad or the roads unusually muddy.

A string of road houses or mile houses developed along El Camino Real to serve the stagecoaches and their passengers. The Abbey House was one of these. The part it played in the peninsula's early political history has already been mentioned.

Perhaps the most important of these houses belonged to Nicholas de Peyster at San Mateo. Here horses would be changed, and the place became known as the Half Way House (because it was about half way between San Francisco and San Jose). It was particularly well-known for its "San Mateo Punch," a local concoction similar to the popular milk punch of the day—a mixture of milk and gin. New York–born de Peyster had seen a business opportunity in the making in 1849, so he established

The San Mateo House, at what is now Second Avenue and El Camino Real. Structure on the right was built in 1851; an expansion with the Colonial Revival building on the left with an encircling porch was built in 1853. Used as an inn by travelers on the wearying stagecoach journey from San Francisco to San Jose, then sold to Captain Edwin Taylor, it served as the Taylor family home until the death of his widow in 1899. It was sold and served, with modifications, as a nurses' home in connection with the development of Mills Hospital. It was demolished in 1964.

American House at Redwood City. Even after the San Francisco-San Jose railroad was completed, stagecoach service to the coast was necessary with lines from Redwood City and San Mateo.

his store and public house in the old mission outpost building. Of course, he was squatting on Mellus and Howard property, the owners of Rancho San Mateo. Finally, after being told to remove himself from the premises, in 1851 de Peyster bought 75 acres just across San Mateo Creek, on Rancho de las Pulgas, and established a proper hotel there, known as the San Mateo House.

Nicholas de Peyster's Half Way or San Mateo House initiated the business community of San Mateo. Other mile houses had similar effect at San Bruno, Belmont, and Menlo Park. Later, these would also become train stops. However, most of the mile houses were primitive affairs that only lasted until the railroad took over. San Mateo County historian Frank Stanger described some of them as simple farm houses ". . . where travelers were entertained as a sideline; many carried merchandise as well. They called themselves hotels, but in the beginning this only meant that the travelers could eat as well as drink, and that he was welcome to stay overnight if he carried his own blankets and didn't mind sleeping in a haystack or under a tree."[1]

Obviously, under such conditions a commute from down the peninsula was impossible. Only a railroad could make the prospect of establishing suburban residence in San Mateo County practical. It did not take too long before schemes began to surface to help the growing business elite of San Francisco consider joining their East Coast counterparts and create estates in the country.

As early as August 1851, various California business interests pledged $50,000 in order to form the Pacific and Atlantic Railroad Company. Unfortunately, enough of the pledges were not honored so that the company fell apart. However, there were some important outcomes to this original company's efforts. It did complete a survey of the land and found a practical route following El Camino Real. It recommended a terminus at Point San Bruno (South San Francisco), where passengers would come off the train and find final passage to San Francisco by steamship. A way to round San Bruno Mountain had yet to be strategically dealt with. In 1853, the Pacific and Atlantic reorganized, but the panic of 1854, which ruined I. C. Woods and other members of the company's leadership, folded the company once and for all.

Finally, in 1859, Peter Donahue, Charles Polhemus, and Timothy G. Phelps helped to form the San Francisco–San Jose Railroad. With approval from the California state legislature, the citizens of the three counties involved voted in favor of issuing bonds in order that the railroad begin construction. San Francisco and Santa Clara counties came up with $200,000 each and the citizens of San Mateo County indebted themselves $100,000. A construction contract was signed with the firm of Charles McLaughlin and Alexander Houston. The firm estimated its work would cost about $40,000 a mile. The estimate was close, the project eventually costing more than $2 million but this included purchase of the locomotives and rolling stock.

Anticipating growth along the tracks, company director Charles Polhemus bought land in the San Mateo area and laid out the original plan that is downtown San Mateo today. Nearby, he acquired land to establish an estate so he could watch his town grow (the place is now Central Park). Timothy G. Phelps purchased land in today's San Carlos.

The company broke ground on May 1, 1861. It started at Redwood City with roadbed crews grading in both directions. Original plans called for a bayshore route; however, at San Bruno Mountain, the railroad chose to build the tracks west of the mountain, following the old mission trail (a cutoff on the bayside of the mountain would not be constructed until 1907, by the Southern Pacific).

The greatest obstacles encountered by the railroad involved trying to build it during the Civil War. Materials from the East were constantly delayed. The Union Army had first priority when rails, spikes, and tools became available. Certain shipments were postponed because of worries of Confederate raiders on the high seas.

Labor was in short supply as well. In California, workers were hard to find before the war. The onset of hostilities only made the situation worse. The directors of the railroad decided to take a chance and experiment with Chinese labor. This attempt was most successful; the first use of Chinese labor for railroad construction in the West had huge impact. When the "Big Four" (Leland Stanford, Charles Crocker, Collis Huntington and Mark Hopkins) began organizing its labor force for the building of the transcontinental Central Pacific, they would remember the success achieved by the San Francisco–San Jose.

On Saturday, October 18, 1863, 400 invited guests, including Governor Leland Stanford, boarded a San Francisco–San Jose train near Mission Dolores and rode it down to Mayfield (today's Palo Alto) for a ceremonial celebration. The next day a daily run was established, and commuter rail traffic was born in the West—no other commuter train service existed west of the Mississippi. Two stops were made: one at San Mateo and the other at Redwood City. They both linked to the coast via stagecoach service. The line was completed to San Jose in early 1864.

By February 1864, the railroad had scheduled two passenger trains and one freight train (with a passenger car as well) each way, every day. The entire trip was only two hours and twenty minutes. Four stops were made in Santa Clara County and seven in San Mateo County, including present-day Daly City, San Bruno, Millbrae, San Mateo, Belmont, Redwood City, and Menlo Park. The success of the company was not missed by other railroads. In 1870, the line was purchased by the Big Four as part of their consolidation of railroads after the completion of the transcontinental railroad the year before. The new name for their company was the Southern Pacific.

Who were the original commuters utilizing the railroad? A look at its 1870 schedule gives some clues. At that time it offered its service three times a day. Its earliest train reached the city at 9:00 A.M. and its last train left the city at 4:40 P.M. This could hardly be of use for a working-class person who labored on average for 10 or more hours a day. Nor could it serve a middle class or professional person who had to work longer hours. Only a member of the elite had the freedom to arrive at the office at 9:30 or 10:00, see how things were going, have lunch at the club, and then return to the train station in the afternoon before 5:00 P.M.

The service was fast and efficient. From the San Mateo station, it took only 55 minutes to reach the city. However, it also cost 75 cents—in the day when the average American worker was making about a dollar a day. From Redwood City, the price was exactly a dollar, and from Menlo Park, $1.15.

One of these original commuters was William C. Ralston, perhaps the most well-known capitalist on the West Coast. He purchased his estate

Stagecoaches, wagons, and carriages met the trains at San Mateo Railroad Station.

in Belmont the same year that the San Francisco–San Jose was completed—1864. This land originally belonged to S. M. Mezes after his successful defense of the Arguello family's Rancho de las Pulgas (as related in the last chapter). Mezes sold a significant portion of the property to Italian nobleman Leonetto Cipriani in 1854. In 1864, Italian King Victor Emmanuel II made Cipriani a count, and he decided to join his old friend and return to help with the unification of his native country. He sold his land in Belmont to speculator Morton Cheesman for $5,500, who three days later turned around and sold it to William Ralston for $6500.[2]

William Ralston, whose mansion in Belmont still stands and is part of the Notre Dame de Namur University on Ralston Avenue in Belmont.

At this time, Ralston was in the process of organizing his Bank of California. He had come to California as an agent for a New York shipping line in 1853. Within ten years, luck, smarts, and aggressive business practices had made Ralston one of the wealthiest people on the Pacific Coast. His plans for his estate at Belmont included making it sort of the White House of the West.[3] He wanted to make the place so alluring that people from the East and everywhere else would see the possibilities of investing in the progress of California.

He therefore greatly embellished the count's estate. He expanded the house into a mansion (which still stands today as Ralston Hall at the College of Notre Dame). Its 50 guest rooms and stable, adequate to accommodate 60 to 100 horses, made Belmont one of the greatest venues in California for fashionable formal parties. During his time there, he entertained Anson Burlingame, the ambassador to China, King Kalakaua of Hawaii, and, in 1872, the Japanese embassy headed up by Sinu Tomomi Iwakura. A dinner for more than 100 guests was served that night. Because of the San Francisco–San Jose Railroad, Belmont was perfect for Ralston's extravaganzas. It took only an hour for his invitees to arrive from San Francisco. Sometimes, with his favorite guests aboard, he would race the train down from the city with his four-horse carriage. Although the train was faster, it had to make its regular stops. Plus, it had to slow down along some parts of the track. Ralston, meanwhile, arranged for change of horses at key points along the way. He proved that he could beat the train.

Certainly Ralston qualifies as the most colorful of the new suburbanites down the peninsula. The many others that came to make this place a summer or commuter home were the families running the business of the West. San Francisco was the dominant city in California for all of the second half of the nineteenth century and into the twentieth. In fact it was the business, political, social, and cultural capital of the West—its queen city, so to speak. And to a great extent, this ruling class that ran the West from their offices in San Francisco, made their suburban homes in San Mateo County. An abridged listing includes the following luminaries:

W. D. M. Howard, West Coast Commerce, San Mateo
Faxon Atherton, Chilean aristocracy, Atherton
Thomas H. Selby, industrialist, Atherton

Four stories, eighty rooms, more than 55,000 square feet, the Ralston Mansion is the only estate—of the many built during the mid to late 1800s—that remains much as it was in the 1870s.

Charles B. Polhemus, San Francisco–San Jose Railroad, San Mateo
William C. Ralston, Bank of California, Belmont
William Sharon, senator from Nevada, Belmont
John Parrott, banking and real estate, San Mateo
Alvinza Hayward, mining, San Mateo
William H. Kohl, Alaska Fur Trade, San Mateo
Henri Barroihlet, international banking, Hillsborough
Gustave Mahe, French Savings and Loan Society of San Francisco, Hillsborough
Ansel Easton, family holdings, Burlingame
Darius Ogden Mills, Bank of California, Millbrae
Charles Lux, cattle king, South San Francisco
Walter S. Hobart, horse breeding, San Mateo
Charles Clark, copper, Hillsborough
Antoine Borel, banking, San Mateo
W. E. Barron, New Almaden Mercury Mine, Menlo Park
Milton S. Latham, Sacramento and Vallejo Railroad, Menlo Park

Train at Redwood City railroad depot (1884). The first train came through Redwood City in 1863. The first passenger depot opened in 1884 on the west side of the tracks near the corner of Brewster and Arguello Streets. This station was on the east side of the tracks, north of Broadway. Photograph taken by James Van Court. Redwood City Library photograph.

Timothy Hopkins, Southern Pacific Railroad, Menlo Park
James Flood, mining, Atherton
Joseph A. Donohue, banking, Atherton
John A. Hooper, banking, Woodside
David Jackling, copper smelting, Woodside
James A. Folger, coffee, Woodside
August Schilling, spices, Woodside
Charles Josselyn, candlery, Woodside
William H. Crocker, Crocker National Bank, Hillsborough
William B. Bourn, Spring Valley Water Company, Woodside
Harriett Pullman Carolan, Pullman Fortune, Hillsborough
John Redington, pharmaceuticals, Hillsborough
Amadeo P. Giannini, Bank of America, San Mateo
Prince Andre Poniatowski, Pacific Gas and Electric, Hillsborough
Herbert Law, patent medicines, Portola Valley
Timothy Guy Phelps, San Francisco–San Jose Railroad, San Carlos
Nathanial Brittan, hardware, San Carlos
Charles Holbrook, merchant, Menlo Park

One would imagine that with the early presence of the railroad, San Mateo County would have been a fast-growing place during the nineteenth century. However, the population of the county only grew from 5,300 in 1860 to 12,000 by 1900. In fact, San Mateo County was the slowest-growing county in the Bay Area in the late nineteenth century. By 1900, Santa Clara County had a population of 60,000, and Alameda County counted 130,000. Even far-off Contra Costa County had 18,000 people.

View of the rear of the Howard home on El Cerrito about 1860; formerly the Rancho San Mateo.

County historian Al Hynding explained: "Oddly, it was the rail-road, that forerunner of progress, that helped discourage rapid growth in San Mateo County. . . ."[4] Hynding contends that the presence of the great estate owners—these original suburbanites—acted as a damper on growth because they took up the best land near the tracks. They hemmed in the small towns developing at the rail stations, discouraging economic activity, agriculture, and expansion of the towns themselves.

Perhaps no better example exists than the story of the land we call Hillsborough. In 1856, W. D. M. Howard, owner of Rancho San Mateo, died. To his 25-year-old wife, Agnes, he left most of the southern half of the rancho (largely San Mateo north of the Creek). He bestowed the northern half of the land (largely Burlingame and Hillsborough) to his father-in-law, Dr. Joseph Henry Poett. Poett, in turn, gave his other daughter, Julia, Mrs. John Redington, a large portion of the western holdings of this

William Davis Merry Howard

land. (John Redington has been credited with becoming Burlingame's first commuter when in the 1860s he built the "pill box station" near the present-day Oak Grove station to provide shelter for him as he awaited the train into the city.) Agnes married W. D. M.'s brother George, and after he died, she wedded Henry Bowie in 1879. The Howard, Poett, and Redington families held tight control over their real estate.

An exception was made in 1866, when Dr. Poett sold diplomat–adventurer Anson Burlingame 1,000 acres of real estate in today's Hillsborough-Burlingame area for $52 an acre. Five years before, President Abraham Lincoln had appointed Burlingame as minister to China. During his stay there he resigned this position and became a subject of the emperor of China. As such, he negotiated the famous Burlingame Treaty, which allowed Chinese labor to enter the country to work on the transcontinental railroad. Burlingame's dealings earned him a powerful position in China from which he gained much wealth. With part of his money, Burlingame wanted to create a large, planned suburban community in the exclusive English style, complete with serpentine roads and country cottages. Unfortunately, he died before being able to realize his dream.

Dr. Joseph Henry Poett

The great William C. Ralston believed in Burlingame's idea and purchased the property with that idea in mind; he commissioned a survey of the place and drew up a map on which he called the future community Ralstonville. As described in the previous chapter, Ralston's flamboyant business style resulted in his being forced from his position as director of the Bank of California in August of 1875. His body was found floating in the Bay the next day.

Ralston's old associate, and his largest creditor, William Sharon, took over Ralston's role at the bank and received most of his former partner's estate, including the Palace Hotel in San Francisco, the mansion at Belmont and the 1,000 acres of Rancho San Mateo property. Sharon had come west to California by wagon train in 1850. He at one time was the Bank of California's agent in the Comstock Mining District in Nevada. Sharon was wiser in his business maneuverings than Ralston and was one of the richest men in the West when he acquired this property.

Sharon also believed that a planned community could work on this rolling wooded country. He changed its name to Burlingame, after the man who had the idea originally. However, Sharon was unsuccessful in trying to promote the concept and therefore sold a portion of it east of El Camino Real to William Corbitt, who established a successful ranch. On the remaining land east of the highway, he situated a dairy to supply his Palace Hotel. Sharon died in 1885 in the midst of a scandalous battle with Sarah Althea Hill, who claimed to be his wife under terms of a contract marriage. The fate of the Rancho San Mateo property was left up to his estate.

Sharon's attorney and son-in-law, Francis Newlands, took control of the situation. He had come to California in 1870 looking for work as an attorney. After Sharon hired him, he married his boss's daughter, Clara Adelaide, in 1874. As Sharon was the largest taxpayer in San Francisco, with holdings extending to Nevada, and all the way to the East Coast, Newlands was a busy man. Now, with Sharon's death, and the Hill case still going on, Newlands wished to liquidate some of the estate's holdings. He got the inspiration to create a planned exclusive community (similar to Burlingame's plan) on Sharon Estate property near Washington, D.C., at a place called Chevy Chase. As the idea gained interest, Newlands took it upon himself to develop a country club there, which he felt would be a desirable adjunct to the suburb. In March of 1893, the Chevy Chase Country Club was estab-

Looking east on Burlingame Avenue to the Bay, circa 1905. The recreational values of the peninsula were well known by the turn of the twentieth century.

lished with financing from Newlands' Chevy Chase Land Company. That same year, Newlands entered upon a political career as congressman from Nevada. He now felt the pressure to do something with the Burlingame property and hoped that the Chevy Chase model would work in California—sell the real estate to an exclusive clientele in exchange for creating a country club.

The concept of the country club was not very old when Newlands proposed it in California. The country club is an American invention. The first was established at Brookline, Massachusetts, in 1882. Brookline, Chevy Chase, and those that followed gave the emerging upper classes of industrializing America the opportunity to participate in the sporting activities of the English aristocracy. While the English had their own country estates where they could play polo and pursue the hounds during the fox hunt, the American elite was largely based in the cities. With country clubs the clannish Americans could go to the country as associates and try to emulate the noble cliques of the old world together.

For Newlands, the time finally seemed right for selling real estate on the property west of El Camino. He was not alone in that assessment. A travel brochure printed in the 1890s explained about the mid-San Mateo area: "Excepting none, San Mateo is much more accessible than any other place of suburban residence around San Francisco."[5]

It pointed out that a commute to any east or north bay community would entail a streetcar ride to the ferry, the trip across the Bay and then another train excursion to get home. To get to Burlingame, by contrast, all that was required was a five-minute ride on the tramway from Market Street to the railroad station, and then in only 35 minutes, one could be in Burlingame.

Good transportation was only part of what the region could offer. Climatically, the peninsula was known as one of the most favorable locations in the nation with mild temperatures existing all year long. San Mateo County was extremely rural with just 10,000 people living here, according to the 1890 census. For sporting enthusiasts, the foothills abounded with deer and other game. The marsh-lands of the Bay were on the Pacific flyway and offered excellent opportunities for hunters. Fishing in local creeks was excellent. El Camino Real (one of the better roads in California) was sprinkled on weekends with bicyclists. In short, the Burlingame area, and really much of the peninsula, allowed young San Franciscans of the upper crust the opportunity to participate in the English country life. *Sunset* magazine made the connection:

> There is not the least hazard in asserting that in no section of the United States—or in this hemisphere, in fact—(is there a place) where an Englishman of sporting proclivities would feel so much at home as in San Mateo County. This section is nearly a counterpart of the most favored parts of the mother country, saving that in place of baronial halls and castles, built centuries ago, there are palatial residences of later date.[6]

To initiate things, Newlands contracted renowned San Francisco architect, A. Page Brown, to build six cottages in 1892 on 16 acres of today's Hillsborough. The project called for serpentine roads and walkways, tennis courts, croquet grounds, fountains, and other embellishments to attract a certain type of buyer. The *Redwood City Democrat* explained: ". . . when the houses are finished and the land in the highest state of cultivation, an offer of the property will be made with such a reserve price that none but those of ample means will care to purchase. . . ." The *Democrat* went on to say that when about 100 homes had been sold, it was the Sharon Estate's intention to establish a country club, as it proposed for Chevy Chase. While the approach was succeeding at Chevy Chase, it did not in California. Newlands, therefore, reversed his thinking and decided that he would first establish the Burlingame Country Club—the first country club in the western United States—and then attempt real estate sales.

He invited a well-chosen group of sporting enthusiasts to a picnic under oak trees near one of the cottages. Drinks were served liberally, and the idea was announced. Newlands hosted a second meeting at the Palace Hotel, and an agreement was worked out. The men present promised to create a club of 50. In exchange, the Sharon Estate would give them use of one of the cottages, with furnishings, and 20 acres of land free for two years. The Palace Hotel would provide all the supplies needed to maintain the cottage—again, free of charge. A staff of servants would be hired. Transportation from the Oak Grove railroad station was guaranteed at 12-1/2 cents a trip. After two years, if the club became indebted, the Sharon Estate would pay up to half the loss.

Under these favorable conditions, the club was organized with a stellar list of the San Francisco business and social elite. Included on its first board of directors was William H. Crocker, the Burlingame Country Club's first treasurer (his New Place mansion is now the home of the club). Crocker's father was Charles Crocker of the Central Pacific's Big Four who built the transcontinental railroad. William ran the family business as president of the Crocker National Bank. As with many of the second-generation wealthy, Crocker had a variety of interests outside of making money. For example, for many years he was also president of the California Academy of the Sciences.

John Parrott Jr., whose father built one of the first business blocks in San Francisco and established his great Baywood estate at San Mateo, was on the board. John Parrott Sr.'s sons-in-law, Christian de Guigne and A. H. Payson, were also active. De Guigne was part of a French banking firm and Payson was manager of the Spring Valley Water Company. Payson gained local notoriety when he became San Mateo's first mayor in 1894.

Another early leader was sportsman and businessman Joseph D. Grant. At the age of 33 he became a life trustee for Stanford University. He was also one of the founders of the Save-The-Redwoods League. Among the first members were Joseph Tobin, president of Hibernia Savings and

Loan for many years. So, too, was George Pope, a lumber and shipping entrepreneur and a substantial contributor to St. Luke's Hospital.

In these early years, the purpose of the club was to provide the members with the opportunity to participate in the popular sports of the day—especially as practiced back in England—and this meant equestrian type activities. No better place could be found for such interests than at Burlingame. Just across the highway from the Burlingame Country Club was the William Corbitt ranch, called Crossways. Some of

The Carolans Mansion under construction.

the best horses in the nation were bred here. Meanwhile, in nearby San Mateo, John Parrott Jr. bred hackneys and Walter S. Hobart specialized in polo ponies.

A great boom for the club occurred in 1901, when Francis Carolan bought Crossways. Carolan was a mere store owner until he met Harriett Pullman, of the Pullman railroad car fortune. With his wife's wealth he became a popular clubman among the elite of San Francisco. He literally allowed Crossways to become an extension of the club, with its top-quality breeding sheds, barns, stables and other facilities made available to the members. Crossways also had a race track and a polo field. Francis later built kennels so the club could have hunts in the style of the English aristocracy. There were also facilities for trap shooting. Later, the Carolans would move up into the hills and build the gigantic Carolands mansion. It is said that Harriett wished to look down on all the Crockers around them.

The early members enjoyed horse racing, and with the great enthusiasm of Francis Carolan, the hunt was also attempted. Because of the lack of foxes on the peninsula, at first the members pursued the longer-legged and faster coyote. Some of these hunts ended up on the fringes of San Francisco without a satisfactory conclusion for the hounds and the hunters.

Of all the early sporting activities, none was more popular than polo. The best of San Francisco's society would turn out to watch the Burlingame polo teams. Newspapers covered these games just as the modern press follows football today. Actually, they sort of combined the society page with the sports section. Reporters dubbed individual players as dashing and debonair, encouraging "bevies of charming young ladies" to come down the peninsula to watch. *Sunset* magazine commented that it had become ". . . part of a debutante's social equipment that she tell a No. 1 in polo from a back and recognize an offside play."[7] The Burlingame players soon developed a national reputation for their skills. That, plus excellent playing conditions and the availability of great horses, made easterners recognize Burlingame as the "Winter Home of Polo." Teams from all over the country were joined by international teams from South America, Hawaii, and even the Hurlingham team from the mother country herself.

Interestingly, golf was not treated, a serious sport among the Burlingame set until 1913, after polo declined in popularity as the players got older. Regardless of the sport, for Francis Newlands the club served his purpose perfectly, as Burlingame members bought properties from him in order to be closer to their beloved club.

As for the members of the club, Burlingame fulfilled its promise of emulating the English style of things. In 1901, *Sunset* magazine noted: "Everything is decidedly English in Burlingame and its immediate neighborhood. Horses anglicized, drags, traps, harness, saddles of English manufacture, the prevailing garb the handiwork of the best London tailors, and graduates of Oxford and Cambridge are here to recount the glories, to tell the tales of college life and pay glowing tributes, in the best English vernacular to great universities." Indeed, Burlingame became a "must stop" for princes, barons, and counts of Europe. American "royalty" also visited, including President Theodore Roosevelt in 1903.

However, not all was right for the membership. Not long after the formation of the club, members found it would become necessary to become politically active in order to preserve the best aspects of their suburban experience.

In 1894, a year after establishing the Burlingame Country Club, the members decided to build a train station nearer to the club's property. Their Burlingame Train Station, designed by George H. Howard, is considered the first permanent building constructed in the Mission Revival style.[8] It was such a great convenience for the members that after the station was built, a few storekeepers and service providers clustered around it.

By April 1906, there were still fewer than 200 people living in the village. The 1906 Great San Francisco Earthquake and Fire changed everything. The disaster in the city forced people out. They took up new residences all over the peninsula, especially in north San Mateo County and Burlingame. Within a year, 1,000 people lived here. By 1910, there were 1,585, and by 1914 it was rivaling San Mateo as the largest town in San Mateo County, with a population of 2,849.

Why Burlingame? Its reputation as the home of the club certainly had an effect. People wanted to be associated with the elite, and when given the choice of where to start over, more than a few selected Burlingame.

Club members watched warily when in 1908, in order to avoid annexation by neighboring San Mateo, Burlingame incorporated itself. Still hungry to extend its borders, in 1909, San Mateo successfully annexed San Mateo Park west of El Camino, alarmingly close to the club. Burlingame then annexed the community of Easton to its north in 1910. Also that year, San Mateo annexed Hayward Park, to its south. Club members knew that both the aggressive towns were looking west, at the lands of the club and the private properties of many club members, for possible absorption. What the members faced was the prospect of being regulated by a local government of which they would be a minority. Even worse, they would be forced to pay taxes for the things they did not want, such as wide streets, commercialism, industry, the leveling of their beloved hills, the cutting down of trees, and the filling of creeks.

Rallying the members to protect their way of life was Arthur H. Redington, of the old Howard-Poett-Redington clan (whose political exploits against consolidating San Francisco and San Mateo County were mentioned in Chapter V). He organized the members and their neighbors. He convinced them that only by incorporating themselves could they avoid being gobbled up by Burlingame or San Mateo. And so in 1910, Redington led them to establish the town of Hillsborough.

Streetcar Suburbs

Yes, to their horror, the members of the Burlingame Country Club were going to have to share their life in the suburbs with new middle-class groups of people. What made this possible? The development of streetcar service plus the Great Earthquake and Fire of 1906 encouraged a new kind of growth for the peninsula. One without the other would not have had the same effect. However, the two together provided convenient ability to commute and motivation for a new class of suburbanites.

The effort to establish a streetcar system down to San Mateo County began in 1890 with the creation of the San Francisco and San Mateo Railroad Company. By 1891, the line had extended from Market and Stuart to 30th Street in San Francisco, and in 1893 the track had reached Baden (part of South San Francisco today).

The original cars resembled San Francisco cable cars. They were of the California type, with both ends open and an enclosed mid-section. The cars used for service down the peninsula were slightly larger than those used in the city. At 28 feet in length, they were powered by two 25 horsepower motors. By 1896, when the original owners of the company sold out to the new San Francisco and San Mateo Electric Railway, there were some 30 cars altogether. The new company purchased another 40 cars. It also replaced the original track with a heavier, stronger kind that allowed the usage of larger and speedier cars. A Baltimore group of investors, in turn, bought the line in 1901. Their United Railroads of San Francisco intended to lay track all the way down the peninsula and eventually reach Oakland. It purchased still larger and faster cars, known as the *Big Subs*. By 1902, United had built the line as far south as downtown San Mateo, but, unfortunately never got further than that.

One of the most important user groups of the early streetcar service were visitors to the cemeteries in Colma. With space for cemeteries running out in San Francisco, the Colma cemetery complex had become the place for city mourners to bury their dead. The Colma cemeteries, created in parklike settings, became destinations for city folk on weekend excursions wanting to visit the remains of past members of the family. When, in 1898, San Francisco forever prohibited any further burials, the streetcar line was guaranteed an increasing clientele.

The Roman Catholic Church consecrated Holy Cross Cemetery in 1887, which became the first of the Colma area cemeteries. Jewish leaders established Home of Peace in 1888. Later the Italian, Chinese, Serbian, Japanese, and Greek communities did likewise. In 1892, Cypress Lawn was established and was immediately proclaimed one of the most beautiful nonsectarian burial grounds in the United States.

Because of the poor condition of the roads from San Francisco to the cemeteries, the streetcar companies provided transportation for funeral parties with direct and private service. Originally, a special, ornate, small car, called the Cypress Lawn, featured a compartment for a casket and possessed wicker chairs for the mourners. The Cypress Lawn had no motor or controls at first, and had to be towed by a work car. After United Railroads took over operations, the car was motorized, and a second car was built for the service.

Between 1903 and 1904, United constructed three more funeral cars. These were designed with a considerable number of improvements catered for their special purpose. They were painted Brewster green with a red roof and gold lettering. Their interiors included luxuriously cushioned seats, richly carpeted floors, dark window drapes, and beautiful woodwork. Lead inserts were

Downtown San Mateo, Depot Square. Businesses developed near railroads and their depots. In this photograph, taken circa 1903, buildings from left to right around the square on Main Street are: the San Mateo Train Station (roof); Union Hotel (behind flagpole); Union Stable (middle); Library Hall II; Goodspeed Corner; St Matthew's Roman Catholic Church on 3rd Avenue (background right).

attached to wheels and gears in order to cut down on noise. Divided into three compartments, these 45-foot-long, 43,000-pound, 32-seat cars were maintained in immaculate condition and were the ultimate in style and class for carrying the dead to their final resting places. The elegant vehicles were widely promoted by United in the newspapers. Ads emphasized quick and courteous service "to all cemeteries in San Mateo County" from three points in San Francisco: the Ferry Building, 18th and Guerrero Streets, and 30th Street and San Jose Avenue. Arrangements for rental of the cars could be made through the undertaker involved. Some larger funerals required the calling into action of three private cars, usually employed to carry groups to the racetrack at Tanforan (established in 1899) and other attractions.

Keeping in mind frequent family callers, Mount Olivet Cemetery provided its own streetcar to transport passengers from the regular line and the cemetery gate to its centrally located depot at no charge. The original Mount Olivet car (a converted horse-drawn streetcar) began transporting visitors to the graves within the first year of the cemetery's establishment (1896). A fire destroyed the streetcar in 1907, so Mount Olivet bought a vintage 1900 California Car as a replacement. The cemetery's superintendent, Mattrup Jensen—known as one of the principle leaders encouraging the incorporation of Lawndale (later renamed Colma) and then a long-time city councilman—used the car for personal excursions. On occasion, he took his family aboard and motored all the way up to San Francisco for an outing. He would stop the car in one of the depots there and spend a leisurely day in the city.

Funeral cars at the turn of the century allowed San Francisco to reach Colma in style.

The presence of the streetcar down the peninsula was a crucial ingredient to expanded growth after the Great Earthquake and Fire devastated San Francisco in April of 1906. The quake registered 8.25 on the Richter Scale, but it was the fire that did the most damage. Officially, some 450 people were killed, but it has been speculated that the loss in life was actually much greater. Hundreds of millions of dollars in property was lost. Oakland took in most of the refugees; they crossed the Bay by ferry and boat. Oakland was relatively lightly hit, with just five fatalities.

The peninsula and Santa Clara County had more problems. In San Jose, at least 20 lost their lives. At nearby Agnew State Mental Hospital, more than 100 (some strapped to their beds) were killed when the building collapsed. In San Mateo County, the greatest human losses occurred at Half Moon Bay, where three died when one of the original adobe dwellings there fell down. At the middle of the San Andreas fault, which runs down the peninsula through the Crystal Springs Valley, the power of the quake was experienced the most. The west half of the county lunged forward several feet. This could be frightfully seen on the Half Moon Bay road to San Mateo at Crystal Springs Lake. Crystal Spring Dam, the largest interlocking concrete dam in the world, held—as a tribute to its engineer, Hermann Schussler. Destruction was evident in the larger towns. In Redwood City, most brick buildings crumbled, including the new courthouse, only completed the year before. San Mateo's business district was about wiped out. Throughout San Mateo County, schools, banks, and saloons were shut. Gas and electric power was mostly curtailed. Pipe damage made fresh water more difficult to obtain. While most San Franciscans fled across the Bay, many did go south. A multitude simply walked out, down the old mission highway. Some 60,000 rode out on the Southern Pacific. Many north county residents opened their doors and took in the homeless. The Western Meat Company in South San Francisco donated significant quantities of food.

Many of the refugees stayed in San Mateo County, especially in the north, where the streetcar could easily get them to work. And there was much work as San Francisco began rebuilding itself. Census records tell us that the county nearly doubled in population during this time, from 12,000 in 1900 to 20,600 in 1910. San Mateo County was still small in size compared to other Bay counties. For example, Santa Clara County grew from 60,000 in 1900 to 84,000 in 1910. Nevertheless, this was the first strong increase that the county had experienced thus far in its history. There is no doubt that the presence of the streetcar was an important contributing reason.

All the towns from San Mateo north that had streetcar service experienced far more growth than the communities south of it. From the emerging town of San Bruno, a commuter could make it to the Ferry Building in San Francisco in 40 minutes. The middle and working classes had an inexpensive means of transportation into the city that left early in the morning and had service into the evening hours. In the opposite direction, students from north county took the streetcar down to San Mateo High and later, to San Mateo Junior College. Old-time San Mateo County residents to this day (2006) remember using the streetcar in the 1930s to rapidly get up to the city in as little as 30 minutes from, say, Burlingame. Many families took the streetcar to the Ferry Building in San Francisco to get to the 1939 World's Fair at Treasure Island. As late as the 1940s, the streetcars were running every 10 to 15 minutes during commute times in both directions.

In North County, sparsely settled dairy country gave way to new suburban development. One of the first places impacted was the Daly City area. Newcomers could buy a lot for $200 to $300. One could then contract to have a house built for about $1,500. Some that could not afford a new house might have the remnant of a partially ruined one dragged down from the city for a few hundred dollars.

Fearing that San Francisco might try to annex the emerging north county, in 1908, some residents began thinking about incorporation of one large town to be called Vista Grande. They envisioned its borders stretching from the Bay to the ocean, from San Francisco to the Mills estate, including today's towns of Daly City, Colma, Brisbane, South San Francisco, and Pacifica, with San Bruno Mountain thrown in. However, many people felt the north county too diverse to combine. Old-time pioneers such as Robert Thornton pointed out that the Daly City area was residential while South San Francisco was becoming an industrial town. Meanwhile, toward the south, agriculture still predominated. Not wanting to get gobbled up by the Vista Grande proponents, South San Francisco incorporated on its own that year. Residents of Daly City did likewise in 1911. San Bruno, little more than a railroad stop before the earthquake, incorporated in 1914.

Robert Thornton, originally a blacksmith, was an early settler of Daly City.

South of north county, the towns of Burlingame and San Mateo were evolving into the suburban communities that would soon characterize suburban growth throughout much of the peninsula. County historian Al Hynding summed it up this way: "Neither rural nor urban, agricultural or industrial, elite or proletarian, the two towns typified the suburban wave of the future. Each boasted a prosperous business district and growing numbers of lawyers, physicians, bankers, and other affluent professional people employed either in San Francisco or in the community. Burlingame and San Mateo best reflected the dominant middle-class values of the period. In both towns, one seemed to notice fewer minorities and saloons, more movie palaces, and automobiles."[9]

Indeed, as San Mateo County grew in the early twentieth century, many of its new middle-class residents wished to emulate the good life pioneered by the estate owners before them. In the days before movie stars and rock and roll musicians, before sports heroes and other media-made personalities, the celebrities most followed by Americans were their new aristocracy—the families who had most benefited from the Industrial Revolution and now set the standards in popular culture. Most people on the peninsula certainly admired the rich at least as much as they may have jealously hated them. Middle-class people wanted to live like them as much as they could—in the way they dressed, the way they played—in all the ways that they could manage.

In the architectural styles of their homes, one could see their quest to mimic the grand houses of the upper classes. Their California bungalows, reminiscent of the country cottages of the elite, featured horizontal lines, heavy porch pillars, visible eaves supports, and natural wood on stone finishes. They also copied the designs of the rich and famous with their ever-popular mission revival or Spanish colonial versions of the bungalow. These homes were characterized by stucco walls, tile-accented roofs, and arched windows and doors. From plan books, builders could construct a single-story bungalow for about $3,500 through the 1920s.

Innovations developed in the new century facilitated the desire to copy the lifestyle of the elite. Besides the streetcar that made it easier to live in the suburbs but work in the city, modern electrical and mechanical conveniences—the washing machine, refrigerator, gas stove, etc.—allowed families more leisure time. The new progressive middle class also banded together to make things better for their communities. They wanted quality public schools and nurturing cultural institutions. Incorporation of cities, professionalization of fire and police departments, and creation of libraries and hospitals were the priorities of the new suburbanites of the peninsula.

Between 1910 and 1920, the population of San Mateo County grew another 79 percent, to 36,800. Once again, compared to other places this still might not seem like a lot. By that year, Contra Costa County was 54,000, Santa Clara County was 100,000 and Alameda County was 344,000. Nevertheless, the suburban rise was

Streetcar service from San Francisco to San Mateo ended in 1949.

happening here, and in the next ten years the population would more than double to 77,400.

Another way to measure the change existed in the number of incorporated towns. Before the 1906 earthquake, only two communities had incorporated during San Mateo County's first 50 years: Redwood City (1867) and San Mateo (1894). In the next 21 years, ten would incorporate:

South San Francisco	1908
Burlingame	1908
Hillsborough	1910
Daly City	1911
San Bruno	1914
Atherton	1923
Colma	1924
San Carlos	1925
Menlo Park	1927
Belmont	1927

Although the middle-class suburban towns of San Mateo County thrived, the history of the streetcar, which began the era, was sadly not successful. No one could have predicted that the slow-moving and dangerous horseless carriage would dominate California transportation so quickly. But for the peninsula's streetcar service, affectionately called the "40 Line" by old timers, a hint of competition to come might have been seen when, in 1914, the Peninsula Rapid Transit Company began internal-combustion bus service through San Mateo County. Because of competition from automobile hearses, the three beautiful funeral cars were taken out of service in 1921 and scrapped in 1926. Over the years, automobiles and buses continuously cut into the profitability of the streetcar. In 1944, San Francisco took over the operation of the 40 Line. Unfortunately, after just five years, it gave up the service. Within a decade, peninsulans found themselves in an increasingly congested transportation bind, and within two and a half decades, energy shortages and environmental concerns would once again make electric mass transportation desirable, but at a tremendous cost.

The Automobile and Postwar Mass Construction

The popularity and affordability of the automobile has had tremendous impact on the history of San Mateo County and how its suburban communities have evolved. Our connection with California automobile history has been an important one from the beginning. For example, in 1902, the first automobile meet in California history had a peninsula connection, since it began in San Francisco and ended up at Crystal Springs Dam.

For all of American history, the building of the first Model Ts by Henry Ford in 1908 allowed more people the ability to buy cars. In San Mateo County, this resulted in a business boom of sorts. Fix-it shops, car dealers, and parts suppliers came into being. While livery stables operators, in general, did not jump on board and mostly stayed with the horse-and-buggy trade, bicycle-shop owners, blacksmiths, and machinists did become part of the new industry. At first there were no gas stations. Those possessing an automobile often could afford an underground storage tank that would be filled by horse-drawn tank wagons. Smaller amounts of gasoline could be bought at hardware and drug stores. Some storekeepers began selling gas out of 50-gallon carts.

Not everyone was happy with the new-fangled invention. Cars frightened horses and splashed pedestrians with oil, dust, or mud. They also made a lot of noise. In 1907, the town marshal of Redwood City distributed a circular warning motorists about the "reckless manner in which the machines

The 1902 automobile meet to Crystal Springs Dam.

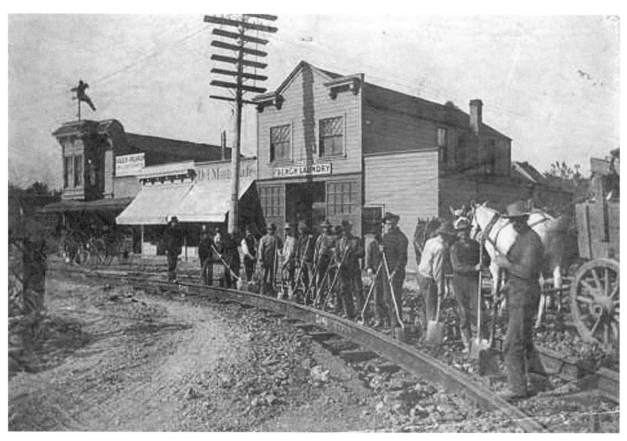

Laying track in San Mateo for the San Francisco and San Mateo Electric Railway at B Street and Baldwin Avenue. (circa 1902).

are being operated through the streets of this town." He therefore set the speed limit at ten miles per hour—four when approaching sharp curves and bridges.

Nevertheless, the age of the automobile had come. In a momentous step in the county's history, and indeed for California history as well, on August 7, 1912, work began on a five-mile stretch of El Camino Real, from San Bruno to Burlingame, that represented the initiation of the California State Highway System for the automobile. The state's initial investment in highway construction suited to automobile utilization was inspired by the coming of the Panama International Exposition at San Francisco in 1915. That it happened in San Mateo County was no accident. Since 1911, San Mateo County elected officials, at the urging of the *San Mateo Times,* had been clamoring for better roads, despite the opposition of the Southern Pacific Railroad. In 1913, San Mateo County voters, willing to buck the political and economic pressure of the Railroad, approved a $1,250,000 bond issue to match state grants to create a variety of roads for automobiles, including the Junipero Serra Highway.

This road construction helped set the stage for a new era. County historian Al Hynding explained: "No development after 1920 rivaled the impact of automobiles and highways in shaping Peninsula history. . . . Everywhere, highways dictated patterns of growth as the railroad had done a half century earlier."[10] Now for the first time since the days of the San Francisco–San Jose Railroad, those thinking of suburban residence down the peninsula did not have to be tied to the rail corridor.

The automobile made it possible to grow suburban development on the bayside up into the hills and down toward the Bay. For middle-class people, the vision of their little piece of the country could now expand. They were no longer limited to finding a place within walking distance of the street-car or train. They could now drive to work or the station. Their home could be more distant from the tracks, allowing more feeling for the country life made popular by the upper crust, and better yet, the piece of property they lived on could be bigger, allowing for more gardening and recreational opportunities, and in the process moving them even closer to their California Dream. Critics would say that this also opened the door for problems associated with urban sprawl, especially in the postwar period.

During the two decades that preceded World War II, the pace of construction for

Ship built and being launched in South San Francisco at Western Pipe & Steel. From 1940-1945, they built 45 ships in 48 months for the Maritime Commission during World War II. The plant became part of United States Steel, and existed as a steel rolling mill until 1983.

roads, highways, and bridges for the automobile was frenetic. For example, in 1922, work began on Skyline Boulevard, and in 1924, it also began for the Bayshore Highway. In 1927, the Dumbarton Bridge was completed. Two years later, so was the San Mateo Hayward Bridge. In 1937, the difficult work to create Highway 1 at Devil's Slide was accomplished.

Skyline in Daly City in the 1920's

As the streetcar was the facilitator and the 1906 Earthquake was the motivator for growth at the beginning of the twentieth century, the automobile was the facilitator and World War II was the motivator for growth at the midpoint in the century. Again, Al Hynding: "No other event, not even the Gold Rush, affected the Peninsula more deeply."[11] The county's significant expansion in population, economy, and infrastructure was certainly not an isolated occurrence. California was undergoing extraordinary growth as well. During the decade of the 1940s, California's population went from 7 million to 11 million, a 64 percent increase. However, San Mateo County did even better, comparatively. In 1940, 111,800 people lived here. By 1950, 235,000 were here, a 110 percent increase. As it did for all of California, World War II brought defense projects, whole industries, and people to San Mateo County.

Because America had a significant Pacific war for the first time, the entire California Coast was fortified against possible invasion by Japan. After the bombing of Pearl Harbor, coastal defense works were installed down the San Mateo Coastside from Daly City to Half Moon Bay. At Half Moon Bay an airfield was installed. The Merchant Marines created a training base at Coyote Point. The Cow Palace served as a gigantic motor pool and barracks. Tanforan first was employed as an "assembly center" for the Bay Area's Japanese-American population destined for internment at interior locations in the western United States. After their removal, the racetrack became an ammunition dump.

South San Francisco experienced a boom in industrial activity. By 1943, 10,000 workers were employed by Bethlehem and other steelmakers. Meanwhile, some 48 ships were built there, including four escort aircraft carriers.

War industries like these brought people to the peninsula from all over the country, including the first sizable number of African Americans from the South. Other ethnic groups attracted included Filipinos, American Indians, and Chinese. Additionally, thousands of military personnel, seeing the peninsula for the first time on their way to overseas duty, liked what they saw and returned here after their assignments, bringing their families with them.

No other single factor equaled the development of the airport off Millbrae in increasing economic activity in San Mateo County. Before the war, San Francisco's airport on the San Mateo County Bayshore was almost a joke. This despite the fact that San Mateo County had a rich aviation history that went as far back as the flight of Fred Marriott's Hermes, a self-propelled/dirigible aircraft back in 1869. The racetrack at Tanforan featured significant air shows in the days before World War I. In 1911, Eugene Ely became the first to land a plane on a ship after taking off from Selfridge Field at Tanforan. He landed on the armored cruiser, USS *Pennsylvania* out in San Francisco Bay, ushering in the era of naval aviation.

By the 1920s, San Francisco felt the need to create a quality municipal airport. The City's air facility at that time existed just east of the Presidio's Crissy Field at today's Marina District. Civic leaders judged this too confined an area to create a proper airport, recognizing that San Francisco was only 44.82 square miles. Thus, another location outside of the city would be nec-

Tanforan Race Track became an assembly center for Japanese Americans used for about 6 months until more permanent relocation camps were constructed. Photo taken April, 1942.

essary. They took the issue to the citizens of San Francisco, who approved the ability of City Hall officials to purchase land to create an airport by a five-to-one majority. While the campaign was still in progress, City Engineer M. M. O'Shaughnessy and staff considered where to place the future utility. A citizen's committee came up with several suggestions for him, including reclamation of shoals off Goat Island, nowTreasure Island, or roofing Civic Center. However, on the day before the election, O'Shaughnessy recommended property down in San Mateo County belonging to the Mills Estate. He reasoned that this was

Mills Field in 1931.

the first place down the bayshore of the peninsula that had suitable weather conditions. It was only 14 miles south of the city and only 22 minutes away from Civic Center by automobile. His investigation found that 160 acres were readily available for development, while there existed another 1,000 acres that could be reclaimed for future expansion. On March 17, 1927, the city leased the property from the Mills Estate, and on June 7, 1927, operations actually began.

However, there was considerable competition from Oakland, whose leadership was determined that its airport be the most important in the Bay Area. In fact, in November of 1927, Boeing, which had been the only airline at San Francisco Airport, moved its facilities to Oakland, leaving San Francisco with only general aviation business. It did not help that in 1929, while on a national promotional tour, the famed aviator Charles Lindberg accidentally got his plane stuck in the mud at what many people referred to as Mills Field. International headlines about the incident embarrassed San Franciscans.[12] The *San Francisco Chronicle* described the airport about this time as ". . . the world's prize mud hole and dust producer."

Nevertheless, the city kept on investing in Mills Field. In 1930, it finally bought the property from the Mills Estate. After some effort, commercial airlines were attracted there. In December 1932 came the good news that United Airlines would base its Pacific operations at San Francisco Airport. However, the Depression of the 1930s had effect. As late as 1934, falling revenues forced the city to reduce its airport staff from 16 to 11.

Dramatic change came with World War II. The military took control after Pearl Harbor and invested $10 million into the facilities there. By 1945, 100 acres had been reclaimed, with yet another 2,000 under development. About 700 acres were already in use, supporting several 16,000 foot runways. San Francisco Airport had become the largest single air link between the United States mainland and the Pacific theater of war. After the war, expansion continued as commercial aviation came into its own. In 1946, more that one million air passengers passed through the terminal of

This small farm, was the site of the future Bayshore Highway looking north of Third Avenue in San Mateo.

Bayshore Highway at 3rd Avenue in San Mateo in the 1920s.

Opening of Bayshore Highway in October 20, 1929 at South San Francisco.

Bayshore Highway at Bay Meadows in the early 1950's.

Highway 101 looking North from the Broadway Burlingame overpass. August 1985.

San Francisco International Airport, nearly one-tenth of the total for the entire United States. By that time, the Airport was providing 6,000 jobs, by far the single greatest employer on the peninsula.

Clustering around it in the postwar period were a variety of other companies that also created jobs for locals. Maintenance yards, shops, parking lots, industrial parks, hotels, restaurants, and many others lifted the economy of San Mateo County and the Bay Region on the whole. During and after the war, the airport helped stimulate the development of an electronics industry on the peninsula. EIMAC in South San Francisco became one of the biggest manufacturers of crucial transmitter tubes during the war. Dalmo Victor and Litton Industries started up in the Belmont/San Carlos area. Ampex got going in Redwood City. The airport, improved harbor facilities at the Port of Redwood City, the creation of freeways, the availability of cheap land, and intellectual talent pools furnished by the two great local universities, Stanford and the University of California at Berkeley, were all important to the success of the electronics industry, which eventually evolved into today's important software and biotechnology industries.

The right ingredients were now in place for the development of San Mateo County as an automobile-based suburbia. Kenneth Jackson, in his important work *The Crabgrass Frontier* (1985), established the criteria for such development. Road and highway systems need to be in place, catering to the automobile. In San Mateo County in the postwar period, the Bayshore Highway was expanded and improved into a freeway. In 1961, construction began on the 19th Avenue, or J. Arthur Younger Freeway, through San Mateo. In 1967, the San Mateo Hayward Bridge was replaced. In 1971, the Portola Freeway or Highway 380 was opened. In 1973, Highway 280 was completed. In 1984, the Dumbarton Bridge was improved and enlarged.

Third Avenue in San Mateo circa 1960.

Jackson tells us there needs to be a healthy economy, and the war brought that as well.

He asserts government needs to be friendly. The federal government in the postwar period offered financing at low interest rates to both home buyers and home builders on the peninsula and beyond. Meanwhile, state and local governments worked hard to provide adequate infrastructure and services to the new housing developments.

He suggests desire for the new suburban lifestyle has to be established, and Menlo Park's *Sunset* magazine would help with that.

Finally, Jackson holds that there also has to be knowledgeable developers—planners and builders—who know about mass construction financing, technique, and building practices. A variety of individuals stepped forward to answer that need in San Mateo County. Most had been well schooled in such activities while working with the federal government on projects during World War II.

Recognizing an acute housing shortage during the war because of the increased industrial activity, the federal government contracted a variety of builders to construct temporary low cost and unsightly projects in Millbrae, San Bruno, and South San Francisco. Among these builders was Henry Doelger.

As the war was ending, Doelger decided to buy up some 1,300 acres west of Daly City to create the Westlake District. Over a 20-year period he built a city for 20,000 people, which was annexed to Daly City in stages. Doelger was involved in other developments in San Mateo County, including

Aerial photograph of the Doelger development of the Westlake district.

Henry Doelger.

Construction at Serramonte about 1963 viewed from Skyline Blvd.

large tracts in Pacifica. He became sort of the prototypical builder in the area and gained considerable attention from admirers and critics as well.

Among those casting disparaging barbs at Doelger was poet and song writer Malvina Reynolds. In her folk song *Little Boxes,* she refers to the "ticky-tacky" houses in his mass construction projects in Daly City. Others would label the work of Doelger and developers around the state at this time as sterile and unimaginative. Defenders said such developments were there when Californians needed them. The nation on the whole believed that the children of the Great Depression who fought and won World War II deserved a reward. Low-interest loans to buy a home—part of the American Dream—were at hand through the federal government, but even with the money, many homes were going to have to be built in a hurry to satisfy the demand. Henry Doelger, and developers like him, answered the need. For the most part, those who bought up Doelger's inexpensive but utilitarian homes in Westlake were satisfied. They had come to own their own home, and without Henry Doelger this may never have happened.

Also working in the Daly City area were Carl and Fred Gellert. Like Doelger, the brothers had gained government contracts during the war. They built a number of projects in the north county area in the postwar era. The results of all this activity on Daly City was enormous. In 1950, it had a population of just 15,000. By 1960, the number stood at 60,000. The Gellerts bought up 1,000 acres of property in the early 1960s to create the Serramonte subdivision, which was also annexed to Daly City in stages. Their development included the construction of the Serramonte Shopping Center. In 2006, Daly City was the most populous city in the county with well over 100,000 people.

David Bohannon was the great builder for the mid-county area. He too worked on government housing contracts during the war, in other parts of the Bay Area. After World War II, he came back to a prewar plan to develop the Hillsdale area in San Mateo. By 1953, he had constructed the 500 apartment units of the Hillsdale Garden Apartments. Meanwhile, he built houses on his property from El Camino Real up to Alameda de las Pulgas and beyond. He also created the Hillsdale Shopping Center, which by 1960 was the site of three major department stores.

An aerial photograph shows an early view of Foster City with large areas of planned but yet undeveloped land. Barges or ships dredging fill for the young city are visible in the lower left portion of the photo.

Perhaps the most challenging development of the era was put in by the T. Jack Foster family. Hailing from Texas, T. Jack Foster Sr. began his career by building housing on southwestern military bases, notably Biggs Air Force Base in El Paso, Texas. He also built housing at Fort Ord in California. After building for the government, he completed civilian housing projects in California, Texas, New Mexico, Kansas, and Hawaii. His exposure to Monterey with his Fort Ord development induced him to retire there in 1958. However, his retirement lasted less than one year, because he decided to bring his three sons in on a development in California. After an extensive search, they settled on Brewer's Island, just east of San Mateo.

Brewer's Island had been drained and diked in 1900, and was the site of the Frank M. Brewer Dairy Farm. The Fosters chose this site for development because of its good size and its location on the Bayshore Freeway and Highway 92. On this land that they purchased from the Leslie Salt Company, the Fosters called for a "planned community" modeled after such developments in bombed-out England. Various engineering, architectural, and social concerns were focused on for the first time in a California development.

However, times were beginning to change for developers on the peninsula. Their plans had to endure much more scrutiny as the 1960s began. The educational establishment of the peninsula stood against the project because of its potential negative effect on taxpayers and the ability of local government and school districts to provide services. Even *San Francisco Chronicle* newspaper columnist Herb Caen jumped in. In 1962, he wrote: ". . . we have this big developer, T. Jack Foster . . . who has bought Brewer Island down the Peninsula and plans to turn the 2,600 acre site into something called Foster City. Now there's a name to wing the heart of a poet. Foster City. Sounds like a company town in Eastern Pennsylvania."[13] Then came the Army Corps of Engineers, who originally required filling the island to the height of 8 to 12 feet for insurance against flood and earthquake. The Corps also estimated that drainage would be a major problem. Something on the order of 200 acre-feet of water would have to be stored between high tide and low tide before it could be released into the bay and Belmont Slough.

The Fosters were into their project for the long haul, however, and answered these challenges. As far as their engineering problems were concerned, the Foster City engineers figured out that by installing attractive lagoons, they could store the water within the Island and not have to engage in the 8- to 12-foot filling operations. Doing so would have necessitated the topping off of some local hilltop, like Mount San Bruno, a disagreeable operation for any number of reasons. The lagoons, instead, would render beauty and recreational opportunities for families who bought lots with their backyards facing the water.

To avoid criticism from the Malvina Reynolds types, the Fosters desired to stay away from boxy home designs. Instead they chose Joseph Eichler as a builder with his varied free and flowing forms. They also employed Duc and Ellison, and Kay home design types.

To finance the project, the Fosters would again have to become creative. Few traditional banking institutions were interested in such a challenging development. So they went to their California state representatives to introduce special legislation to create an improvement district. The Estero Municipal Improvement District was signed into law in 1960. Nothing quite like it existed before or after. With the complete backing of the San Mateo County Board of Supervisors, who believed if the Fosters did not succeed nothing would happen to the property, this Estero Act created a self-governing district with power vested in a Board of Directors appointed by private parties who had invested in the development—in other words, the Fosters for the most part. Thus, state funds were loaned to the project to make Foster City a reality.

The Fosters' plan called for the creation of a city of 30,000 by 1976. This was to include 5,000 single-family houses, 1,600 townhouses, 4,400 apartments and condominiums, 9 elementary schools, 2 junior high schools, 1 high school, 230 acres of parks, 40 acres reserved for houses of worship, and 2,000 trees. The innovative plans were deemed so futuristic that they were placed on display at the Museum of Modern Art in San Francisco in 1963. Except for the schools (only two elementary and one junior high school would actually be built), most of what the Fosters imagined did become reality.

In 1964, when the houses went up for sale, prices ran from $22,950 to $40,000. The first 115 Kay homes sold in two weeks. Soon, some 2,000 names were on waiting lists to buy houses.

Not surprisingly, within six years the citizens of Foster City began to debate their future. Their options included staying as the Estero District, trying to annex themselves to San Mateo, or incorporating into a new city. Continuing as the Estero District with a less than democratic system seemed to be no one's choice. Annexation to San Mateo would have to meet with agreement from the citizens of San Mateo, who would have to accept the bonded indebtedness of the Estero of some $62 million. Thus, incorporation was the only real alternative. After a vote, 2,265 marked ballots were in favor of incorporation and only 38 said no.

Foster City was a marvelous success in the way that it was financed and built. It was also a success in the way that it was marketed. One real estate advertisement read: "In the age of many miracles, wouldn't it be infinitely better to dream-build a new city than to redesign and over-extend an old one? . . . Can a dream like this become a reality? Yes, indeed! At this very moment the dream of a perfect city is being translated into steel and wood, concrete, and glass. This is Foster City, a daring concept of an all-inclusive, self-supporting urban community. This is Foster City where a man may build his castle and raise his family in the finest of all possible worlds! . . . Foster City—a need fulfilled, a dream come true. . . ."[14]

The Fosters had employed in their marketing use of the word *dream*, as it applied to the *California Dream* and its accompanied term, *California Living*. Historian T. H. Watkins explains this concept of California life in the postwar period as "affluent, consumptive, credit oriented, extremely mobile, and leisurely self-indulgent." He tells us it's a lifestyle "wedded to the outdoors,"—not the wilderness, but one's backyard. By "stepping out the back door on a balmy weekend" one could appreciate one's patio, swimming pool, redwood furniture, freshly cut lawn, plants, and trees. Watkins tells us: "Its finest moment might be said to be illustrated by the picture of a man standing on his patio on a Saturday evening, a drink of good Scotch in one hand and a spatula in the other, barbecuing a few . . . steaks while his wife prepares a cool green California salad, his children cavort on the lawn with the dog and the patio lights dance on the chlorine blue surface of his kidney-shaped swimming pool."[15]

No better oracle inventing and promoting this type of lifestyle can be found than Menlo Park's *Sunset* magazine, "the magazine of Western Living," which succeeded in making the California Dream a national obsession. The Southern Pacific Railroad started *Sunset* in 1898 as a promotional piece, trying to encourage people in the East to visit and settle in the West. In 1928, Laurence Lane purchased the publication and established a new editorial philosophy that the magazine would be "for the West, not about the West."[16] While it would stand for certain values and ideals, its primary purpose would be to provide a program of action on how to achieve the best of western life. Through the years *Sunset* won its place as a guide to better suburban living for westerners. For the growing numbers of people from other places who read the magazine, it represented what the West was all about and—for many—the reason they would eventually come to the West to live.

In 1951, Lane and his two sons, L. W. "Bill" and Melvin, defined their vision of suburban life further by moving their operations from San Francisco down into the suburbs at Menlo Park. Home designer Cliff May planned the new building, and landscape architect Thomas Church laid out the gardens. Their intention in creating the headquarters was to construct a large-scale ranch-style complex encompassing the best aspects of the new western suburb.

From these offices, the Lanes and their editorial staff could better focus on the four major categories that were the hallmark of *Sunset*. One of these was home improvement. Beyond how-to-do instructional articles, this category also allowed the magazine to become the first of its kind to extol western architectural values. Because of this promotion, the western home design became popular across America.

Another area centered on the garden. Recognizing the mild climate in California, the magazine discussed "year-round gardening calendars." A third area was travel. Westerners are mobile, and the West is a great jumping-off place for adventure to the islands of the Pacific, to Alaska, Mexico, and other lands far away and closer at hand. Finally, there was food and entertainment. *Sunset* pioneered the development of the modern American kitchen. This former hidden work space for servants and/or the solitary mother figure of the family became a creative place for the whole family—a room for parents and offspring to come together. At the Menlo Park headquarters, large kitchens, equipped with the latest and best cooking devices, became the "the Laboratory of Western Living," as recipes were tried and invented on site.

By exploring these four categories, the Lanes made sure that *Sunset* would not become a women's or men's magazine. Home improvement was, by and large, directed at male readers, and the food sections were largely for females. Gardening and travel were for all. Although the Lane family sold *Sunset* to Time Warner in 1990, the magazine continues to this day to be the leading voice about how Californians—indeed how Americans—view the ideal suburban lifestyle. From a historical standpoint, there could be no better place to situate the headquarters of such a magazine as in San Mateo County, where the San Francisco to San Jose Railroad started the suburban life of the West in 1864, and where California's statewide commitment to the automobile began with the state's highway construction project of 1912.

The railroad, streetcar, and automobile made the current development of San Mateo County possible. In recent years the automobile, in particular, has given the peninsula its appearance and character. This is one of the most desirable places in the world to live, but the gadget that has made it all possible, the automobile, has also given this county and all of California's urban and suburban communities problems. Pollution and congestion are preeminent among the issues. Statewide, and within San Mateo County, elected officials agree that public transportation needs to be increased in order to answer these vexing questions.

Private operators began exploring bus systems early in the twentieth century. In 1914, Burlingame Mayor William Pearson and partner Harry Regan started the Peninsula Rapid Transit Company, which featured service from San Francisco to San Jose with stops in San Mateo County. In 1916, a competing line, Pacific Auto Stages, began operations. The Greyhound Corporation of Chicago acquired both systems in 1930. Meanwhile, Peerless Auto Stage started service to the coast in 1920. The old horse-drawn coaches were still in operation until 1910. Typical time to reach San Gregorio from Redwood City was seven hours. The Peerless time was five and a half hours—better, but this slow time indicates that the conditions of the roads to the coast still needed considerable attention.

Although these companies offered some service, the period was one completely dominated by the automobile at the expense of the alternative forms of transportation. As an example, the ridership of the Southern Pacific commuter line on the Peninsula that saw 30,000 users a day in the 1940s was down to 16,000 a day in the early 1970s.

The 1973 national energy crisis brought on by the Arab Oil Embargo prompted San Mateo County officials to react. In August of 1974, they asked voters to approve forming the San Mateo County Transit District (Sam Trans), which would integrate 11 existing city bus lines into a uniform system. In January of 1975, the newly organized Sam Trans board appointed John T. Mauro as its first general manager. In 1977, Sam Trans accomplished the buy-out of Greyhound's local fleet, and by 1980, Sam Trans had more than 200 buses, accommodating 20 million annual passengers, some five times the capacity of 1975.

Meanwhile, in 1977, the Southern Pacific announced that decreasing revenues were driving it to consider abandoning commuter service on the peninsula. In 1980, Cal Train agreed to take-over the service, and in 1992, the Peninsula Corridor Joint Powers Board became involved as the contractor to run the system. In 1998, Cal Train posted record ridership, with a tally of 8.8 million in that year—the best showing since 1954.

Rapid rail transit in the form of BART (Bay Area Rapid Transit) has had a slower history, largely because in 1962, local business leaders such as Hillsdale Shopping Center owner David Bohannon, San Mateo attorney Tom Casey, and San Mateo County Development Association director Bud Bostwick opposed the tax measure that would have included the peninsula in the original BART plan. They convinced the San Mateo County Board of Supervisors that the project was wasteful and ill-conceived. Nevertheless, Alameda, Contra Costa, and San Francisco counties successfully pushed ahead with a $792 million bond issue. Much of the system came on line in 1973—during the energy crisis—and many in San Mateo County began to wonder if a big mistake had been made. Seventeen years later, an agreement was reached to build an extension from BART in Daly City (terminus of the original system) to the San Francisco International Airport. Building stations at Colma, South San Francisco, San Bruno, Millbrae, and Burlingame became part of the new plan.

Chapter 7 Footnotes

1. Stanger, *South*, p. 65.
2. Elaine Thomas, "Leonetto Cipriani: The Count of Belmont", *La Peninsula*, vol. XXI, No. l, Fall 1981, p. 26.
3. George Lyman, *Ralston's Ring*, Charles Scribner's Sons, 1937, p. 96–98.
4. Hynding, *From Frontier*, p. 61.
5. Postel, *History of the Burlingame Country Club*, p. 10.
6. Ibid. p.11.
7. Ibid. p. 5.
8. San Mateo County Historical Association, *Burlingame: Its Railroad Station*, May, 1971, p. 3.
9. Hynding, *Frontier*, p. 209.
10. Ibid. p. 256.
11. Ibid. p. 269.
12. Mitchell P. Postel, "San Francisco International Airport: 1869–1942," *La Peninsula*, vol. XXVII, No. 2, Winter 1991–92, p. 12.
13. Mitchell P. Postel, *Peninsula Portrait*, Windsor Publishing, Inc., 1988, p. 72.
14. T. H. Watkins, *California: An Illustrated History*, Weablisvane Books, New York, p. 454.
15. Ibid. p. 455.
16. Kevin Starr, "Sunset and the Phenomenon of the Far West," *Sunset Magazine: A Century of Western Living, 1898–1998*, Stanford University Libraries, Stanford University, 1998, p. 53.

Chapter 8

The Immigrant Experience

oday, San Mateo County is frequently cited as one of the most racially and ethnically diverse places in the United States. The county's character is enriched by the many cultures represented here, while challenges are heaped on educators and social service agencies trying to help newcomers adjust to life on the peninsula. The concept that this is a very diverse place is hardly new. Since Gold Rush times, people from all over the world have chosen to settle here. By 1880, when the population of the county was about 8,700, about a third of the people had been born in another country, hailing from about 15 different countries. When counting their second-generation children, one can surmise that at least half of the people of the peninsula had an immigration experience in the family's recent history.

By far, the single-largest group in the nineteenth century were the Irish. As early as 1880, 900 had come to live in San Mateo County. In other words, more than one-tenth of the people here had been born in Ireland. Second among the foreign born, according to the 1880 census, were the Chinese, with a population of about 600, or around 7 percent, the highest percentage it would reach in local history. Other European people included the Germans at 341, the English at 202, the Scandinavians at 98, and the Scottish at 65. There were also Portuguese and Italian people here, and their

Pescadero School, October 26, 1897, showing the ethnic diversity of the students.

First Roman Catholic Church on the Peninsula. Dedicated in 1853 on property of Dennis Martin in the south county.

numbers increased dramatically after the Chinese Exclusion Act of 1882. During the entire second half of the nineteenth century, immigrants would provide San Mateo County with most of its unskilled and skilled work force.

The Irish

The story of the Irish on the peninsula goes back farther than even Gold Rush times. During the days when Mexico still controlled California, Irishman John Copinger came to own an original land grant here and became one of the most influential men in the region.

Maria Louisa Soto Copinger Greer with Greer sons.

Born the son of Alderman John Copinger of Dublin in 1811, he became a sailor, ending up in Monterey, California, in 1836. He befriended Juan Bautista Alvarado, the assistant inspector of customs there. Copinger helped Alvarado organize a revolt against the Mexican governor of California, using the slogan "California for Californians."[1] Alvarado appointed Copinger to the rank of lieutenant, and as such, Copinger helped win a skirmish against a small garrison at Monterey.

In 1839, Copinger wished to make good on his status as a veteran of the revolt by requesting a land grant from his friend, now Governor Alvarado. He did three things to help himself in pursuit of a rancho. He became a Mexican citizen, converted to the Catholic religion, and married into one of the old Spanish families. Maria Louisa Soto's grandfather was one of the original soldiers on the Anza expedition. As Copinger's wife, she had much influence in his being awarded Rancho Canada Raymundo in August of 1840. This land today would take up a good part of the southern watershed lands owned by the city of San Francisco. There he built an adobe house (which stood until the 1906 Earthquake), raised crops and cattle, and improved his property with fences, a gristmill, and a dam.

He continued to stay active in public affairs. In 1842, he was named justice of the peace for the Redwoods by the Mexican government. His jurisdiction included the coast ranchos and other territories south of Mission San Francisco, about half of what is now San Mateo County. He died in 1847. Maria then married Woodside legend John Greer.

After the Gold Rush began, Irish immigrants came in numbers. They mixed with American farmers on the coast and in present-day north county growing cabbage, potatoes, and grains. In general, the Irish who came to the peninsula and, indeed, to all of California, had a much better experience than those on the East Coast. They rapidly moved ahead economically, socially, and politically. The reasons were many.

For one thing, the Irish that arrived in California generally had an immigration experience already. Whether from Australia or the big cities of the East Coast, the Irish that came to California tended to have the know-how to succeed in this new land. They also tended to be a bit better educated, had a little more money in their pockets, and had perhaps a larger spirit of adventure than, say, their counterparts stuck in the confines of the big cities in the East. Unlike almost everyone else, American or foreign, the Irish intended to stay here. In general, all other groups had it in mind to make a fortune in California and return home. For the Irish, the potato famine and the polit-

The Parrott Estate, one of the large estates of San Mateo. The land parcel had been sold for a housing development when the mansion was destroyed by fire in 1928.

ical oppression of the homeland made this an undesirable choice. And so, unlike most of the other people they encountered, the Irish took a long-range interest in this new place. Its economy and politics were important from the beginning. The Irish appreciated all the freedoms they had here that were denied back home and were anxious that California have a sanguine future. They therefore participated in civic affairs and politics more than their neighbors, on average. Finally, although they encountered prejudice, the immigration experience in California was far less hostile than almost any other place the Irish landed.[2]

In the world of politics, this meant representation far ahead of the East Coast. That David Broderick could become a U.S. senator in 1857 was a California phenomenon. Chris Lilly's assumption of so much early political power in San Mateo County at the time of the Consolidation Act is a local example. That the San Francisco vigilance committee of 1856 chased Lilly and his gang out of California did not mean that Irish political interests were snuffed out on the peninsula. To the contrary, Irish political might in San Mateo County was important throughout the nineteenth century and beyond.

In part, this was due to the fact that many of the founding pioneers were Irish, such as Dennis Martin. Martin's father, William, decided to leave Missouri in 1844 after a priest convinced him and his family that California would be a better place for people of their religion. They became part of the first wagon train to pass over the Sierra Nevada Mountains. After gold was found, Dennis Martin came to the peninsula to become engaged in the lumber industry. In 1853, he helped establish St. Dennis Church at Searsville, the first Catholic Church organized in San Mateo County.[3]

Another example is Patrick Maloney and his wife Hanora, who arrived on the peninsula in the early 1860s and began farming at Menlo Park. In the meantime, Patrick Cullen came to Redwood City in 1862. He established the Cullen Feed & Fuel store in 1882. In 1900, Maggie Maloney and Cornelius Cullen married and merged these two important families. Today, hundreds of their descendants still reside in San Mateo County.

By 1860, Irish communities existed in north county, on the coast, San Mateo, and Redwood City. Their presence in the county was made obvious by the churches they established. St. Matthew's was founded in San Mateo in 1863, and was followed by Catholic churches in Half Moon Bay (1868), Pescadero (1868), Menlo Park (1877), La Honda (1883), and Redwood City (1887).

The common folks were joined by some of California's elite personalities. Joseph A. Donohue established his 40-acre suburban estate in 1868. His Holm Grove featured a three-

Artist rendition of the Flood Estate, known as "Linden Towers."

story Victorian mansion, complete with chapel and hydraulic elevator. Also in 1868, and also at Menlo Park, attorney John T. Doyle built his 400-acre Ringwood with its two-story house.

Of all the early mansion builders, Irish or otherwise, none matched James Flood. Born in New York in 1826, shortly after his parents arrived from Ireland, Flood became known as the "Silver King" after making a fortune in the Comstock mining district. Along with other members of the Irish elite, he decided to create his estate at Menlo Park. Here he built Linden Towers, which became known as "the wedding cake" because of its ornate construction. When completed, it stood as the largest mansion in the West, with 43 rooms and bathroom fixtures made of Comstock silver.

Perhaps the most generous of the Irish elite on the peninsula was Abigail Meagher Parrott. Born to Irish parents in 1829, she came to California in 1853 after marrying John Parrott. Their 377-acre Baywood estate in San Mateo was vastly improved in 1868 with additions made to the mansion there. In 1884, John died, but stipulated to his wife that the hungry and homeless should always find comfort at Baywood. In the latter part of the nineteenth century, El Camino Real was a major road for transient men trying to find work. The Baywood estate was close to the highway, and many knew of John's instructions to his wife. Abby was never known to turn anyone away. She was said to serve as many as a hundred transients on a single evening, and she always prepared for them the same fare that her family and social guests would receive. Abby was also a major donor to St. Matthew's Catholic Church in San Mateo and St. John's Cemetery.

The mansion building on the peninsula attracted yet more Irish. When the Baywood project got underway in 1868, 23-year-old carpenter Robert Wisnom from Ballycarry County, Ireland, decided to settle at San Mateo. That first year he worked for the Parrotts, but then he bought a parcel of land on B Street between Third and Fourth Avenues. Here he established a lumber business and continued to buy property. As an esteemed member of the community, he was elected as one of the original trustees of San Mateo after it incorporated in 1894. His family remains well known and admired to this day.

By the 1870s, at least a tenth of California's population was Irish. Clearly in San Mateo County this was also the case. In 1883, when a history book about the county was published, of the 125 leading residents who sponsored the undertaking, 20 were Irish. Not surprisingly, almost all of them had an experience in another state before coming to California.

Belmont Park, now Twin Pines Park.

The Irish story in San Mateo County also includes large visiting parties. In the 1860s and 1870s, the Fenians, a political organization devoted to Irish causes, used various spots in San Mateo County along the railroad tracks for their picnics. Special trains were hired for the occasions. During these outdoor events, Irish families, mostly from San Francisco, were told of the situation back home. Money was raised for Fenian projects. The families discussed local issues that affected the Irish, as well as who to vote for in the next election. The Fenian picnic at San Mateo drew 15,000 people in 1866. The Belmont Park event in May of 1868 attracted 10,000, and the Redwood City picnic of 1870 was said to have been attended by 12,000. All this in the day when the population of Redwood City, the largest town in San Mateo, did not exceed 1,000. In fact, the population of the entire county in 1870 was not more than 7,000. The sheer enormity of these events, as compared to the capabilities of local law enforcement agencies, required the Fenians to hire their own special police to control fights and other forms of misbehavior.

San Francisco Irish were also responsible for some of the largest work projects on the peninsula during the nineteenth century. They were the labor force that built the Crystal Springs Dam between 1887 and 1889, the largest interlocking concrete block dam ever constructed.

In 1883, as Irish workmen helped build the Holy Cross Cemetery at Colma, Irishman Patrick Brooks opened the Brookville Hotel to assist in housing some of the construction crews. As the cemetery complex of Colma grew, so did Brooks's business. During Prohibition times the place had a rowdy reputation. In 1929, Frank Molloy purchased the Brooksville. Born in Donegal, Ireland, Molloy had started out as a busboy in San Francisco restaurants. When Frank's son Lanty returned home after service in the Korean War, he took over operation of the hotel and renamed it Historical Old Molloy's, a north county social institution to this day.

The Germans

Early on, German pioneers came to the peninsula, acquiring farms and launching into other businesses. As German brewmasters dominated beer making throughout America in the nineteenth century, they did so in San Mateo County as well.[4] Michael Kreiss founded the County's first brewery in 1865—the Pioneer Brewery at Redwood City. Also at Redwood City, Claus Hadler owned the Eureka Brewery.

Kreeis's Pioneer Brewery, Redwood City. German immigrants ran all the early breweries in San Mateo County. From Moore and De Pue's *Illustrated History of San Mateo County,* 1878.

The only brewery on the coast was operated by Edward Schubert at Half Moon Bay. All three men had been born in Germany, and they represented the entire ownership of breweries in nineteenth century San Mateo County.

In the realm of politics, August Eikerenkotter became a well-known county supervisor. He came to California from Prussia during the Gold Rush. He operated a San Francisco boarding house until 1853, when he moved to Searsville and established a small hotel. By 1858, he had added a tavern and store. About that time Eikerenkotter launched his political career when he was named postmaster to the area.

Of all the early Germans, with the exception of Charles Lux (see the next chapter) none was better known than Carl Janke, the creator of Belmont Park. He recognized the potential for renting out a picnic complex for the immigrant populations in San Francisco. Only two years after the completion of the San Francisco–San Jose Railroad, Janke obtained property in today's Belmont for that purpose. Besides the Fenians, other Irish groups used his Belmont Park, including the Hibernians. German organizations and other ethnic communities came to Belmont Park by the thousands, as well. The

Irish News of May 16, 1868, reported that the 10,000 Fenians that attended the picnic at Belmont Park came down the peninsula on a train half a mile long, powered by three locomotives.

Janke patterned his park after a Hamburg biergarten. Its entrance was located a few hundred feet southwest of today's Sixth and Ralston Avenues. The park ran west up Ralston along the creek nearly to today's College of Notre Dame. Bayleaf, oak, and buckeye trees covered the 12-acre property. It featured a dance pavilion that could hold 300 people. The pavilion included large glassless windows, a barroom, ice cream parlor, and lunchroom. The bar, fashioned into a circular configuration, was memorable for the keg of beer that sat in its middle. Other amenities included a shooting gallery and running track. Its picturesque wooded pathways were connected by bridges. The park remained popular throughout most of the nineteenth century, but as the years went by, the place began acquiring a reputation for rowdiness and violent behavior among the groups attending the picnics there. Janke installed a jail under the dance floor, and the various parities were encouraged to police themselves; nevertheless, before 1900, the Southern Pacific refused to cater to the destructive crowds anymore, and Belmont Park closed down.[5]

By 1900, the German population of the county had reached 500. They had achieved, by that time, a successful reputation on the peninsula, matched by none for their accomplishments in small businesses across the county.

The Chinese

The Chinese came to California during the Gold Rush era; however, not too many were originally noticed in San Mateo County. Later, they gained notoriety when they were employed to construct the San Franisco–San Jose Railroad in the early 1860s. Their success as hard workers was noticed by the Big Four who were building the Central Pacific, or the western section of the transcontinental railroad. After that railroad was completed in 1869, the thousands of Chinese who had worked for the Central Pacific were released from their jobs. Many came back to California, where they found work in a variety of places, including San Mateo County.

By 1880, at least 600 were present here. It was difficult to distinguish between the resident Chinese and those only here temporarily for work. They tended to avoid the census takers for fear of persecution and/or taxes. The majority were young, single men from the southern regions of China. Their plan, in most cases, was to make some reasonable amount of money here and then return to China. They were therefore like most other recent arrivals in California, but they tended to hold onto that intention for longer.

They performed most of the low-paying gang labor on the peninsula during the 1870s and 1880s. That type of work was many times limited to the duration of the project, so they tended to be transient, moving in and out of the county as jobs became available. They worked successfully as shrimp fisherman, as discussed in Chapter VI. They toiled in lumber camps, pealed tan bark, and gathered wood. They labored on the farms of others, particularly in north county and on the coast. It was noted that at the small agricultural community of San Gregory, a Chinatown of sorts existed. The laborers lived in town and were employed by the various farmers around them as needed. They also worked on the great estates on the bayside. Darius Mills and Alvinza Hayward used Chinese labor to reclaim marshes and dig ditches. In fact, Hayward used them to lay water pipe for San Mateo. The 1880 census listed 50 of the Chinese as residing at Menlo Park. Here, ten worked at a washhouse and a few of the women became domestic servants.

Some, by that time, operated small shops and owned or leased farms. By 1898, Chinese had entered the flower-growing industry. At Baden (part of South San Francisco, today), Chinese growers were noted for cultivating violets.

According to county historian Alan Hynding, despite the fact that locals disapproved of their gambling habits and they were subject to the racial prejudices of the day, the Chinese in San Mateo County were generally treated better than in other parts of California.[6] Hynding cites the experience of merchant Ah Kim of Pescadero, whose success allowed him to employ 12 of his countrymen. He also relates how, in 1874, William Ralston was able to hire 70 white men and 80 Chinese to work together to build a 100,000-gallon water reservoir behind his Belmont mansion. Of course, peace was maintained only because Ralston promised to pay the Chinese less.

Suggesting social acceptance is the story of the popular Gong Gong, a cook on a Millbrae ranch, who married Ah Ho in 1878. Reverend H. E. Tewett conducted the wedding, western style, at the Tremont House in Redwood City. County luminaries such as Coastside Supervisor Alex Gordon, Judge James Bicknell, and Sheriff George Green attended the ceremony.

Despite such local forbearance, the situation statewide for the Chinese was horrendous. After 1852, when the numbers of Chinese started to swell, Californians, behind doors and quite openly, questioned whether the Chinese should be allowed into the state. That year, Governor John Bigler initiated a doctrine, believing in a "Yellow Peril,"[7] that became an excuse for hatred for three decades. In short, he believed that the Chinese, as temporary visitors, were depressing the white working classes, had allegiance only to their mother country, and would overwhelm California in sheer numbers unless something was done. By far, the majority of Californians agreed with him for the rest of the century.

The sad story of the shrimp fishermen of San Francisco Bay is an example of the oppressive nature of government officials against the Chinese. The reader may recall that in Chapter V of this book we discussed the

Chinese shrimp fisherman mending nets on the bayshore, circa 1890.

James Van Court's photograph of a Chinese lady in Redwood City, circa 1890.

successful shrimp fishing operations off San Mateo County's bayline. In short, by the latter portion of the nineteenth century, a quarter of all the shrimp marketed in California came from the Chinese camps here. Opposition grew against the fishermen until they were forced to abandon their operations.

By the 1880s, white fishermen in the San Francisco area were blaming Chinese fishermen for decreasing catches of fish in the Bay. State law already banned the Chinese from catching most varieties of fish. However the complaints were leveled at the shrimp fishermen because, it was alleged, their highly effective bag nets also caught small commercial fish and the food of the commercial varieties.

Chinese shrimp boat.

The rancor coincided with a worldwide concern about decreasing catches of food fish. The United States created a Commission of Fish and Fisheries in 1870 to, in part, study the matter. In 1881, federal investigator Richard Rathbun found that the Chinese were not only depleting shrimp from the Bay but were catching small fish and eggs of fish. He suggested that the state act to end abusive Chinese practices. However, California had appointed its own team of experts, the Commissioners of Fisheries, to delve into the subject. In the meantime, a State Senate report, published in 1874, stated that after witnessing haul after haul of bag-net catches, the Senators could determine that nothing but shrimp were being caught. In an 1879 publication, the State Commissioners declared the white fishermen as guilty as any for overfishing the Bay. They pointed out that pollution from organic waste was the more likely reason for the decreasing productivity of the Bay, and that this should be the focus of attention to improve the situation.[8]

Despite the findings of these state officials, federal authorities continued to be critical of the Chinese practices. This encouraged local newspapers of the Bay Region to enliven the "Yellow Peril" discussion with yet another example of the "Chinese Scourge." The state commissioners remained firm in their beliefs, withstanding severe pressure. Sadly, in 1883, all three of the original members died. The new board bent to the popular pressure. In 1884, they organized a Bay patrol to crack down on any illegal practices being used by the Chinese. Between that year and 1900, a virtual war was at hand on the Bay as the Chinese tried to avoid the law. In just the period 1885 to 1886, 600 arrests were made.

From today's vantage point, we wonder about all this focus on the Chinese when the Bay's ecology was being truly threatened by other causes. In the Commissioner's Report of 1891–92, deputy patroller John Babcock wrote this:

[W]e went down the bay and arrested two Chinamen who were catching sturgeon with sturgeon lines (an illegal act), and took them to Redwood city (sic.) to await trial. . . . We have made almost weekly trips to the Chinese shrimp stations during the season of 1891–1892, and the constant howl that we do not enforce the law as regards to the Chinese is done for some other purpose than is apparent upon the surface. These camps are regularly and systematically overhauled, and all that we can do with the means at our hands is being done, to see that they do not destroy the young of fish. The drying beds at all of these camps are mostly free of small fish. I do not believe that the law is violated to the extent that is complained of.[9]

Ah Sam Florist Shop, an El Camino Real landmark in San Mateo for decades.

For years, the Chinese shrimp companies in San Francisco tried to deal with state officials in the usual way—by bribing them. In 1900, however, the state unleashed a crackdown more intense than any one previously. Shrimpers at San Rafael rioted in response. The companies then hired a team of lawyers to defend their men, and most of the prosecutions failed. Then in 1901, the state passed a law banning commercial shrimp fishing from May until September. Once again, the Chinese sent their lawyers into action. They claimed that the seasonal restrictions invaded the property rights of the companies and interfered with the practicing of a legitimate business. The dispute made it as far as the U.S. Supreme Court, where the Chinese lost in the 1905 case of *Ah King* v. *the Superior Court of San Francisco*. The seasonal law, plus other types of pres-

Mabel Leong. Susan Gilbert, Photographer.

sure, reduced the shrimp business of the Bay quite a bit. The big blow came in 1910, when the state outlawed the bag net. For five years shrimp disappeared from the California market. Although the bag net was made legal again in 1915, the shrimp camps of San Mateo County were never revived.

The larger story of the Chinese in California is no more uplifting. Substantial pressure from California's working classes, particularly the Irish, resulted in the Chinese Exclusion Act of 1882, which basically stopped Chinese workers from entering the United States. In 1892, the Act came up for renewal and was extended ten years. In 1902, it was made permanent, until the Act was finally repealed in 1943. The effect on California was a drastic drop in the manual labor supply. Immigrants from Italy, Portugal, Japan, and many other places gradually filled the vacuum. For the Chinese of California, they faced a life separated from family. If they intended to stay here, because most had come as single men, they might not ever get a chance to marry. Throughout California, and San Mateo County as well, the population of Chinese people decreased as the years went by.

Nevertheless, some families endured and became important to the cultural fabric of the peninsula. The Lee family of San Mateo is one example. Six brothers from China came to work on the transcontinental railroad together. They found their way to San Mateo after the railroad's completion and decided to pool their money to lease land to open a laundry business. In 1908, the aging brothers sent for their 15-year-old nephew, Albert Chow Yee, for help in order to continue the business. After three years, Albert decided to return to China to marry Dere Shea, by family arrangement. Because of the Exclusion Law, many people from China wanting to enter the United States had to be processed at Angel Island out in San Francisco Bay. Dere was detained there for two years while being interrogated and physically examined. After being released, she helped the Yee family grow in San Mateo. Today the Yees still own their Ching Lee Laundry.

Another family of note, also establishing a San Mateo business, are the Leongs. Shun (Sam) Leong and his wife Wong Shee arrived in California in 1913. In 1931, they decided to move down to San Mateo, where Shun purchased a fruit and vegetable delivery route. Their son, Gordon, founded the Ah Sam floral shop in 1933 when he was only 18 years old. Gordon named the small store at the edge of town in honor of his father, Ah—meaning sir or mister in Chinese—and Sam—the anglicized version of Shun. The business blossomed into one of the great family-held retail operations in San Mateo County. In 1983, due to its terrific reputation, Ah Sam was chosen to create the floral decor for England's Queen Elizabeth's state visit to the Bay Area.

The Portuguese

Among the groups that filled the labor vacuum in California after the Chinese Exclusion Act of 1882, were the Portuguese, and among them, principally people from the Azores. However, there were Portuguese in San Mateo County at least as early as the 1860s, mostly settling out on the coastside. A few picked up farming, but most of the early Portuguese engaged themselves in coast whaling.

California's coast whaling operations consisted of largely Portuguese crews, waiting at various stations along the coast for California Grey and Humpback whales to migrate close to the shore. After the whales were spotted, the whalers would launch their long boats and pursue the animals. The Portuguese would harpoon the whales and then haul their bodies back to the station. The blubber would be stripped off the whales and boiled down in try pots. A full grown whale would render between 30 and 50 barrels of oil. In the nineteenth century, whale oil was used in a variety of ways, including utilization as a fine lubricant and fuel. No large ships were involved in the activity, with the principle production processes completed right on the beach. Two whaling stations existed in San Mateo County, one at Pillar Point and the other at Pigeon Point.

In 1869, a visitor staying at the Swanton House in Pescadero, Col. Albert S. Evans, observed the operation at Pigeon Point. He wrote: "Here, on the high headland, are clustered some dozen cottages, inhabited by the coast whalers and their families. These men are all . . . from the Azores. . . . They work hard, and are doing well in business." He described their boats as "sharp" and "single-masted" with "odd-looking sails." On the day that he witnessed the activity, he noted that the men in the boats were aided by others on land who used flag staffs and signals to guide those at sea to the approach of the whales. Excitement grew when some humpbacks were spotted. The boats were "run out with sails set." Aboard the boats: "All was bustle and excitement . . . the harpooners standing the bows ready to strike, and every man at his post." Evans noticed that one of the signalers knew a little English, and he spoke to him about the pursuit of one of the humpbacks. When this particular

I.D.E.S. Hall in Half Moon Bay circa 1911.

animal escaped the harpoons, the signal man " . . . proceeded to curse in good Portuguese, honestly and squarely, for fifteen minutes, and I felt my respect for him rising almost to the point of admiration." Evans described a row of casks filled with oil testifying "to the success of the business." He wrote about how messy the work was with "flukes and wreck" lying on the beach. The oil seemed to saturate everything with the "stinking fluid" even running down "the face of the bluff to the water's edge, and whole the place was redolent of the perfume."[10]

Whaling fell off as the nineteenth century wore on, mostly because the number of whales off the California Coast declined. Portuguese families continued to arrive, however. Increasingly, they pursued agricultural interests. For example, Antone de Brun left the Azores at the age of 16, arriving in New England where he worked as a servant. He fought in the Civil War and then decided to come to Pescadero where he had relatives. He grew beans and other crops and married Mary Lawrence (also born in the Azores). Their daughter Lena married John Souza (whose family, again, was from the Azores) about 1913. The Souza family was quite well-known in the San Gregorio Valley, where they did the thrashing for other farmers. As a leader of his community, John served on the boards of Half Moon Bay High School and the Bank of Italy.

Chinese Exclusion meant more opportunity to Portuguese immigrant laborers, and after 1882, most of the menial work done in San Mateo County was performed by either Italian or Portuguese men. By 1890, about 500 Portuguese lived in the county. Of these, 125 had already become citizens. About 80 percent of these new Americans lived on the coastside where about four-fifths of them listed their occupations as farmer or dairyman. Only 15 of those that had taken out their papers said that they were common laborers.[11]

The largest grouping of Portuguese not living on the coastside came to South San Francisco. Between 1912 and 1914, something on the order of 17 families from the Azores came to make a life in that industrializing town. They mainly worked in the steel mills there, and in the meat-packing plant and at Fuller Paint as well.

The Portuguese of California, and especially those on the San Mateo County Coast, were more anxious than most to assimilate into their new country. They were quick to anglicize their names. They found the coast the great "melting pot" that was the American promise. Here the old Spanish families had already mixed with pioneers from the United States and with the Irish. Coming in increasing numbers were Italians who shared certain traits with the Portuguese, including their Catholic religion.

Despite their wishes to be assimilated, they did hang onto certain cultural traditions. Perhaps best known is The Holy Ghost Festa originally organized on the West Coast by Rosa Brown, reportedly the second Portuguese woman to come to live at Half Moon Bay. In 1871, at her home at Frenchmen's Creek, it is said the Charmarita folk dance was performed in what is considered to be the oldest celebration of its kind in California history. The festival has its roots in either the thirteenth or fourteenth century, when famine gripped the island of Pico in the Azores. On the morning of the Pentecost (the seventh Sunday after Easter), a ship arrived unexpectedly with a cargo of food,

William P. Cunha. The Cunha family's influence on Half Moon Bay is noted by street names, a school, and other sites that honor these early immigrants to the coast.

answering many prayers. The ship's captain fed the people, but accepted no payment in return. When Queen Isabel of Portugal heard of the generous act, she led a procession in honor of the Holy Ghost through the streets of Lisbon. At the cathedral there, she left her crown on the alter as an offering of thanksgiving. Thus, the people of the Azores treated the day as one of thanksgiving and sacrifice ever since. Besides folk dancing, a free lunch to everyone who wishes one became a tradition for the Half Moon Bay and Pescadero Portuguese communities.

In order to keep the festival alive, in 1896 the Brotherhood of the Holy Spirit (Irmandade do Espirito Santo—or I.D.E.S.) came into being at Half Moon Bay. That year, one of its members, Manuel Phillips Dutra, traveled throughout the county collecting silver coins for melting to create a 30-pound, 24-inch crown for the society's observances. Two years later, Dutra and his wife donated property in Half Moon Bay for the celebrations to take place. In 1911, the Brotherhood built its first hall. In 1928, the hall that stands today in downtown Half Moon Bay was completed. An I.D.E.S. hall was also built at Pescadero, and it still stands as well.

Besides its I.D.E.S. hall and annual festival, the Portuguese have another beloved institution in Half Moon Bay—Cunha's Country Store. Brothers Joseph and William Cunha opened the store on Main Street in 1924. Since that time, it has become a piece of Half Moon Bay community tradition that people truly care about. When a fire destroyed a major portion of Cunha's in 2003, the entire community came together to help the family rebuild the retail landmark in record time.

The Italians

Between 1882 and 1920, the largest group of immigrants to come to San Mateo County hailed from Italy. Like the Portuguese, while the big numbers came after Chinese Exclusion, there were Italians here before 1882.

Perhaps the first Italian to live in San Mateo County was a count who bought up acreage from S. M. Mezes in May of 1854. Leonetto Cipriaini was born into an aristocratic family in 1811. His family sent him away from Italy to the West Indies, partly to manage their holdings there and partly to remove the young, hot-headed patriot from the politically broiling unification movement then consuming the Italian peninsula. After the death of his father, Leonetto returned to Italy in 1837. Because of the lack of progress made on unification, Cipriani looked at foreign adventure again in 1851. The California Gold Rush was on; and so with much cargo, including a prefabricated house, off he went to San Francisco with two friends and two servants. Just before leaving, his political ally, Victor Emanuel II, appointed him the first Sardinian Consul to the new state. Once on the West Coast, Cipriani engaged himself in a series of adventures, including a combined scientific exploration of the West and a cattle drive that crossed the country from Missouri to California.

A. P. Gianninni, founder of Bank of America, financier of local governments during the Depression, and of many small business enterprises.

After his return from the cattle drive, he entered into negotiations with his cousin Ottavio Cipriani's law partner, S. M. Mezes, who had defended the Arguello family in their fight to hold onto Rancho de las Pulgas. He purchased property from Mezes in the then-Canada de Diablo, now a central portion of Belmont. Here he built a fine home and landscaped the area with oak trees. One of his traveling companions, Alexandro Garbi, joined him there, and, as bachelors, the two were often said to be in company of "society ladies" at Angelo's Inn or the Belmont Hotel near El Camino Real.[12]

During the 1850s, Cipriani kept up his involvement with other Italians of distinction in San Francisco. With Nicola Larco and Domenico Ghirardelli, he helped organize the Societa Italiana di Mutua Benificenza, which built a hospital in the city (the organization still exists today as the Italian Cemetery at Colma). Cipriani's heart was never very far from Italy. He visited frequently and participated in the unification movement. Finally, in 1864, his old friend Victor Emmanuel became the first king of Italy and made Cipriani a count. He then sold the property, which eventually became the Ralston place, and returned to Italy.

Of course, the larger story of Italian immigrants is not about aristocrats, but rather about a people tied to the land, who were most interested in becoming farmers. By 1870, there were already 350 Italians living in San Mateo County, mostly in the north county. They were encouraged about the peninsula as a place to grow crops. The environment here was similar to that of Italy. The big difference about the land was that it was available. For an agricultural nation, Italy was developing a large population. In California, a farm could be bought or leased much easier than back home. For many, the idea was to make a fortune in this new place and then return to Italy.

As with the Irish and other European immigrants, for the Italians California and San Mateo County allowed for more success than the eastern portions of American. Again, most Italians had had an American experience when they arrived here and knew certain things about getting along. Being mostly from northern Italy, Italian immigrants in San Mateo County generally had a little more

money and were a bit more educated than their counterparts back
east. Best of all, there was far more
opportunity to become engaged in
agriculture. By 1880, 422 Italian
immigrants lived in San Mateo
County.

The Chinese Exclusion Act of
1882 brought hundreds of poorer
and less-educated Italians to fill the
labor vacuum. All over the county,
they accepted the most menial
employment. Many were transients
and moved around to where the
jobs were. Mostly, they harvested
hay on the coastside and picked
potatoes in north county. This
group was largely made up of single
young men, so after a few years

The Lagomarsino family on their farm.

many did return to Italy. Those that came in family groups tended to stay. Some single men who saw
promise in this new place sent for their families to join them.

The success of those that could lease land or even buy their own farms is discussed in Chapter VI.
By introducing new crops, they dominated the agricultural activity of the county from the 1890s until
World War II. They grew spinach, cabbage, lettuce, cauliflower, brussels sprouts, and radishes. They
introduced garlic, broccoli, eggplant, zucchini, bell peppers, and artichokes to the California market.
At the end of their harvesting, they packed up their produce and sold it at the Colombo Market, created in 1876 by Genovese merchants to streamline the selling process. It might take a Pescadero
farmer two days to drive his harvest to San Francisco, but once there, he did not have to worry about
merchandising the vegetables himself. Instead, the Colombo Market, perhaps the greatest in the
world when it was introduced, offered an entire city block of organized, clean concrete-floored stalls
for selling produce.

By 1900, there were 939 Italians in San Mateo County, and by 1920, about 3,500 were here.[13] In
other words, by 1920, nearly one-tenth of the people who lived in San Mateo County had been born
in Italy. By that time, Italians in the county were branching out into other businesses. They ran
hotels, restaurants, and stores.

The most famous Italian American of San Mateo County, perhaps the most famous resident of
San Mateo County of any ethnicity, was A. P. Giannini. Although not foreign born (he was a native
of San Jose), his Genovese parents had brought him up to believe in the traditions of the old country.
He married Clorinda Cuneo in 1892, the daughter of a coastside land owner. Her family introduced
Giannini to the world of banking. He established his own Bank of Italy in 1904. The couple first
rented a home on Elm in San Mateo and then purchased a beautiful Tudor Revival style home, called
Seven Oaks, at 20 El Cerrito in 1905.

Giannini became known among the immigrant Italian people and other small investors as the
man who catered to the "little guy." In the world of banking, he is known as the man who created the

branch banking system. Two of his earliest branches were established in San Mateo County—at San Mateo and South San Francisco. In 1930, he changed the name of his institution to Bank of America. By 1945, it was the largest private bank in the world.

The most dramatic local story about Giannini concerns his fast and effective actions during the Great Earthquake and Fire of 1906. After he learned that the main offices of the Bank of Italy in San Francisco were directly in the path of the fire, with the assistance of some of his employees, he took $80,000 in gold plus valuable bank documents from his vault and placed the treasure under crates in a horse-drawn wagon. That night, he and his men joined the many refugees walking down the peninsula. They reached San Mateo at dawn and hid the gold and the papers in an ash heap in the fireplace in his El Cerrito home. With these funds and records, after only seven days, Giannini reopened his San Francisco banking service in the ruins of the city. He was able to give people their savings and made loans to those trying to rebuild their lives.

Other well-known actions on the part of Giannini involve his rescuing of the Hetch Hetchy Project in 1928 with a crucial loan,[14] financing of many local governments on the verge of bankruptcy during the 1930s, lending money to Walt Disney toward the production of his first full-length animated motion picture, *Snow White*, and helping make the Golden Gate Bridge possible. In the year 2000, *Time* magazine named Giannini one of the top 100 most influential personalities of the millennium. After his daughter Clare Hoffman died, the Giannini home, Seven Oaks, was almost torn down. Intervention by the City of San Mateo and the San Mateo County Historical Association prevented its destruction. In 2005, exactly 100 years after Giannini moved into it, a new owner purchased the house and is dedicated to its preservation.

For Italian Americans of San Mateo County, and throughout American, the severe restrictions imposed against further Italian immigration to the United States in 1924 came as a blow. Many felt that the rise of Benito Mussolini might elevate the status of Italy and Italian people the world over. However, the onset of America's entrance into World War II dried up any support for the dictator on the peninsula. Nevertheless, because Italy was an enemy of the United States, the first few months of the war were difficult for Italian people living in California and, more specifically, here on the coastside of San Mateo County.

In what some have referred to as the *Secret Story*, restrictions were placed on Italian people living on the coast. Federal law held that people born in Italy, not citizens of the United States, could not live west of Highway 1 for fear that they would be in contact with the enemy. Other regulations required such individuals not own flashlights and radios.

Recently Leo Giorgetti, of a long-time San Mateo County family, discussed the humiliating nature of such laws with San Mateo County History Museum staff:

As an "enemy alien" my mother, who had lived in Half Moon Bay since 1918, had to leave the family home because it was west of Highway 1—a prohibited zone. Like others on the "dangerous" list, she had to carry an "enemy alien" registration card, obey a strict 8 p.m. to 6 a.m. curfew, stay within five miles of home, and had to give up "contraband," including short-wave radios, cameras and flashlights. It was shameful and embarrassing.

Giorgetti lamented how Italian prisoners of war held at the Presidio of San Francisco had more freedom than immigrants like his mother. The prisoners were released on weekends. Many attended dances and paid visits to local Italians, who would have them for dinner.

Coastside farmer Guido Giusti left Tuscany in 1921 and came to the Half Moon Bay area, where he originally worked as a cook on the Petrocci Ranch. In 1924, he went as far as filling out his American citizenship papers but did not send them in. By 1930, he saved enough money to go into a partnership on a farm. At the beginning of World War II, he was considered an "enemy alien," and was not permitted to live or work west of Highway 1. He was forced to leave his farm to work on other lands he owned at San Gregorio. When his 16-year-old son, Aldo, was hurt in a car crash and taken to the nearby hospital, west of Highway 1, Guido was not allowed to visit the teenager. Later, Aldo served in the military during the War. Guido and his wife did become citizens when the war ended.

Unlike the experience of Japanese Americans who endured official restrictions and incarceration throughout the war, the regulations affecting Italian Americans were lifted after a few months on October 12, 1942—Columbus Day.

After the war, many Italian farmers, especially in North County, sold their properties to busy developers. However, as a community, Italian-American people of the county have taken much pride in their history and culture. A variety of cultural institutions and events still practiced with great enthusiasm testify to the continued interest of these people in their immigrant past.

The Japanese

The Japanese draw to California was in many respects similar to that which attracted the Italians. They were people attached to the land, wishing to continue to have an agricultural life but facing decreasing farmland available to do so. They then looked to far-off places to make a fortune with the purpose of returning to the homeland and using their new fortune to make a better life for themselves and their families. Again, the Chinese Exclusion Act of 1882 created opportunities in California.

However, like the Italians, the Japanese beginnings in San Mateo County started with aristocracy. In 1872, Japanese Ambassador Tomomi Iwakura with 48 officials and 59 students (including 8 women) visited William Ralston at Belmont in order to reach an agreement for minting gold coins. This Japanese contingent was impressed enough with Ralston (who they considered the "Emperor of Belmont") and the peninsula that some years later Japanese boys were sent to William Reid's prestigious Belmont School to learn of western ways.

The larger story, of course, is about young single men, looking to make it big in the new place and then improve their family's position back in Japan. The Japanese community calls the immigrants that originally came over the *Issei*. Their first jobs in nineteenth century San Mateo County included work as servants and gardeners on the big estates. At the turn of the century, they were the primary labor force for the salt makers on the Bayline, making 90 cents a day, during a 12-hour day, six days a week.

Some did start their own businesses. There was a Japanese-owned bathhouse in San Mateo as early as 1891, and a tailor and laundry shop by 1901. An oriental grocery store was in operation in San Mateo in 1906. Japanese families would eventually operate nine laundries in the county before World War II. In the beginning, the Japanese faced severe challenges in the laundry business from white competitors. Up in San Francisco, an Anti-Japanese Laundry League organized in 1908, and put pressure on the white clients of the Japanese to not use Japanese services.[15]

Japanese pioneers faced less opposition working on the farm. At first, they toiled on lands of others, then they leased or sometimes even purchased property of their own. They grew crops successfully, but their greatest achievements came with the flower industry. As discussed in Chapter VI, this story begins about 1900 when I. Takahashi, a professor of horticulture at the University of Tokyo, opened a nursery at Montara and began the strawflower industry in San Mateo County.

At Redwood City, in 1904, Henry L. Goertzhain developed a new way of growing chrysanthe-mums by using cheesecloth to protect the flowers from the powerful rays of the California sun. By 1907, the Enomoto family in the Redwood City area was making extensive use of this technique. In 1915, Sadakusu Enomoto astounded the floral industry by successfully shipping a railroad car of Turner Chrysanthemums to New Orleans for the All Saints Day celebration. The cut-flower business in San Mateo County had now gone national. Growers all over northern California took note. Japa-nese on the peninsula were already active in Redwood City and North County, but spread operations into the Belmont and San Mateo areas.

While Italians and others participated, it was the Japanese of the county who were most recog-nized as initiators of what became the county's most successful industry tied to the earth. By 1939, 38 percent of the 140 independent flower growers of Japanese heritage in northern California were in business in San Mateo County.

Despite their successes in the flower industry, the experience of the Japanese in California was replete with open racial hostility. Much of the "Yellow Peril" type hate rhetoric once applied to the Chinese was now used against the Japanese. After 1900, the Issei were barred from becoming citizens. After 1913, those judged ineligible for naturalization could not buy property. This forced the Issei to place the title of their land in the names of their children (the Nisei), or lease their farms instead of owning them. A "Gentleman's Agreement" in 1907 between United States President Theodore Roo-sevelt and the Japanese government severely limited Japanese immigration to the United States. In 1924, an exclusion act was passed in Congress that shut the door completely.

The intensity of anti-Japanese feelings on the West Coast inspired Issei leaders to create a national organization to challenge the hostile environment. In 1900, they formed the Japanese Asso-ciation of America. Its programs included assistance to immigrants looking for advice on American customs and also provided charitable aid to the newly arrived. The major focus was, however, to offer resistance to the various anti-Asiatic leagues and their strong lobbying efforts. In 1906, 50 members of the Japanese community in San Mateo formed a branch of the Japanese Association of America. The group was mostly remembered for the social outlet it enabled its members—especially the picnics.

By 1910, there were 358 Japanese in San Mateo County. Most of these were single men. With the inevitability of the exclusion law coming, many of the Issei began to consider what the alternatives were. Was their long-overdue return to Japan now possible? For most, this was a negative response. One more harvest might make the sacrifice of all of their tough years worth it—or maybe two. How-ever, as time went by, having a family seemed more remote. As the year 1924 approached, many Issei men called on their families back in Japan to arrange marriages for them. Photographs were exchanged between the Issei men and young women back in Japan. In Japan, all the ceremonies were executed by the two families, and off the girl would come to America. Some of the brides were surprised at the advanced age of the husbands who greeted them at the dock.

Nevertheless, a new generation was on its way. When it came time to give birth, many of the Issei women were reluctant to seek out white doctors for help. In San Mateo County, midwife Kamechiyo Takahashi was greatly responsible for bringing the local Nisei population into this world. Between 1917 and 1930, she drove her old car (that she had to crank up to start) throughout the county, deliv-ering baby after baby. By 1930, the Japanese population of the county had more than tripled, to 1,169.

This included a growing farm community in Pescadero. For the newly arrived Issei women, this life on the coast could be hard. Chiye Shintaku Yoshifuji recalled that soon after her arrival at Pescadero: "During a peak harvest season, I cooked for 30 farm hands and got little more than two hours of sleep at night. The demands made upon me were great and required tremendous physical stamina."[16]

Issei parents hung on to the idea that one day the family would return to Japan. Some of the children, who they called Kibei, were actually sent to Japan for their educations. Most of the Nisei were educated in San Mateo County public schools. However, their schooling was augmented by Japanese language schools. By 1930, schools had been organized in San Mateo, Pescadero, Belmont, and Redwood City. The children

Nobuo Higaki (right) checking the carnation crop in one of the first greenhouses in the country, circa 1913.

were not only taught the Japanese language, but they were instructed in aspects of Japanese culture as well—all of this in preparation for the eventual return to the homeland.

The population of Japanese Americans in San Mateo County by 1940 was 1,218. By that time, many within the Nisei generation were entering their teenage years and even early 20s. A generational split was evident between the Issei and the Nisei. The Nisei, who by birth were automatically considered citizens of the United States, did not share their parents' hopes for the eventual return to the homeland. After all, most of them had never been to Japan. They had been educated alongside American kids and enjoyed social opportunities afforded American young people, including the ability to choose a spouse. They also could vote, when they came of age, and own property. It was largely the Nisei generation that formed a new national organization in 1930, the Japanese American Citizens League (JACL) to promote equal rights for American citizens of Japanese ancestry. In other words, it was an organization formed to advance their generation's interests. The San Mateo branch of the JACL was organized in 1935, not surprisingly over the objections of some of the Issei parents. As World War II approached, the JACL found itself increasingly having to defend Japanese Americans as loyal citizens. Their float in the September 1940 San Mateo County Fair parade was a gigantic American flag carried by dozens of members of the League. A year later, they took out an entire-one-page ad in the September 17, 1941, *Burlingame Advance Star* to declare: "We too, are Americans." In this message, the JACL proclaimed the loyalty of "American citizens of Japanese parentage" and plainly stated that the Nisei were as ready as anybody to defend the United States in the event of war.

Sadly, no statement of loyalty was strong enough to resist the hysteria in California caused by Japan's bombing of Pearl Harbor on December 7, 1941. Almost immediately, Issei leaders were arrested by the FBI. Franklin Roosevelt's Executive Order 9066 allowed local military commanders the authority to intern people because of their ancestry. General J. L. DeWitt at the Presidio of San Francisco made the decision to round up the Japanese Americans on the West Coast.

By May 9, 1942, all of the Japanese Americans of San Mateo County had been taken to the Tanforan racetrack, which had been converted into an "Assembly Center." Nearly 8,000 people from throughout the Bay Area were detained there for four months. Then, the whole group was loaded into railroad cars to Camp Topaz in central Utah, where most of them had to wait out the war.

It has long been recognized that constitutional rights were ignored and racial prejudice allowed to rule the day. Among the injustices was the requirement that all possessions had to be sold off within a 30-day period. For the flower growers, this was disastrous. Some would lose everything gained by the work of two generations. Some of the Japanese Americans were helped out by friends and business associates, who protected their holdings during the war. Banker J. Elmer Morrish of Redwood City was one of those who arranged for the Mori family and others in the area to keep their flower businesses intact.[17]

One of the most amazing stories about the internment at Topaz was the reaction of the Nisei men to U.S. Army recruiters that visited them. Incredibly, despite the fact that their own constitutional rights had been violated and their families were suffering the hardships of living in the Utah desert, they volunteered in overwhelming numbers. What is more, their war record was outstanding. Some served with military intelli-

Family of Japanese ancestry arrives at an assembly center at Tanforan Race Track. Evacuees will be transferred later to War Relocation Authority centers where they were housed for the duration of WW II. Photograph by Dorothea Lange, April 29, 1942.

gence, translating Japanese papers and interrogating prisoners. Most enlisted into the 442nd Regimental Combat Team that saw action in Italy, France, and Germany. It was, for its size and length of activity, the most decorated unit in all of American military history. There has never been a full count made, but at least 27 Nisei from San Mateo County were in the Army during World War II.[18]

When the war finally ended in 1945, the Issei and Nisei in the camps had to come to grips with the question, what now? There was no government program to help these people reestablish their lives. Many of the Issei became lost to despair. However, while things were far from perfect, perhaps their return to San Mateo County was easier than in other places such as the Central Valley, where Japanese farmers more closely competed economically with whites. As the years went by, most were able to regain a livelihood, although they could never forget the injustice perpetrated against them. In 1966, symbolic of the healing process, Japanese Garden in San Mateo's Central Park was dedicated to mark the sister-city relationship between San Mateo and Toyonaka, Japan. Many Japanese Americans of the area donated thousands of volunteer hours to see that the project was successfully completed.

World War II and the Influx of Newcomers

Shipbuilding at South San Francisco and an assortment of other industries brought many new people to the peninsula during and after World War II. This included the first sizable numbers of African Americans.

However, African Americans had been here long before the 1940s. One of the earliest to stay and make a mark was Thomas Rolls, an ex-slave from Virginia who arrived in California in 1858 and settled in San Mateo County in 1873. In 1875, he began operating the Star and Garter roadhouse in present-day San Bruno. He eventually changed the name of it to Uncle Tom's Cabin. The building served as Rolls's place of business, his home, and the local post office. Uncle Tom's Cabin became a sort of local legend for its food, drink, and assorted entertainments. Rolls died in 1879.

Another well-known African American of historical note was San Mateo restaurateur Noah Williams. Williams came from a long line of famous chefs from the "Old South." He cooked for the Southern Pacific until

Noah Williams created one of the most popular restaurants of the county in the 1920's.

1921, when he opened a restaurant on B Street in San Mateo. He would bake up to 20 Missouri hams a day at his Noah's Cafeteria. Motorists made his place a must stop, until Sunday at Noah's meant a waiting line around the block. In 1924, he moved into a bigger building on Third Avenue. His new Noah's Ark had a decor featuring the biblical saving of the animals. Unfortunately, the Depression of the 1930s killed off the business.[19] However, his family went on to important things. One son, Barney, became a well-known Boy Scout leader. Another son, Les, was a prestigious Tuskegee Army airman during World War II, and then a renowned local dance instructor.

After World War II, the many racial covenants on real estate forced African-American newcomers into segregated neighborhoods. At first, a few urban renewal projects accounted for some blacks coming down the peninsula to live at East Palo. Into the 1950s, white home owners began moving out as more African Americans moved in. After the Bayshore Freeway was constructed through the area, it became increasingly difficult to find local employment. By the early 1960s, East Palo Alto was a troubled place, with a 40 percent unemployment rate and a feeling of despair among the people similar to Watts and other West Coast urban black enclaves. Frequent trouble occurred at the community's Ravenswood High School. East Palo Alto incorporated in 1983 as the community wrestled to get control of its many problems.

Testifying to the progress being made in East Palo Alto, and for the peninsula's African-American community in general, in 1999, Rose Jacobs Gibson joined the San Mateo County Board of Supervisors as its first African-American member. In March of 2004, the people of the county elected her to a second four-year term. She began her political career as an East Palo Alto City councilwoman, serving from 1992 until 1999. During that time she became recognized as turning the community's social environment and economy in a positive direction. As a member of the board of supervisors, Gibson has concentrated on long-range planning, youth-related issues, housing, health care for the under-privileged, and economic growth in poorer communities.

The Filipino population of San Mateo County is on the rise, both in numbers and cultural impact. In 1970, they numbered only 5,676. After only ten years, in 1980, the Filipino population had more than quadrupled. Filipinos are mostly concentrated in the north county, especially in Daly City, which has gotten the nickname of "New Manila." By 2006, Daly City had more people of Filipino ancestry than any other city in the continental United States.

Once again, the story of the people here goes back before the time usually associated with their coming to San Mateo County. For exam-

Augustin De Ocampo was in the U.S. Navy during World War I and moved to Menlo Park soon after. Here he is seen in his Navy uniform, posing with friends.

ple, Augustin De Ocampo was perhaps the earliest Filipino resident of Menlo Park. He came to the area after World War I and met and married a Portuguese girl, Mary Frances Borba. During the 1920s, they had two sons, Tony and Frank. Augustin worked as a builder, ran a chicken farm, and raised dogs. In general, Menlo Park seemed a good place to live. Augustin was an avid boxer and set up a ring in his backyard. His realization of the American Dream was especially evident in the success of his son Tony. He graduated from Sequoia High School and then joined the Menlo Park Police Force at the age of 22 in 1946. Records are sketchy on these types of issues, but Tony's mixed Filipino and Portuguese blood probably made him the first person of color to join the force. In fact, he may have been the first person of color to join any law enforcement agency in San Mateo County.

Among the cultural contributions of Filipino people to San Mateo County are the numbers of talented DJs or record-playing preformers coming from Daly City and other north county communities. Their popularity has been noticed nationally and was the subject of an exhibit created by Melanie Caganaut at the San Mateo County History Museum in the fall of 2002.

Since 1965

The Immigration and Naturalization Act of 1965 replaced the old quota system of allowing immigrants into the United States. On the West Coast, and for San Mateo County, this has meant a considerable increase in the number of people coming to live here. During the 1960s, as the white population of the county was increasing at a rate of 19.4 percent, the nonwhite population was gaining at a rate of 153.2 percent. This was especially true within the Hispanic community. In 1960, they numbered 19,722. By 1970, their population was 63,039. By 1990, it stood at 114,627.

Of course, Hispanic people have been around these parts since 1769 (see Chapter V), but their percentage of the population was shrinking until more recent years (only 4.4 percent in 1960). Farmers of the coast were still using Mexican farm labor, however. When a labor shortage confronted California farmers during the war year of 1942, the federal government set up the Bracero Program that brought in Mexican labor during planting and harvesting times and bused the workers back down to Mexico during the off season. The United States discontinued the program in 1964 and left many farmers wondering where the workers would come from next. The situation inspired coastside farmer and World War II veteran, Aldo Giusti to invent a brussels sprouts harvesting machine. Over time, Mexicans, here legally and illegally, helped to bridge the gap and continue to be an important part of the county's agricultural labor supply to this day (2006).

Today the presence of immigrant Hispanic people is felt all over San Mateo County. On the bayside they have taken jobs as gardeners, domestics, restaurant workers, hotel employees, baby sitters, and assembly-line workers. Of all the places in the county, there is no better appreciation for these immigrants than in Redwood City, where every elementary school notice is required to be bilingual.

An interesting relationship exists between Redwood City and the town of Aguililla. This Mexican village of 25,000 residents has witnessed, over some 56 years, a migration of 10,000 people to Redwood City and its adjoining

Umang Gupta is a leading high-tech entrepreneur in San Mateo County.

neighbor, unincorporated North Fair Oaks.[20] Johnny Garcia and his cousin Abel Bustos are considered to be the first Aguilillans to come to Redwood City, sometime around 1950. They had been working farms around Salinas, Stockton, and Sacramento for some years and then found restaurant jobs through a Sacramento friend in Redwood City. In 1953, Harry Kramer, owner of Harry's Hof Brau, hired Garcia to work at his Atherton restaurant. Garcia continued to visit Aguililla, telling his former neighbors about the good pay and accommodating nature of the Redwood City area. He married an Agulillan girl on one of his trips and decided to return to Redwood City and make it his permanent residence. Many followed his lead, encouraged by Garcia's descriptions and the kindly assistance of Harry Kramer, who not only hired Aguilillans but at times acted as their benefactor and protector.[21] To this day (2006) strong ties exist between the two towns. Aguililla is situated in the State of Michoacan, due west of Mexico City. It has gained the nickname, "the other Redwood City."

Another immigration of recent years has come from the Pacific Islands—principally Samoa and Tonga. This migration to the peninsula began in 1951, when the U.S. Navy shut down its operations in American Samoa. At that time, Samoans were allowed to find new jobs in California and began coming to San Mateo County. By 1976, it was estimated that between 6,000 and 10,000 Polynesians resided here. Samoans tended to settle in Daly City, South San Francisco, and San Bruno, while Tongans chose San Mateo, Burlingame, San Bruno, East Palo Alto, and Redwood City. Dr. Caroline Naufhu, the first Tongan woman to receive a Ph.D., has done social work among her people in the county. She tells us that the reasons for Pacific Islanders leaving their homes revolves around finding more lucrative work and securing better education for their children in California. As with most groups who have come here, they generally do not expect to stay, but to go back with money enough to make a better life back home. By the early 1980s, when 90,000 Tongans had already migrated to the mainland United States, 50,000 lived in California, and of these, 25,000 were in San Mateo County. Many of the Pacific Islanders found employment at San Francisco International Airport.

The end of the Vietnam War saw an increase in Vietnamese and Cambodian people to the peninsula. By 1977, there were 412 Vietnamese in the county, with most residing in East Palo Alto. By 1980, the number increased to 902, with most of the people living in San Mateo, Foster City, Redwood City, East Palo Alto, Menlo Park, and parts of north county.

The census of 2000 tells us that over 32 percent of the population of San Mateo County are foreign born (interestingly, nearly exactly the percentage of 1880). Of the immigrants, Latinos and Asians are the fastest-growing groups. However, they continue to come here from all corners of the world. Russian people are here, coming in numbers after World War II. Jews who suffered the Holocaust are on the peninsula in numbers that exceed proportional logic. The author apologizes for not giving a history on every group of people to arrive. Their stories are important. They should be, and will be, told fully in future studies.

In summary, the reader may ask why so many immigrants from so many places have looked to the peninsula as a new home. Economic opportunity, our beautiful weather, and wonderful natural environment certainly have much to do with it. There has also been a tendency among peninsulans to be comparatively more accepting and fair than those in other places, even in California. A recent example emanates from the terrorist attacks on New York on September 11, 2001. Hysteria swept the United States in a way reminiscent of the early days of World War II. As a place that honors toleration of people—that is the home of such organizations as the Jewish-Palestinian Living Room Dialogue—county officials were quick to remind people that San Mateo County would not be a place allowing hatred for hatred's sake. When outside political pressure was applied on Sheriff Don Horsely to round up Middle Eastern men for questioning, he refused to disregard their constitutional rights. Horsely had the mainstream support of the people of the peninsula in that decision. The mistakes of 1942 would not be repeated in San Mateo County .

A fitting recent example of the immigrant experience and San Mateo County is the story of Umang and Ruth Gupta. They came to the United States during the immigration wave of the late 1960s and 1970s, he from Delhi, India, she from Watford, England. After a few years studying and working in Ohio, they moved to San Francisco in 1978, got married in 1980, and soon settled down in San Mateo County.

Since coming to the Peninsula, Gupta has become one of the earliest India-born technology entrepreneurs in Silicon Valley, with a number of firsts to his credit. In 1981, he wrote the first business plan for Oracle as a vice-president during its initial days. In 1984, he became one of Larry Ellison's first executives to leave Oracle to found and build a successful company of his own, Gupta Corporation, which became well-known in the high-tech industry for client/server computing. He took the company public in 1993, thereby earning the distinction of becoming the first India-born entrepreneur to found a successful public global software company. In 1997, he invested in, and soon took over, a new company called Keynote Systems. He built it into a leader in the technological field. Its mission is to improve the performance of clients' utilization of the Internet. He successfully offered Keynote stock to the public in 1999. He currently (2006) serves as the chairman and chief executive officer of Keynote.

As a boy in India, Gupta developed a love of technology. He recently said: "As a kid, I always enjoyed building things and making things out of kits." He pursued a chemical engineering degree at the Indian Institute of Technology in Kanpur. He then found that: "I was more interested in building organizations that built products than in building the products themselves."[22] Gupta decided that he ought to come to the United States and obtain a master's degree in business administration. In 1971, he enrolled at Kent State in Ohio. He graduated in 1972, and a year later began his career with IBM at its Cleveland office. There he met his future wife Ruth, also an immigrant, but from Great Britain.

Umang and Ruth couldn't have had a more different family background. His parents were socialist intellectuals who had both participated in India's struggle for independence against Great Britain. She was born into an upper-crust British family.

After the two were married in 1980, they bought a home in San Mateo. As Umang started his entrepreneurial career, a daughter, Clare, was born. In 1987, they tragically lost their two-year-old developmentally disabled son, Raji. As a result, they helped form Raji House, a respite home located in Burlingame under the auspices of the nonprofit organization, Parca.

Their third child is Kashi, who is Hispanic by birth and was adopted from Honduras when he was just a baby boy, thus making the Guptas one of the truly unique immigrant families of San Mateo County, with each member being born on a different continent.

Today (2006), the Guptas give back to the peninsula community in a variety of ways. Ruth works to support the activities of Raji House and Parca. Umang sits on the board of the nationally honored Peninsula Community Foundation. He is also chairman of the San Mateo County Historical Association. His major interest there is to create two new galleries in its museum in Redwood City—one focusing on immigration history of the peninsula and the other on entrepreneurs of San Mateo County. His Keynote Systems is additionally involved with a variety of nonprofit organizations.

Chapter 8 Footnotes

1. Gil Richards, *Crossroads*, Gil Richards Publications, Woodside, 1973, p. 14.

2. R. S. Burchell, *The San Francisco Irish 1848–1880*, University of California Press, Berkeley, 1980, p. 4.

3. James O. Clifford, Sr., "Irish in San Mateo County", *La Peninsula*, vol. XXXIV, No. 2, Winter/Spring, 2003/2004, p. 10.

4. Holly Warnke, "A Profile of Several German Immigrants Who Settled San Mateo County (1850 – 1890)," manuscript within the San Mateo County History Museum Archives, p. 4.

5. Mitchell P. Postel, "Belmont Park", *La Peninsula*, vol. XXXIV, No. 2, Winter/Spring 2003/2004, p. 22.

6. Hynding, *Frontier*, pp. 165–167.

7. Robert F. Heizer and Alan F. Almquist, *The Other Californians*, University of California Press, Berkeley, 1971, p. 155.

8. Postel, "Lost Resource," p. 34.

9. *Report of Commissioners of Fisheries for the State of California for 1891–1892*, p. 21.

10. Col. Albert S. Evans, *A la California: Sketches of Life in the Golden State*, A. L. Bancroft & Company, 1873, pp. 44–46.

11. Stanger, *South*, p. 141.

12. Thomas, "Leonetto Cipriani," p. 25.

13. Elaine Thomas, "In Pursuit of a Dream: The Italians of San Mateo County", *La Peninsula*, Fall 1981, vol. XXI, No. 1, p. 7.

14. Kevin Starr, *Endangered Dream: The Great Depression in California*, Oxford University Press, New York, 1996, p. 288.

15. *1877–1942: A Community Story*, Japanese American Citizens League, San Mateo Chapter, 1981, p. 30.

16. Ibid. p. 57.

17. Nicole Neroulias, "Japanese-American War Experience Remembered," *San Mateo County Times*, February 16, 2005, p. 1.

18. Gayle K. Yamada, and Dianne Fukami, *Building a Community—The Story of Japanese Americans in San Mateo County*, Japanese American Citizens League, San Mateo Branch, 2003, p. 157.

19. Mitchell P. Postel, "San Mateo's African American History", La Peninsula, vol. XXX, No. 1, Summer/Fall, 1996, pp. 19–20.

20. Edwin Garcia, "Living in Two Worlds," *San Jose Mercury News*, December 27, 1995.

21. Dean Missar, "Aquililla, Mexico," manuscript collection of the San Mateo County History Museum Archives.

22. Pete Christensen, "Following His Heart," *Silicon Valley Biz Ink*, January 30–February 4, 2005.

Chapter 9

San Mateo County History Makers: Entrepreneurs Who Have Changed the World

*I*t makes for a marvelous transition to go from Umang Gupta and San Mateo County's immigrant experience to a discussion of entrepreneurialism on the peninsula. Gupta is a great example of the significant business spirit here. San Mateo County has been a cauldron of creativity for entrepreneurs who have lived here or established their activities here. Especially in recent times have their businesses influenced not just people of the peninsula, but folks the world over.

Webster's Dictionary defines entrepreneur as: "One who takes the initiative to create a product or establish a business for profit; generally, whoever undertakes on his own account an enterprise in which others are employed and risks are taken." While organizing its exhibit gallery on local entrepreneurs, San Mateo County History Museum staff, with guidance from some of our area's business leaders, wrestled with this definition and how it pertains to the entrepreneurs of the peninsula. We added that an entrepreneur is a risk taker with the skills and initiative to look at the world in an original way. They revolutionize patterns of business by introducing technologies for producing new commodities, or at least producing old commodities in new ways. They might reorganize old industries and create new ones by finding undiscovered sources of materials or new outlets for products. They help make life healthier, more affordable, more fast-paced, and more fun. Entrepreneurs see what is missing. They make things better. Their innovations build communities, industries, and economies.

Today, San Mateo County businesses, from their offices at Oracle in Redwood City, Genentech in South San Francisco, and so many more, make international headlines on a regular basis. At no time in its history has San Mateo County been more important to people everywhere than right now, due to local entrepreneurs creating and building the world's future. This sesquicentennial history book can only pay slight homage to this important aspect of our county's past. A single volume devoted just to this topic could not cover it all. The following descriptions of human endeavor are meant to be examples and highlights of a much bigger story.

A Heritage of Entrepreneurial Spirit

While discussing the giants of wartime and post–World War II San Mateo County is the more compelling part of our entrepreneurial past, the peninsula's entrepreneurial heritage goes back much further. In Chapter VI, we listed the many famous families of the nineteenth and early twentieth

centuries who made fortunes in all kinds of businesses from offices in San Francisco and then retreated to suburban estates down the peninsula. Some of those important people also had a long-lasting influence on San Mateo County because of their endeavors.

For example, there is Timothy Guy Phelps, who county historian Frank Stanger listed as the peninsula's "most famous citizen."[1] A forty-niner and self-made man, Phelps watched his father suffer a series of financial disasters before coming to California. At the age of 25, he failed as a gold miner but became wildly successful as a San Francisco grain speculator. He learned of fertile lands down the peninsula, and in 1853 began buying property in the San Carlos area, eventually acquiring some 3,500 acres. In 1857, he decided to run for office and became San Mateo County's first state senator. As an antislavery man, he cofounded the Republican Party on the peninsula in 1860. He served in the United States Congress during the Civil War and became a personal friend of Abraham Lincoln. While a congressman, in 1861 he helped to organize the San Francisco–San Jose Railroad. In fact, he was one of that railroad's original directors. Later he was president of the Southern Pacific before it was taken over by the Big Four of Central Pacific fame. His ties to the railroad establishment and Republican Party placed him in a good position to run twice for governor of California. He lost both times.

Timothy Guy Phelps, an early San Mateo County entrepreneur, was a director of the San Francisco–San Jose Railroad which was completed in the midst of the Civil War that raged in the east and delayed some of the construction materials.

He had dreams that his railroad might make his San Carlos properties the site of a town, but he was a little ahead of history. So he created a dairy and farm there. By the 1870s, he had some 500 cows at San Carlos and is said to have worked the fields with his men. He continued his dairy operations until 1887, when he sold some of the land to make room for the little community emerging around the train station. Meanwhile, he served on the board of the University of California for 19 years. He also founded the county's first financial institution, the Bank of Redwood City. He died in a freak accident in 1899, when he was knocked down by riders on a bicycle built for two.

Another nineteenth-century entrepreneur of note was Charles Lux, a partner in the West's most extensive cattle empire, who came to own some 1,500 acres of Rancho Buri Buri property within today's South San Francisco. Lux was born in Germany in 1823, where he was trained as a

The Charles Lux home in today's South San Francisco.

wheelwright, but he emigrated to New York at the age of 16. Here he worked as a butcher's apprentice until he heard of the Gold Rush. Once in California, he opened a butcher business instead of becoming a miner. His success allowed him to buy the Buri Buri property from Isidro Sanchez in 1853 for $10,000. He called the place Baden Ranch and built a home. He married Miranda Potter in 1857, and also went into his famous partnership with Henry Miller that year.

Miller had been a competitor in the butcher business, but Lux proposed that they buy 1,600 head of cattle together to feed the growing population at San Francisco. The partners began purchasing sizable ranch lands in 1863. Their lands eventually included 600,000 acres in Merced County, 60,000 in Monterey County, 114,000 in Kern and Tulare Counties, and another 50,000 in other states. The cattle from the many ranches were driven to the Lux place in San Mateo County, where they were rested and fed before being brought to San Francisco for butchering. Cattle, at the rate of 1,600 a month, were delivered to three slaughterhouses owned by the partners in what became known as the "Butchertown" neighborhood of the city.

William P. Kyne, founder of Bay Meadows racetrack.

The Miller and Lux partnership lasted 30 years. Lux preferred city life and handled the finances and business end of the endeavor. Miller enjoyed the country and managed the operation of the ranches. Their joint venture was further cemented when Miller married Miranda's sister.

Lux died in 1887. One year later, G. F. Swift came to the area, looking for a site to establish a Pacific Coast meat-packing center. He liked what he saw and established the Western Meat Company in 1892. South San Francisco was thus initiated as an industrial city.

Although discussed in the last chapter concerning the immigrant experience in San Mateo County, no summary of early entrepreneurs on the peninsula would be complete without mention of A. P. Giannini of San Mateo. He founded the Bank of Italy, which became the Bank of America, in 1930. He is remembered mostly for bringing banking services to the "little fellow." One of his more memorable quotes was: "Any banker can make a sound loan for a million dollars. But you can't get real constructive banking until you put up five hundred dollars for some fellow who has nothing but imagination and ambition." With this as his philosophy, within one year of his bank's 1904 founding, depositors had invested more than $700,000. By the beginning of World War II, his Bank of America was the biggest bank in the world.

The story of Bay Meadows racetrack is largely about entrepreneur William P. Kyne, one of the greatest equestrian enthusiasts in California history. By the time of his death in 1957, he was known for the creation of the daily double, night racing, quarterhorse racing, Bay Meadows track itself, and the legalization of parimutuel betting, which made it all possible.

Kyne's original career goal was to become a priest, but after seeing his first horse race at Emeryville Racetrack in 1900, he determined that he wanted to be a part of the "sport of kings." In 1910, California banned horse racing. Kyne then traveled to other states and even to Mexico, working as a bookmaker. In the early 1930s, he led the campaign to legalize parimutuel wagering in California. This allowed for the creation of a state-controlled betting system that featured a monetary return to the track and the state on every bet. It also established a California Horse Racing Board to oversee tracks throughout the state.

Kyne won his fight in 1933, and then began searching for a site to open his own track. He settled on lands a little south of San Mateo, where Curtiss-Wright maintained a flying field. Bay Meadows opened for racing a year later. It was an immediate success, with $100,000 wagered on its first day.

Under Kyne, Bay Meadows became a leading force in horse racing. It was the first in California to use the "tote" adding machines, simplifying parimutuel betting. It was the first to use the photo finish. It was the first to install an electric starting gate. Some of the most famous horses in the world raced at Bay Meadows, including Charles S. Howard's Seabiscuit, who twice won the Bay Meadows Handicap. Also the English horse, Noor, first raced in America at Bay Meadows.

While William Kyne was creating Bay Meadows, Bernard "Mike" Doolin was struggling to energize the effort to create an airport at Mills Field. In 1932, the citizens of San Francisco had voted in favor of creating a Public Utilities Commission that would oversee the nearly completed Hetch Hetchy project, the Municipal Railway, and, among other things, the airport. The Commission named as its first manager "the Terrible Tempered Mr. Bang,"[2] of City Hall, Edward G. Cahill. Cahill had a big job, and the airport was certainly on his mind as a problem. By 1932, the utility had accumulated a $223,000 debt. Its monthly payroll (of 17 employees) equaled all of the revenue produced. Cahill's first action was to fire Airport Superintendent Roy Francis and half the staff. He reduced the monthly payroll to $1,375. He then hired Doolin.

Mills Field as it appeared in 1931—not much development along the peninsula.

Doolin was born in Berkeley in 1897. His first experiment with aviation occurred when he was 11 years old, when he attempted to fly a glider he had built. Although never getting past the eighth grade, he tested successfully for acceptance into the Air Corps during World War I. He trained with Jimmy Doolittle and other famous flyers of the day. Once in France, he was assigned to the 22nd Fighter Squadron. He earned one confirmed "kill" before being shot down himself in 1918. In the crash he lost most of his teeth and later suffered from a mustard gas attack that burned off all his hair. Gradually, he regained his strength and saw all his hair grow back. Although in his early twenties, his hair was now gray and would remain so for the rest of his life. After the war, he worked as a mechanical draftsman. Then in 1926, Standard Oil hired him to fly gas to rural airfields. In 1928, Standard promoted him to chief pilot, a position he held until Edward Cahill hired him for the airport job on June 1, 1932.

With a staff of only seven employees, Doolin had much to do. However, he had public relations talent and made friends with the media. On November 14 of that first year, the *San Francisco Chronicle* ran a story about him titled "Twelve Hat Doolin," referring to all the tasks he had to undertake and claimed that every time he was performing a certain job he wore a different hat. He also began to attract airline business to the young airport. When he began at San Francisco, the airport was principally a general aviation field. However, Doolin recognized that the future of aviation rested in commercial airline traffic. His first success was signing Valley Air Lines, a San Francisco to Stockton to Sacramento carrier, to the airport. He then signed Cardiff and Peacock Airlines, also a within-California company.

Another publicity coup of late 1932 was a grand hangar dance he organized to raise funds for an air show the next day. Naval Reserve pilots and aircraft took part, along with seven Army pursuit planes under the command of Henry "Hap" Arnold, an old friend of Doolin's from his World War I days. Arnold routed the planes through San Francisco as a favor to Doolin. Mike himself flew in a dog- fight demonstration. Some 20,000 people visited the airport and witnessed the spectacle.

Certainly the best thing to happen in Doolin's first six months was the signing of a contract with United Airlines on December 27, 1932. The future of the airport would be tied to this emerging carrier from that day onward. In early February the next year, Transcontinental and Western Air (later Trans World Airlines or TWA) became a tenant. Between December 1932 and July 1933, 11,735 passengers used the airport, a significant increase.

All this progress was not lost on the voters in San Francisco. On November 17, 1933, they passed a $270,000 bond issue to improve airport facilities. The revenue measure was the first in a long time passed to help the utility. The bond was matched two to one by the federal government. To Doolin's credit, the issue succeeded by a wide margin: 101,339 for and only 40,277 against.

Recognizing his accomplishments, the Civil Works Administration appointed Doolin supervisor for California. In that position he oversaw the improvement, with federal and state funding, of 32 airports in the state, including his own.

In November of 1937, San Franciscan voters showed a much larger measure of confidence when they approved a $2,850,000 bond issue. That year, a beautiful 90-by-225-foot terminal was built in Spanish Revival style architecture. Designed to handle 1,700 passengers a day, the terminal was criticized for overconstruction. However, eventually it would serve three times that number. This building, which became synonymous with San Francisco aviation history and Mills Field, was torn down in 1966.

As told in Chapter VII, World War II had a dramatic effect on the peninsula. Nowhere was this felt more than out at the airport. Things began brewing in 1940 when the Coast Guard created a base there. Also that year, United announced that it would build its main maintenance base at San Francisco.

Once World War II actually started, the federal government took control of the airport, while asking Mike Doolin and his staff to continue their functions. Under the auspices of the Army, the airport was to have three main services; it became a base for patrol operations; it provided facilities for training pilots and crew; finally, and most importantly, it operated as an airport for commercial airlines, which had taken on substantial war-related duties. The airlines were given responsibility for flying transport routes, and with San Francisco being the closest major airport in the continental United States to the Pacific theater of the war, a great amount of activity could be expected.

In 1942, all records were broken when 112,641 takeoffs and landings were logged. As the war progressed, the federal government spent millions of dollars to improve facilities. Doolin became a formidable lobbyist, calling on his military friends and securing some $10 million. By the end of 1944, the annual payroll at the airport was $4 million. The book value of the place had increased from $6,685,000 in 1941, to $19 million in 1946. Fewer than 127,000 passengers flew from San Francisco in 1940. More than 526,000 did so in 1945. The 112,641 flights of 1942 were made small in comparison by the 722,000 of 1945.

World War II advanced the cause of commercial aviation manifold. With bigger and safer planes, made possible by wartime technology, the public accepted air travel more readily. Doolin now envisioned many more improvements necessary in the new age. A $20 million bond issue was presented to the voters of San Francisco in November of 1945, and passed. About this time Doolin began dreaming of what the future airport would look like. He devised the idea of a central terminal, flanked by two more, to the north and south, with a large place for parking automobiles in the center. This is essentially the San Francisco International Airport's design to this very day.

Meanwhile, the beat went on. In 1946, 1,025,000 passengers used the airport. The utility now employed some 5,800 employees, with a $19 million payroll. As the old Spanish Revival terminal building of 1937 seemed to be bursting at its seams, in November of 1949 another $10 million bond was passed by the voters. This one would be matched by $6 million from the federal government. The construction slated now would replace the 1937 building with a new terminal—to become the Central terminal—in 1954.

Sadly, Mike Doolin would not be manager at the celebration in 1954. Early in 1950, he became embroiled in a political skirmish with San Francisco Mayor Elmer Robinson. Doolin was quickly forced out of his job. California Governor Earl Warren then appointed him state director of aeronautics to assist the cause of general aviation. To this day, Doolin is still regarded among insiders as "father of the airport."[3]

No roster of prewar entrepreneurs would be complete without mention of Rod McLellan. After receiving degrees in botany and economics from Stanford University, he took over his father's Burlingame floriculture business, the McLellan Company, in 1926. He moved the business to South San Francisco, and in 1937, began developing the gardenia as a corsage flower. Under McLellan's guidance the gardenia soon became the top-selling corsage in the United States. Certainly the expansion of the nearby airport had much to do with his success. By 1945, 3 million gardenias were being shipped annually.

In the meantime, McLellan began cultivating orchids as houseplants. Orchids up until that time were thought to be too difficult to grow for mass markets. However, McLellan believed otherwise and made his company, renamed Acres of Orchids, the greatest orchid grower in the world. McLellan registered his first hybrid orchid with the Royal Horticulture Society in England in 1944. By 2002, his company had registered more than 3,000. As McLellan's business expanded, his facilities at South San Francisco became one of the most popular tourist destinations in San Mateo County. Recently the McLellan family sold the South San Francisco location and, in 2005, divested itself completely from the flower business. Nevertheless, the legacy of Rod McLellan as an entrepreneur endures in the many innovations enabling enjoyment of gardenias and orchids to this day and beyond.

Rod McLellan

World War II Entreprenuers

World War II was a total war. It was a war fought with the aid of technology. Because of the airport and the talent of students from the two great universities of the region, Stanford and the University of California at Berkeley, San Mateo County became the site of a variety of important businesses that aided the war effort. Then in peacetime, they transformed themselves to cater to the electronic needs of the American public. No better example of the local entrepreneurs who changed local business can be named than Charles Litton.

At the age of 10, Charles Litton had already shown his aptitude for things electronic by building a ham radio set. In 1932, he opened Litton Engineering Laboratories, a manufacturer of tube-making equipment in Redwood City. With the war, Litton saw the need for expansion and moved into larger quarters in San Carlos. With his 40 employees, he created a radar tube so effective that he was given awards for excellence by the Army and the Navy. After the war, the company grew exponentially, becoming one of the world's largest electronics concerns. A variety of radio-related businesses spun off from Litton. Eventually, most of its Bay Area holdings were sold.

Alexander M. Poniatoff, founder of Ampex, (on the right) with project engineer Harold Lindsey with the first professional quality magnetic tape recorder. Ampex created many of the major innovations in commercial recording technology, credited by many as revolutionizing the radio industry. In the 1950's Ampex created the first commercial videotape recorder which radically changed the staging and production of television programs as well as making it possible to record TV signals.

Litton Engineering still exists in Grass Valley, California, where it operates as a family business.

Alexander M. Poniatoff, another great in the electronics industry, established Ampex in 1944. Born in Kazen, Russia, in 1892, Poniatoff was a pilot flying for the Imperial Russian Navy during World War I and the Russian Revolution. During the fighting, he found himself in a boxcar as a snowstorm raged outside. With temperatures diving below zero, a friend described to him the San Francisco Bay Area with its beauty and temperate climate. He was sold, but a variety of adventures lay before him first. Forced to leave Russia by the new Bolshevik government in 1920, he traveled across Siberia to the Sea of Japan. Engineering education gained before the war at the University of Kazan, the Imperial College at Moscow, and the Karlstruhe Technical College in Germany allowed him to gain employment with the Shanghai Power Company in China. He obtained an American visa in 1927 and finally came to California. Poniatoff landed a job with the Dalmo Victor Company in San Carlos. He move into a home in Atherton.

In 1944, Poniatoff decided to start his own business manufacturing airborne radar motors and generators for the U.S. Navy. As he started his business in a San Carlos warehouse, he began to consider what the name of his company should be. He came up with Ampex—a combination of his own initials and ex for excellence.

In 1946, Poniatoff's Ampex began developing the first professional-quality magnetic tape recorder, enabling tape recording of radio broadcasting. In 1948, the American Broadcasting Company (ABC) used an Ampex Model 200 audio recorder for the first ever American tape-delayed radio broadcast—a recording of the *Bing Crosby Show*. That year, Bing Crosby became an Ampex distributor, selling the recorder to radio stations, networks, and recording studios.

As the company grew, Poniatoff decided a bigger plant was needed and moved Ampex to Redwood City. Then in 1956, the company realized another big breakthrough. It introduced the first videotape recorder. Before this time, nearly all television shows were live programs. The industry was forever changed. The next year Ampex was given an Emmy Award by the television industry for this important technological innovation. Through the next two decades, Ampex continued to set standards and be a leader in the tape recording business from its headquarters in Redwood City.

Postwar and Beyond

In the field of medicine, one of America's great innovators and entrepreneurs is Dr. Thomas Fogarty of Portola Valley. Born in Cincinnati in 1934, his was not an easy path to success. At the age of eight his father, a railroad engineer, passed away. Additionally, he was not always a very good student, and for a while toyed with the idea of being a professional boxer. However, there was no denying that he had a certain gift about fixing and making things. As a youngster he designed and built soapbox derby racers. He crafted model airplanes that were so detailed he could sell them to other neighborhood kids. In his own words: "I had a natural inclination and inquisitive nature about how 'things' worked. Taking apart broken toys and appliances, then putting them back together was an enjoyable challenge. Often during this process, I would attempt to make new or better things."

One of Fogarty's jobs, which he undertook to help his family, was working as an orderly at Good Samaritan Hospital in Cincinnati. Here he met his lifelong mentor, Dr. Jack Cranley. Cranley talked young Fogarty out of the boxing idea and encouraged the lad to take up a career in medicine. He had to work three jobs while going to college, but one of the positions he held was as a scrub tech. As such, he began to consider various ways to make surgery easier on patients. One of his ideas was to create the balloon

Dr. Thomas Fogarty. Photo courtesy of Thomas Fogarty Winery.

embolectomy catheter to safely remove arterial blood clots. First used in 1961, this devise has saved the lives of millions of patients. After completing his medical school experience and becoming a doctor, Fogarty went on to work on another 60 patents that have been utilized by some 20 companies.

In 1969, he patented his catheter and began his tenure at Stanford University Medical Center. That same year he developed an interest in wine making. He planted his first vines in 1978, and established his commercial winery—Thomas Fogarty Winery—in 1981. His estate and winery now take up 325 acres in the hills west of Portola Valley.

In the realm of finance, no bigger story can be told than that of Charles Johnson and Franklin Templeton Investments. The organization was founded in New York in 1947 by Rupert H. Johnson Sr., who admired Benjamin Franklin's business philosophies. His son, Charles B. Johnson, became president and chief executive officer in 1957, when the company had assets of but $2.3 million. He felt that mutual funds would become the best way for average investors to reach their financial goals, and headed the company in that direction. In 1972, Johnson with brother Rupert led his $225 million firm from New York to San Mateo. While Franklin grew steadily during the 1970s, it was in the 1980s that it experienced phenomenal success. In 1984, the company had $3.6 billion in assets. By 1985, it had $10 billion, prompting *Forbes* to declare Franklin the "Best Small Company in America."[4] By 1986, the firm had amassed $15 billion in

Charles Johnson, in center, who has guided Franklin Templeton to one of the world's most respected investment companies.

assets, and by 1988, it had a staff of 1,700, making it easily the largest employer in the city of San Mateo. By 2005, with Johnson still at the helm, the company had extended its expertise beyond mutual funds and expanded its global footprint with offices in 27 countries, and was managing more than $400 billion. No longer the "Best Small Company," Franklin Templeton is a recognized global leader in investment management.

In the field of computer software, no Bay Area name is bigger than Larry Ellison and his Oracle Corporation. Yet another San Mateo County entrepreneur without a privileged background, Ellison was attending the University of Illinois when, during finals week, his mother died. He quit school. In 1966, he ended up in Berkeley, California. He was in his twenties, with a weekend job at IBM as a systems programmer, while during the week he went hiking, rock climbing, kayaking, or bike riding. He then went to work for Amdahl in the Silicon Valley, but was laid off in 1973. At that point, Ellison joined Ampex, which was working on a memory system for the Central Intelligence Agency (CIA), with the code name of "Oracle." Ellison worked for Omex after Ampex and received his first title as vice president of research and development. Here he met Bob Miner and Ed Oates, and in 1977, the three decided to form their own company, Software Development Laboratories—later Oracle. The first customer for their relational database type systems was the CIA. Oracle's specialty became storage of massive amounts of information for institutions.

It is said that Larry Ellison's favorite saying comes from Genghis Khan: "It's not sufficient to succeed; everyone else must fail." With that as a part of his belief system, he molded Oracle into an international software giant within ten years. In 1989, he completed the first of six office buildings on a 66-acre site in Redwood Shores, the former grounds of the Marine World/Africa USA theme park. The award-winning design of the campus included a fitness center and four parking garages. Most of the construction was completed in 1998.

By 2006 Oracle was the second largest software maker in the world, only behind number one, Microsoft. The company is consistently one of San Mateo County's top employers.

Larry Ellison, himself, is frequently rated among the nation's ten richest people. He loves yacht racing and is devoted to Japanese culture. Japanese samurai armor from

Larry Ellison, Oracle Corporation founder.

the sixteenth century is counted among his collections. His Woodside house cost him an estimated $100 million to build and is a replica of a Japanese village. On 33 acres, it was constructed with pegs in the traditional tongue and groove style. It is said that not one nail was used on the entire estate. It was crafted together by artisans from Japan, especially brought in for the job. The compound includes at least 12 houses and a man-made lake.

Another important entrepreneur in the world of software within San Mateo County is Thomas Siebel. He was born in Chicago and received a BA in history, an MS in computer science, and an MBA from the University of Illinois. In 1984, he took an entry-level position at Oracle. Within

The futuristic architecture of the Oracle Headquarters in Redwood City has made these buildings a peninsula landmark.

a year he was named the company's top salesperson, worldwide.

He decided to spin off his own company in 1993, acquiring space in East Palo Alto. The venture was funded largely by Siebel and some of the original employees. They sat and worked on used furniture. Some went months without pay, but Siebel Systems made a name for itself as a software company dedicated to enabling organizations to apply information technology to managing everyday business communications with customers. By 1995, the company was profitable, and by 1999 it was exceeding $800 million in annual revenue. In 2000, it exceeded $1.79 billion. In 2000 and 2001, Siebel was named one of the top 25 managers in the world by *BusinessWeek*. In 2002, he was named "CEO of the Year" by *Industry Week*. Today (2006) Siebel employs 5,000 people who serve 4,000 clients, including IBM, Microsoft, and General Motors. From its new offices in San Mateo it has become a provider of services in 29 countries. At the time of the writing of this book, Tom Siebel is engaged in selling his company to Larry Ellison's Oracle.

In 1971, former Ampex employee and Woodside resident Nolan Bushnell had become the world's first professional computer-game designer.[5] His Atari company sold the Pong game and set in motion a major new industry for the Silicon Valley. Although widely successful (by the end of 1977, Atari was a $400 million company), internal conflict ruined it. In 1978, Bushnell broke from Atari, and it disappeared not long thereafter. However, another company, initiated only four years later, put San Mateo County firmly in the computer gaming arena.

Tripp Hawkins, the founder of Electronic Arts (EA), is certainly a different kind of entrepreneur than Larry Ellison. He recently was quoted as saying: "I hate the dog-eat-dog aspect of business and copying what everyone else does. I want to invent something truly new." He did just that in 1982, when at the age of 28, he left Apple Computer to get into the computer gaming business. Hawkins actually created his first games as a teenager, including a minicomputer football simulator that was only one point off in predicting the score of the 1974 Super Bowl.

Hawkins decided to create EA after meeting with Don Valentine at Menlo Park's famous venture capital firm, Sequoia Capital. Valentine actually offered the use of his offices to help Hawkins get his start. And so in May of 1982 Hawkins moved in and hired his first handful of employees that fall, after authoring the company's first business plan on his Apple II computer. Hawkins personally financed the company for most of the first year. Pinball Construction Set was one of the first products released in May of 1983. Hawkins and his entire staff of 30 went to the company's warehouse to handpack and ship the first orders. It was he who introduced new packaging strategies that sold the games like record albums. Before this time, computer games were simply sold in zip locked plastic bags. It was also Hawkins who decided to use celebrities and athletes in videogames. Such personalities included John Madden, Doctor J (Julius Erving), and Larry Bird.

When EA entered the marketplace in 1982, it had 135 competitors. Within just a few years, EA was number one among them. The company moved to Redwood Shores, and Hawkins left it for other interests, including the founding of a new venture, Digital Chocolate (located in San Mateo). Nevertheless, today (2006), EA is the world's largest videogame publisher with titles like *Madden NFL*, *Harry Potter*, *Lord of the Rings* and *Need for Speed*.

In recent years San Mateo County has become acknowledged the world over for its significant biotechnological contributions. No company better represents the achievements made in that area than Genentech. In 1976, this firm was established by two individuals, Herbert Boyer and Robert Swanson.

A high school biology class in Pennsylvania inspired Herbert Boyer's fascination with genetics. When he applied for graduate school at the University of Pittsburgh, a new faculty member interested him in microbial genetics. In 1973, as a professor of the University of California at Berkeley, Boyer combined energies with Stanley Cohen at Stanford University to pioneer a new scientific field called recombinant DNA technology, opening the door to "cutting and pasting" DNA with the potential of improving the health of people.

This information found its way to Robert Swanson, who was working for the Venture Capital firm of Kleiner Perkins in Menlo Park. Swanson had worked at a chemical company during college. He pursued degrees at MIT, completing both a BS in chemistry and an MBA in business management—all in five years. Swanson took the job with Kleiner Perkins with the intent of discovering a great idea and then creating his own company. In January of 1976, Swanson called Boyer and asked for a 10-minute meeting. A three-hour meeting took place instead, and the two decided to start up Genentech.

With financing through Kleiner Perkins, Boyer and Swanson obtained office space in a building in San Francisco and hired one employee.

"Biotech in Bronze" Artist Larry Anderson depicts the story of the founding of Genentech in this life-size bronze statue which is on permanent display in Genentech's Founders Research Center in South San Francisco. The sculpture recalls the first meeting of founders Swanson and Boyer which set in motion the beginning of Genentech and the biotechnology industry.

After its first year, Genentech achieved its first breakthrough, a way to produce a brain protein. In 1978, the firm moved into a warehouse in South San Francisco. It chose this location because of its proximity to the airport and its nearness to the two great universities at Berkeley and Palo Alto. That same year, Genentech cloned human insulin, and in the process improved the lives of millions. Before this time, insulin was obtained from the pancreas of pigs and cows. Many diabetics were allergic to this form of insulin. Genentech insulin was perfectly suitable for the human body. This first product, making use of recombinant DNA, was approved by the Food and Drug Administration (FDA) in 1982.

Investors anticipated the company's success. In 1980, after only one year of profitability and with no real product on the market, Genetech became the first biotech firm to offer stock to the public. It opened on Wall Street at $35 a share. Within 20 minutes it was selling at $88—a record showing.

More success came in 1985, when the FDA approved Genentech's human growth hormone, Protropin. This product is used to combat short stature in children who have hormonal deficiencies. Before this development, hormones from the dead were employed—sometimes with fatal results. Genentech's most recent major accomplishment came in 2004 with the FDA's blessing of Avastin, a cancer-fighting product.

Once again the author asks to be forgiven for all of the great entrepreneurs associated with San Mateo County not mentioned. Among those not detailed in this short essay are luminaries such as the following:

The Levy Brothers—stagecoach transportation and retail stores
Antoine Borel—banking and peninsula land owner
Russell and Sigurd Varian—klystron tubes
Stanley Hiller—helicopters

The Moore family helped establish Pescadero. This is the community circa 1900.

Tim Moseley—Dalmo Victor
Paul Cook—Raychem
Ray Dolby—Dolby sound systems
Carl Djerassi—the birth control pill
Reid Dennis—Institutional Venture Partners, venture capital
Miller Ream, Hal and Ron Fick—Borel Bank and Trust Company
Thomas J. Ford—real estate
Bill Somerville—Venture Philanthropy
Guy F. Atkinson—construction
Paul Saffo—Institute of the Future

Gordon Moore: Epitome of San Mateo County Entrepreneurship

For all the entrepreneurs associated with the peninsula, perhaps none has an experience more closely identified with San Mateo County than entrepreneur, scientist, and philanthropist Gordon Moore. His is a California family story that begins before the Gold Rush.

The Moore family came across the plains to California in 1847. Theirs was the second covered wagon party to use the Oregon Trail. Think for a moment what our western world was like in 1847. They were traveling over conflicted territory. Much of the land was still part of Mexico, while a war between Mexico and the United States was raging. Along the way there were no stops for relief. There was no Denver, no Salt Lake City. There were plains and deserts and forests. There were buffalo and elk and antelope. The Plains Indian tribes were intact and powerful—referred to as the greatest light cavalry the world had ever known. The winter before, the Donner party had been stranded in the Sierra Nevada with disastrous results. California was a place in flux because of the Mexican

War. With no more than 10,000 Mexican citizens stretched out from Sonoma to San Diego and the coast to the base of the mountains, California itself was part of the great American frontier.

As the Moores came across the country, climbed the Rockies, and walked across the Great Basin, what concerns must they have had? How difficult would crossing the Sierra Nevada be? What condition would they be in once they arrived in California? Who would win the Mexican-American War? How would they be received by the natives and fellow newcomers? What was their recourse if they didn't like what they saw in California? (There were no wagons east!)

From that long trip (from May until October of 1847), the family kept several souvenirs. These included their single-shot rifles, a bullet pouch, complete with bullet molds and percussion caps, and two powder horns. Along the way, they also acquired an Indian bow and—perhaps most mysteriously in the Utah wilderness—a broken European-style cadet sword. (How that got to Utah in 1847 can be anyone's guess!) The family generously gave all these things and more to the San Mateo County History Museum in 1957.

The Moores first settled in Santa Cruz County, but San Mateo County's original 1878 history describes how in 1852, Eli Moore, Gordon's great, great grandfather

> . . . came on horseback, by trails through the mountains. . . , rented a portion of the Pescadero Valley and afterwards put his sons upon it. . . . At the period of the settlement mentioned, there were no wagon roads in this part of the country, mails came at long intervals across the mountains from Searsville. Wolves and grizzly bears were disposed to possession of the beautiful valley, and the only reminder that it was a habitable country was of Indians and the native Mexicans.[6]

The Moores became the first non-Hispanic settlers of Pescadero, and as such, Alexander Moore, Gordon's great grandfather, established the first school. It was 14 by 16 feet in size. He also hired the first teacher with money from his own pocket. Mrs. Shield Knight taught that first year for $400. A San Mateo County History from 1883 tells us: "She had but seven scholars, four of whom were from Mr. Moore's home, and the others were Spanish children."[7]

Gordon Moore's grandfather was born in Pescadero, as was his father, Walter. What must it have been like for Walter, that kid of the isolated San Mateo County Coast, to serve in the 363rd Infantry Regiment during World War I? The 363rd was nicknamed the "Prune Pickers." They were mostly Californians and fought in Belgium and France. Walter himself went "over the top" (that is, charged from trenches in the face of the enemy) four times during the war.

After World War I, at the age of 28 in 1923, Walter entered the law-enforcement profession by becoming constable for the coastside between Tunitas Creek and the Santa Cruz County line. Of course that was the day of the bootlegger and rumrunner. Little ships would anchor off the south coast and boat in cases of "hootch" from Canada. Many locals from the poor farming community participated by loading whiskey onto trucks bound for San Francisco.

Walter's dedication and abilities in this difficult situation was not lost on Sheriff J. J. McGrath, who appointed Walter deputy sheriff. By the 1930s, the county was in the grip of organized gambling syndicates. Corruption at all levels of local government prevailed. However, during the 1930s and 1940s, Walter became locally famous for his efforts to stop organized crime on the peninsula.

As chief deputy during the 1950s, he, in the company of reform-minded officials such as Louis Dematteis and Keith Sorenson, finally achieved a permanent clean-up. Walter retired in 1960. Perhaps his prized possession was his collection of historic law-enforcement badges (about 300 of them).

After Walter's death, his family gave them to the County Sheriff's Department, which has allowed the San Mateo County History Museum to display them.

Walter and his wife, Myra, of another pioneer Pescadero family the Williamsons, had three sons, Walter, Gordon, and Francis. The young family lived at Pescadero. Recently, Gordon remembered how he would get his hair cut at Durates, a local restaurant and saloon. The family moved to Redwood City just before World War II. The boys went to local public schools. At age 11, Gordon and a friend decided they would become chemists. They dangerously experimented with mixing chemicals into explosives.

Gordon Moore graduated from Sequoia High School (the oldest high school in the county), went to college, and met and married Betty in 1950. He had a Ph.D., but there were few tech jobs on the West Coast. Therefore, Moore moved east and worked on Navy missiles at John Hopkins' Applied Physics Lab. In 1956, eager to return to San Mateo County, he accepted a position with Dr. William Shockley, the inventor of the transistor, at Shockley Semiconductor Laboratory. While working

Gordon Moore

for Shockley, Moore met Robert Noyce. They, along with six others, left the often-difficult Shockley (he referred to them as the "Traitorous Eight") to form a new company, Fairchild Semiconductors.

In 1965, *Electronics* magazine asked Moore to predict the future of technology. He said that the power of the silicon chip would double almost annually, with a proportionate decrease in cost. This quote became a guiding principle for the computer industry and is universally known as *Moore's Law*. Another frequently repeated quote, this one about being an entrepreneur, reads like this: "If everything you do works, you're probably not trying hard enough."

In 1968, Moore and Robert Noyce left Fairchild and established Intel, a producer of microchips. Venture capitalist Arthur Rock, who had helped fund Fairchild when it was being organized, lined up $2.5 million to help create Intel. He was able to raise this money in less than two days. In 1969, Intel created the first microprocessor, creating whole new industries.

Within ten years, the microprocessor was hailed as one of the most important inventions in American history. In 2003, Intel shipped its one-billionth processor. Today (2006), Intel of Santa Clara County, is a multibillion-dollar company, creating thousands of jobs and opportunities. Common appliances and household devices—from the washing machine, to the television set, to the microwave oven, to the cell phone—are improved or made possible by the processor.

Gordon and Betty still live in San Mateo County and have long been noted for their tremendous philanthropy. However, in September of 2000, they took their generous spirit to new levels by creating the Gordon and Betty Moore Foundation. Dedicated to making a significant impact on the condition of the world, the foundation focuses on science, higher education, environmental issues, health care, and regional projects.

Chapter 9 Footnotes

1. Stanger, *South*, p. 63.
2. Mitchell P. Postel, "A History of San Francisco International Airport," 1988, p. 41 in the manuscript collection of the San Mateo County History Museum Archives.
3. Ibid. p. 74.
4. Postel, *San Mateo*, p. 267.
5. Terry Borrell, "Still Playing After All These Years," *Upside Magazine*, October, 2001, p. 112.
6. Moore and DePue, *Illustrated*, p. 24.
7. Alley, *History*, p. 217.

Part *Three*

Regional Histories

The history of San Mateo County is a broad topic. The parts of this book that precede this one split the story into the major topics important to the overall development of San Mateo County. Even at that, much could be added about the political beginnings of the county, the natural resources used to build San Francisco, the suburbanization of the peninsula, the immigrant experience, and great entrepreneurs of the peninsula. Although these areas were chosen by the author to explore in a general way how San Mateo County came to be what it is today, more topics could and someday will be added to make the picture more complete.

In order to show some of the diverse local history here, Part III of this sesquicentennial work will discuss the different regional stories of the county. The coastside is very different from the bayside. The north county likewise is unlike the south. Each incorporated city has an individual story to tell. Here, then, are highlights of the history of these places.

Aerial view of San Mateo, c. 1931.

San Mateo County

Formed 1856
Population as of 2003: 717,000

The human story of San Mateo County begins at least 5,500 years ago. Recent archeology on the coastside near Montara has revealed human habitation going back that far. At the time of European contact with the natives (1769), it has been estimated that about 2,000 California Indians occupied the San Francisco Peninsula. They were part of a group of 10,000 people anthropologists call the Costanoans or the Ohlones. These Stone Age, prehistoric, hunting–gathering people lived in unchanging conditions for thousands of years. By most accounts, they maintained a caring way of life that valued generosity within the small communal triblets. Likewise, they had a light touch on the environment. They took only what was necessary from it. They periodically burned the underbrush to encourage grasses for large game. They practiced birth control in ritual and by allowing abortion.

Their unchanging world changed dramatically when, in 1769, Gaspar de Portola marched up the coast. It was from today's Sweeney Ridge, which separates the cities of Pacifica and San Bruno, that Portola discovered the San Francisco Bay.

The discovery of the Bay became pivotal in the Spanish plan for colonizing California. Within seven years, a mission and presidio were built at the northern tip of the peninsula at today's San Francisco. The Franciscan padres found this a challenging place to situate a mission. The sun never seemed to shine. The soil, in most places, was sandy. The little fresh water was brackish. There were no good stands of trees for lumber. Finally, most the potential neophytes lived down the peninsula. And so they found it necessary to build agricultural outposts in what is today's San Mateo County. The two most important were built at San Pedro Creek (at Linda Mar Boulevard in Pacifica) and San Mateo Creek (in the downtown San Mateo area). The establishment of these outposts was essential to the success of the mission community and presidio at San Francisco.

After the San Francisco mission lands were secularized in 1835, 17 land grants were carved out of what would become San Mateo County. The grants were awarded to favorites of the new Mexican–California government. The Arguello family owned the largest on the peninsula—35,250-acre Rancho de las Pulgas. The powerful Sanchez family came to own three of the grants—Rancho Buri Buri, Rancho San Pedro, and Rancho Feliz. Francisco Sanchez led the Californios against U.S. Marines at the Battle of Santa Clara (1847), which happily resulted in no casualties but achieved a truce.

Before the California Gold Rush began, a number of Americans and other foreigners inhabited the southern hill country of today's San Mateo County. They initiated an infant logging industry, which became significant after gold was discovered (1848) and San Francisco emerged into the most important city on the West Coast. R. O. Tripp and other early pioneers recognized the potential of a port at Redwood City. Some 14 mills cut up the giant redwood trees of the Woodside and Skyline regions. Tripp established the Woodside Store to cater to the lumberjacks and others who came to the area. Meanwhile, Redwood City got its start as the most significant population center on the peninsula's bayside.

San Mateo County was not one of California's original counties when the state was created in 1850. It was organized in 1856 through political compromise. At the time, most of the area now called San Mateo County was part of San Francisco County. San Francisco, was becoming a haven for corrupt politicians, and reformers reasoned that it was easier to cleanly manage one local government than two. They wished to combine San Francisco county and city political leadership and services into one entity. However, those enjoying the status quo had many political allies, and when the issue was taken to Sacramento by State Assemblyman Horace Hawes, "he had to make terms with the thieves," as one contemporary observer wrote. In a compromise, it was agreed that San Francisco government would be consolidated, but there would be two counties.

As discussed in detail in Chapter II, those "thieves" hoped they would have a political base by seizing control of the more rural San Mateo County, which had a population of only about 2,500 residents. From San Mateo County they could wait for the reform-minded citizens of San Francisco—who were mostly middle-class businessmen—to tire of their efforts. In time, they could recover their former power in the city.

They rigged the organizing election of 1856, seemingly ensuring that San Mateo County would serve as the new base for political corruption. However, two days after the election, James Casey shot and killed James King of William, a San Francisco newspaper editor. This resulted in the formation of a San Francisco vigilance committee numbering 8,000 individuals. Targeted were a few dozen old confederates of Casey, including his cronies who had just taken over San Mateo County. Most of the crowd fled the area after the vigilantes hanged Casey and took control of San Francisco. Local leaders in San Mateo County then had the opportunity to stage new elections.

Nevertheless, San Mateo County was slow growing for the rest of the nineteenth century, and this had three major ramifications.

First, its industries such as logging focused on providing San Francisco with resources to keep the city the dominant metropolis of the West. Agriculture, oyster cultivation, shrimp fishing, shore whaling, and waterworks all provided for the city to the north.

Second, the San Francisco–San Jose Railroad completion, in 1864, allowed San Mateo County to become the first rail suburb west of the Mississippi. Emulating their East Coast brethren, the new elite of San Francisco's industrial and commercial circles wished to rescue their families from the unhealthy and immoral conditions of San Francisco by establishing estates down the peninsula. Families like the Mills, Floods, Haywards, and Parrotts controlled the economic resources of the West from their offices in the city, but called the peninsula their home. Clear into the first third of the twentieth century, these suburban estates and the many that followed took up much space and retarded growth, giving San Mateo County a distinctive character.

Finally, the rural nature of San Mateo County made it a place where certain activities could take place that could not in the city. Although San Francisco was largely known as a wide-open city for most of its history, for many years it was also known that if you couldn't get away with some activity in the city, you could do it by crossing the county line.

Dueling, for example, outlawed everywhere in California, was practiced here. The most famous of all California duels occurred in 1859, when California Supreme Court Justice David Terry shot to death U.S. Senator David Broderick just inside the county line in today's Daly City. Gambling, prostitution, and other activities were only slightly regulated by the county's weak local law-enforcement agencies. By the turn of the century, activities illegal in San Francisco but legal in San Mateo County (notably prize fighting and horse racing) enhanced this legacy. During prohibition, the county became famous for rum running and speakeasies. During the 1930s, flagrant illegal gambling operations prompted one gangster to declare the county the most corrupt in California.

The twentieth century brought considerable growth to San Mateo County. The San Francisco Earthquake of 1906 resulted in a great migration to the peninsula. A newly constructed streetcar system, from San Francisco all the way to San Mateo, allowed for the hamlets along the line to become home to a new middle-class suburbanite. The affordability and popularity of the automobile through the 1920s and 1930s continued this growth.

However, it was World War II that sparked the creation of a great portion of the built environment of the County. The airport east of Millbrae, termed a mud hole by San Francisco newspapers before the war, was improved to such an extent by the U.S. Army that by 1946, it was handling nearly a tenth of all the air traffic in the United States. All around this San Francisco utility sprang up warehouses, hotels, and other supporting businesses. Partially because of the growth of the airport, a wartime electronics industry exploded on to the scene. Firms such as EIMAC, Varian, Dalmo Victor, and, in the postwar, Ampex became huge employers.

Building homes for the growing population became the responsibility of a new breed of housing developers. Schooled in mass building techniques during the war, Henry Doegler, Fred and Carl Gellert, David Bohannon, Andy Oddstad, Jack Foster, and others constructed thousands of tract homes through loans made possible by the federal and state governments.

The original electronics companies are mostly history today, but they gave rise to the peninsula's computer software and biotech industries. They make international headlines daily and call San Mateo County home.

SAN MATEO COAST
Pacifica to Miramar

In many ways, San Mateo County history begins on its north coast. It was from Sweeney Ridge in present-day Pacifica that Gaspar de Portola made his fateful

Ocean Shore Rail Road.

discovery of the San Francisco Bay in 1769. Portola, a Spaniard just recruited to New World duties, didn't think much of the discovery. In fact, he recorded that he had "found nothing." However, an observant Franciscan padre, Juan Crespi, was also in the party and saw more to the discovery. He convinced Spanish authorities that further investigation was warranted.

Within seven years the Spanish established a mission at the northern tip of the peninsula. Between 1785 and 1786, the padres also built an agricultural outpost in the San Pedro Valley (today's Linda Mar district in Pacifica), just southwest of the Bay's discovery site. At one point, with 2,760 yards of fencing erected, the padres had 36 acres of wheat and nine acres of corn under cultivation. Pear and peach trees and grapevines rendered fruit.

Taken from a watercolor of Rancho San Pedro by artist A. Cros in 1865.

After secularization of the mission lands, Francisco Sanchez acquired much of the property now included in the City of Pacifica. In 1839, he built a temporary dwelling shortly before receiving title. Between 1842 and 1846, he constructed a grand adobe home on the ruins of the old mission outpost.

Like his father Jose, who lived on the other side of the hill, Francisco was a leader. At age 32, he was chosen captain of the regional civic militia, and in 1842, at the age of 37, he was made alcalde of Yerba Buena (San Francisco). Francisco led the Californios against American Marines and volunteers at the Battle of Santa Clara in 1847. After the Mexican War, while all his rancho neighbors gradually lost their properties to lawyers and bankers, Francisco managed to keep his land until the day he died, in 1862, after falling from a horse.

For the rest of the nineteenth century the north coast remained a rather quiet place, isolated by the Pacific Ocean with no good natural harbors on the west and the coastal hills to the east. However, on May 18, 1905, all this was to be challenged with the incorporation of the Ocean Shore Rail Road Company. The scheme was to link San Francisco with Santa Cruz by rail and open the entire coast to real estate development.

Good progress had been made with construction when the April 18, 1906, Earthquake caused significant damage. Nevertheless, building continued. Five future communities were laid out at today's Pacifica—Edgemar, Salada Beach, Brighton Beach, Vellemar, and San Pedro Terrace. A tunnel was punched through at Devil's Slide, and the railroad began serving the coast while planning the communities of Montara, Moss Beach, Princeton, El Granada, and Miramar.

It was at El Granada that the railroad's leaders held their greatest hopes. Here they hired nationally renowned architect D. H. Burnham to lay out a town and hotel resort, which they pronounced the future "Coney Island of the West." Sadly for the Ocean Shore Rail Road and its promoters, rebuilding San Francisco became the major focus of serious local investment. While construction of

El Granada Hotel in the early 20th century.

El Granada Station. It was quite an excursion to get to and go on the Ocean Shore Rail Road.

the railroad along the San Mateo Coast was completed all the way down to Tunitas Creek, a crucial 26-mile gap between Tunitas Creek and Swanton in Santa Cruz County was never completed. The railroad stopped service in 1920, and the north coast remained largely an agrarian area until after World War II and the beginning of the California postwar real estate boom. Even at that, the only community to incorporate on the north coast is Pacifica, in 1957. Today its population is about 39,000.

SAN MATEO COAST
Half Moon Bay to Año Nuevo

San Mateo County's first community was established on the south coast at Pilarcitos Creek. When hostilities began between Americans and the Californios during the Bear Flag Revolt (1846), two San Francisco land grant families decided to move to their coastside ranchos to avoid the violence. The Vasquez family built a few adobe structures north of the creek that separated their lands from the Miramontes family, who constructed some buildings on the south side of the creek. Other Californios moved to this remote place as well. They called their community San Benito. Over the hill, the Americans called it Spanishtown. Later it became know as Half Moon Bay. After a century of slow growth, town leaders incorporated the place in 1959. Today, with a population of more than 12,000, it is the only incorporated community on the south coast.

Just south of Half Moon Bay, James Johnston of Ohio purchased 1,162 acres from Candelerio Miramontes to create one of the first dairy farms in the state during the 1850s. Johnston had struck it rich during the Gold Rush and became a part owner of San Francisco's famous El Dorado Saloon. From his dealings at the saloon he came into contact with a few of the old California families and came to know and then marry Petra de Jara in 1852. It was through Petra that Johnston was able to meet Miramontes to acquire the land. Following Johnston's lead, other dairymen established ranches all the way down to Año Nuevo.

South of the Johnston place was the village of Purisima. By the 1860s, Purisima consisted of a saloon, hotel, schoolhouse, store, livery stable and post office. Founded by American, Irish and German immigrants, many thought that Purisima would become the leading community of the coast, but Half Moon Bay's better location on the road to San Mateo gave it the advantage, and Purisima slowly disappeared. Only a cemetery marks this place today.

In the 1850s, two other towns got started on creeks south of Half Moon Bay. San Gregorio and Pescadero supported the agricultural community around them. Although San Gregorio at one point even boasted a little Chinatown, it was Pescadero that rivaled Half Moon Bay, and, by the late 1860s,

Main Street in Half Moon Bay, circa 1911.

The Vasquez adobe, home of some of the earliest settlers in the Half Moon Bay area, was destroyed in the 1906 earthquake; three people died.

Ladies walking down Stage Road in Pescadero in the latter part of the 19th century.

had become the fourth largest town in the county.

However, when California counties were originally established in 1850, Pescadero laid in Santa Cruz County. Farmers and towns people complained that it was too difficult to reach Santa Cruz and, in 1861, began a campaign to become annexed to San Mateo County, which finally occurred in 1868.

Throughout its history, the South Coast has maintained its character as agrarian. However, early on its rough coastline also

Rockaway Beach Railroad Station in Pacifica was one of the stops for the Ocean Shore Railway.

gave it a dangerous reputation among sailors. Año Nuevo Island, Franklin Point, and Pigeon Point have all witnessed maritime disasters. A major wreck occurred in 1853 when the *Carrier Pigeon*, a new clipper ship, ran aground at La Punta de la Ballena. While no one was killed, the entire 1,300 tons of cargo was lost. So memorable was the incident that the point was renamed for the wreck—Pigeon Point. Twelve years later, a little north of Pigeon Point, the *Sir John Franklin* went down with the loss of 12 seamen—and Franklin Point got its name.

Recognizing the risk to maritime interests, in 1870 the federal government purchased Año Nuevo Island and Pigeon Point for $10,000 for the purpose of establishing lighthouses. They became operational in 1872. At that time, Pigeon Point was already serving as a station for Portuguese shore whalers. Año Nuevo Island would become famous in the next century for its marine animals, becoming part of an important wildlife reserve in 1976.

The Montara Point Lighthouse. Originally a fog signal station (established in 1875), the current lighthouse was added in 1928. In the photograph above, it is seen as a military station during World War II, when it housed military units including a mobile artillery unit and a K-9 corp which patrolled the beaches below. In the early 1970s, the fog horn was replaced by an offshore horn bouy and the light was automated. Since 1980 the lighthouse has served as a youth hostel.

Prewar, 1939, Half Moon Bay was sparsely populated.

San Mateo County Hill Country

From Woodside over Kings Mountain almost to the coast, and from the southern county lines to the San Mateo to Half Moon Bay Road, lies a hill area in the county dominated by a variety of forest vegetation, including gigantic redwood trees. Beginning in the 1830s, a variety of American and other "foreign" drifters came to inhabit the hill country and worked as sawyers and hunters. Most had jumped ship at Yerba Buena or Monterey. They found themselves continually at odds with Mexican officials for dodging taxes and building illegal stills. Moreover, whenever they were in the hills hunting, traveling, or building stills, they were in constant danger from the numerous grizzly bears.

This relatively quiet world changed dramatically in 1849. No gold was found in the hills, but San Francisco was fast becoming an important city and needed lumber to build its wharves, hotels, warehouses, and saloons. By 1853, there were 14 mills active in just the Kings Mountain area.

At the center of the hill-country community was the Woodside Store. Dr. R. O Tripp and his partner, M. A. Parkhurst, are recognized as pioneers of the logging industry. They also initiated the store. Their emporium stocked every imaginable type of commodity. It also functioned as a post office and community meeting place. Parkhurst died early on, but Tripp lived until 1909, becoming one of the county's most memorable historic characters.

While the logging industry went into decline by the 1880s, the creation of a water-storage and delivery system for San Francisco increased in importance. From today's San Bruno to Woodside, the man-made lakes of the peninsula's interior have given San Mateo County a special appearance.

A reliable freshwater supply at San Francisco had been the settlement's greatest resource issue since mission times. With the Gold Rush, the problem was exasperated. During certain times of year, water had to be barged in from Marin County. Water barrels were strapped to the sides of mules, and water peddlers roamed the streets selling the liquid for as much as a gold dollar a bucket.

In 1858, the Spring Valley Water Company incorporated to create reservoirs in San Mateo County as a better resource for the city. By 1900, it owned 20,000 acres of peninsula land.

German-born, Swiss-trained engineer Herman Schussler designed most of the system. His greatest achievement was the building of Crystal Springs Dam, located just under today's Doran Bridge on Highway 280. This 150-foot-high engineering marvel was constructed with concrete interlocking blocks and was the largest of its kind in the world when it was completed in 1890. The success of its construction can be measured against the earthquakes it has endured. From the great 1906 disaster clear to the Loma Prieta Earthquake of 1989, the dam has held without a crack.

Although Crystal Springs Dam was undamaged by the 1906 Earthquake, the Spring Valley Water Company's water deliver systems were crippled. Broken pipes meant no water to

Back of stables at Filoli.

put out the fires in San Francisco. After the disaster, many blamed the Spring Valley Water Company's deferred maintenance for much of the city's losses. Previously, the city had adopted a new charter allowing it to purchase its own water system. San Franciscans began eyeing the Hetch Hetchy Valley for a reservoir that would satisfy their needs into the next century.

Recognizing that the city would one day purchase the Spring Valley Water Company's holdings as part of the great Hetch Hetchy system, entrepreneur William Bourn bought the banged-up company in 1908. Bourn's sale to the city was not completed until 1930. In the meantime, he built a substantial estate just south of his watershed properties. He called the place Filoli, and it still stands today as a historic house and garden operated by the National Trust for Historic Preservation.

Daly City, Colma, and Brisbane

During the nineteenth century, much of north San Mateo County was collectively called Colma. Most of the population of the Colma area clustered close to Mission Street. A variety of gambling and drinking houses were the main business. Some said that this stretch of Mission Street featured "the finest mile and a half of eating and drinking found anywhere in the country." By 1890, of the 20 businesses present on the business portion of the highway, six were saloons.

By the turn of the century, the north county had attracted a variety of activities that San Francisco had either outlawed or outgrown. For example, dog tracks and boxing arenas drew thousands of San Franciscans across the county line.

In addition to having a reputation for catering to the leisure activities of San Franciscans, the Colma region was also known for agriculture and dairy ranching. First Irish and then Italian farmers came in numbers. Close proximity to the big city gave farmers easy access to a substantial market.

Because of San Francisco's shortage of real estate, the north county also became a place to bury the city's dead. The Roman Catholic Church consecrated Holy Cross in 1887. It was followed by the Jewish cemetery, Home of Peace, in 1888. Later the Italian, Chinese, Serbian, Japanese, and Greek communities

Daly City's Parkview Avenue can be seen in the foreground, with a sign advertising lots for sale. This photograph was taken about 1920.

The Italian Cemetery in Colma. South San Francisco hills can be seen in the background of this photograph taken December 31, 1981 by Evelyn Ihrke.

wanted resting places. In 1892, Cypress Lawn began operations and was immediately recognized as one of the most beautiful, nonsectarian burial grounds in the country.

For years this section of the county was known as Lawndale. When it incorporated in 1924, it became Colma. Today (2006) this "City of the Dead" has a living population of about 1,200.

The Great San Francisco Earthquake and Fire of 1906 had tremendous impact on north county. Refugees fled across the county line. Dairy rancher John Daly provided shelter and later subdivided his property to allow for suburban development. In 1911, Daly City incorporated.

The city received a boost in development with the California post–World War II real estate boom. In 1945, Henry Doelger purchased 1,300 acres west of Daly City and began creating Westlake. Over a 20-year period, homes for 20,000 people were constructed there, and Westlake was annexed to Daly City in stages. Similarly, Fred and Carl Gellert purchased 1,000 acres after the war and created the Serramonte subdivision.

No place in the county was more affected by the postwar boom. Between 1950 and 1960, Daly City's population grew

Widening Mission Boulevard in Daly City.

The intersection of San Bruno and Visitation Avenues in Brisbane, 1955.

from 15,000 to 60,000. It is now the county's largest city, with more than 104,000 people.

Today's Brisbane and the north side of San Bruno Mountain were originally part of Rancho Guadalupe la Visitacion y Rodeo Viejo. The 9,000-acre land grant was owned by Jacob Leese, an American who married into California General Mariano Vallejo's family.

Although real estate development on the mountain had been considered as far back as 1908, it was not until the 1930s that Brisbane as a town began to take shape. Many of the original settlers were of poor Depression-era families that established a rather dilapidated community. As with other places in north county, it experienced considerable suburban growth in the postwar period.

In 1961, the people of this place decided to incorporate in order to better defend their immediate environment. San Francisco intended to expand its nearby dump. Many Brisbane residents organized their own action committee, "Garbage A-Go-Go," to fight off this bay fill initiative. The environmental victory, with the creation of the San Francisco Bay Conservation and Development Commission in the middle of that decade, was, in part, due to many groups such as Brisbane's. Today the city numbers about 3,600 people.

Mills Estate

D. O. Mills

San Bruno and Millbrae

San Bruno, Millbrae, South San Francisco, the southern portion of Mount San Bruno, and the northern part of Burlingame all were part of Jose Sanchez's Rancho Buri Buri. Within 15 years of the American takeover of California, the Sanchez family was forced to yield all but 5 percent of the property to bankers, attorneys, and the taxman.

During the latter part of the nineteenth century, at what we would call San Bruno today, there existed little more than some farms, a couple of well-known roadhouses, and a railroad stop. The area's greatest claim to fame was the Tanforan racetrack. Polish Prince Andre Pontiatowski financed the 120-acre development in 1899. In 1902, the California Jockey Club bought the track from the prince for $82,000.

The club had only modest success with the track in its first year, and then leased it to the California Auto Club in 1903. Car racing became popular, with

Celebration for the incorporation of San Bruno September 7, 8, and 9, 1914. Queen of the occasion was Edith Schmidt, center.

General store and Post Office at Millbae and El Camino, circa 1906.

speeds reaching more than 60 miles per hour. However, interest dropped off considerably in 1908 when California outlawed gambling at tracks.

For awhile, Tanforan's major attraction shifted to air shows. At one of these shows in 1911, daredevil Eugene Ely did much to demonstrate the feasibility of the aircraft carrier by taking off from Tanforan and landing on the *USS Pennsylvania* out in the Bay. The warship had a deck built out over its aft. Gunnysacks filled with sand were tied together across the 130-foot wooden deck. Ely's Curtis biplane had grappling hooks that caught the ropes, slowing him into the first successful landing of a plane on to a ship.

During World War I, Tanforan served as a military training field. It returned to horse racing in 1923 with limited success. Finally, with the legalization of parimutuel betting in 1933, the track became quite successful. With the outbreak of World War II, Tanforan was utilized as an assembly center for Japanese-American residents of the San Francisco Bay region. After spending some time here during the early part of 1942,

Lomita Park's first school on St. Helena Avenue in San Bruno.

Millbrae City Hall after incorporation.

Japanese Americans were placed in internment camps in the interior of the country until the end of the war. Today Tanforan is a major regional shopping center.

San Bruno as a suburban community began growing after the San Francisco Earthquake and Fire of 1906. The railroad and the streetcar afforded good transportation into the city, and former refugees from the city became commuters. Lots sold for as little as $225 each, payable in $5 monthly installments. The muddy roads of the instant town demanded improvements. San Bruno incorporated in 1914 to answer this and other needed improvements. Today's San Bruno has a population that exceeds 40,000.

South of San Bruno, there was not the same activity. This was due to the presence of the Mills estate and the family's reluctance to sell its properties. Back in 1860, banker D. O. Mills had bought up 1,500 acres to establish the northernmost of the great estates in San Mateo County. Here he built a lavish three-story mansion and called it Millbrae. His lands included a dairy, a eucalyptus forest, water reservoir, and a huge, glass-covered greenhouse. After D.O.'s death the family mostly moved back east, but the land stayed part of the family's estate.

The Millbrae area did experience some suburban development after World War I, but did not incorporate as a town until 1946. Today, Millbrae's population is about 21,000.

South San Francisco

South San Francisco is perhaps the most unique of all the peninsula's incorporated communities because it began as a company town. By the time it incorporated in 1908, the city of nearly 2000 people had ten industries—including a meat-packing plant, Fuller Paint Company, two steel mills, a tannery, brickyards, and a lumber company.

Before the arrival of these companies, much of what would become South San Francisco was a ranch. Charles Lux purchased the land in 1856. He built a substantial home here, and in 1858, formed a partnership with Central Valley cattle rancher, Henry Miller, creating the West Coast's largest livestock company of its day. For more than 30 years Miller and Lux cowboys drove thousands of cattle from massive Central Valley ranches up El Camino Real to Lux's spread. The cattle were kept here before being butchered at San Francisco.

Lux died in 1887. A year later, Gustavus Swift, the Chicago meat-packing giant, surveyed the property for the purpose of establishing a West Coast site to expand his business. Swift joined forces with other meat packers and bought up some 3,500 acres, including Lux's ranch, setting up what they called the South San Francisco Land and Improvement Company.

Grand Avenue, South San Francisco, 1894.

During the 1890s other companies established operations, and a residential area, built for employees of the companies, began to take shape. By the time of the 1906 Earthquake, the place's population was quite diverse. The foreign-born included Irish and Portuguese workers, along with a large contingent of Italians.

During both World War I and II, shipbuilding took place at South San Francisco. However, after the Second World War, the old smokestack industries went into decline. Their place has been taken by other endeavors—most notably Genentech, Inc. This firm, organized in 1976, moved into a South San Francisco warehouse in 1978. Since that time it has become one of the world's most important biotech firms, making international headlines for its work in fighting cancer and for other advances.

Grand Avenue, South San Francisco, 1926.

Today's South San Francisco still features a diverse economy and a diverse population. It numbers more than 61,000 people.

San Mateo

About 1793, the San Francisco Mission fathers established an agricultural outpost at San Mateo Creek. This *asistenian* was constructed near the spot Padre Pedro Font had recommended the creation of a formal mission back in 1776. The outpost was a great success for the Franciscans. They eventually had 10,000 head of sheep here. Christianized Indians, some local but including people from many triblets of the Bay region, did the work.

At the time of the Mexican Revolution (1822), there were about 30 native Californians at San Mateo. A year after Jose Sanchez received title to his Rancho Buri Buri (1835), his son, Jose de la Cruz Sanchez, petitioned for the lands south of Buri Buri to San Mateo Creek, which became known as Rancho San Mateo. This property basically included the southern portion of today's Burlingame, Hillsborough, and the northern part of San Mateo. The request was not honored. The Mexican authorities cited the presence of the Indians as the reason. South of San Mateo Creek, southern San Mateo, all the way down to San Francisquito Creek, was granted to the Arguello family.

In 1839, the entire San Francisco Mission Indian community moved to San Mateo, and the population increased to about 90 people. Finally, in 1846, the last Mexican governor of Alta California, Pio Pico, who knew very little about the situation at San Mateo, awarded the rancho to Cayentano Arenas of Los Angeles as payment for a debt. With the uncertainties of the Bear Flag Revolt and then the Mexican-American War, Cayentano's father, Luis, sold San Mateo to the American mercantile firm of Mellus and Howard. Eventually, W. D. M. Howard bought out his partner Henry Mellus, with the intention of creating the first of the peninsula's great estates.

Meanwhile, recognizing a business opportunity in the making, in 1849, Nicolas de Peyster moved into the abandoned mission-outpost building at Rancho San Mateo and opened it as the first roadhouse between San Francisco and San Jose. Of course, he was squatting and was ordered off the property, but he stayed there for two years. In 1851, he bought up 75 acres of Arguello land just across the creek and built a new roadhouse to accommodate the increasing stage travel.

The San Francisco–San Jose Railroad reached San Mateo in 1863. One of the railroad's organizers, Charles B. Polhemus, laid out a town east of the stage stop on both sides of the creek. The town slowly took shape. In 1894, the issue of incorporation reared up. Some 150 San Mateans voted in favor of it, with only 25 against.

San Mateo became the terminus of the streetcar line from San Francisco in 1902. Following the 1906 Earthquake, the town grew at a faster rate and became the focus of a variety of projects. Some were doomed to failure—like Pacific City, an amusement park at Coyote Point. Others, however, made San Mateo one of the leading cities of the region between San Francisco and San Jose. They included the creation of San Mateo Junior College (1922), San Mateo County Community Hospital (1923), San Mateo Hayward Bridge (1929), Bay Meadows Race Track (1934), San Mateo County Fair (1935), and the San Mateo County Historical Museum (1941).

After World War II, a variety of developers helped San Mateo grow. Most notably was David D. Bohannon, who built the Hillsdale shopping center and also constructed apartment houses and single-family homes from El Camino Real to the western hills. Today, San Mateo is the second-largest city of the peninsula, with a population of more than 94,000.

Early view of B Street in San Mateo.

South San Francisco's first store, 1893, at the northeast corner of Maple and Grand Avenues.

El Camino at Central Park in San Mateo in the 1930s.

Kohl Mansion, now part of San Mateo's Central Park. (This photograph is of the entry driveway of the mansion.)

Burlingame and Hillsborough

W. D. M. Howard, owner of Rancho San Mateo, died in 1856. To his wife, Agnes (who was not yet 25), he left the southern half of his property (mostly north San Mateo today). The northern half (roughly southern Burlingame and Hillsborough), he gave to Agnes's father, Dr. Joseph Henry Poett, who, in turn, gave the western portion of his holdings to his other daughter, Julia (Mrs. John Redington). For decades the Howard, Poett, and Redington families controlled most of Rancho San Mateo, establishing the Peninsula's original great estates.

In 1860, Dr. Poett sold diplomat-adventurer Anson Burlingame more than 1,000 acres of land in what we would call the Hillsborough and the Burlingame Avenue area today. Five years before, Abraham Lincoln had appointed Burlingame minister of China to secure labor to help build the transcontinental railroad. His dealings with the emperor of China proved lucrative. With some of this money, he bought his San Mateo property for $54,757 (about $52 an acre).

On his more than 1,000 acres, Burlingame planned a residential park after the English style with a view to establishing a grand manor of his own. However, he died in 1870, probably never seeing this property more than twice.

William C. Ralston bought the property from Burlingame's widow. Ralston, California's most famous capitalist of that time, believed in Burlingame's dream and planned his own country community which he wanted to call Ralstonville. Sadly, Ralston's Bank of California underwent hard times in August of 1875. He was removed as the bank's chief executive, and the next day, his body was found floating in the Bay, perhaps as the result of a swimming mishap.

William Sharon, Ralston's greatest creditor, received much of Ralston's estate, including his San Mateo County properties here and at Belmont. Sharon also felt Burlingame's country community idea was feasible. He had the area surveyed and he published a map of a residential community to be called Burlingame. After a few years, Sharon realized that time was not right for this development. He then sold the portion of his property east of El Camino Real to William Corbitt, who established a successful stock ranch. On the remaining land he created a dairy to supply his Palace Hotel in San Francisco.

Golf at the 3rd Burlingame Country Club, built in the late 1890s, designed by George Howard.

Lots in Burlingame were advertised at $650 in 1907, with easy access by electric train from San Francisco.

Sharon died in 1885, and his able son-in-law, Francis G. Newlands, came to manage the huge Sharon estate that extended from San Francisco's financial district to the silver mines of Nevada to Washington, D.C. Among Newlands's initial projects was creation of one of the first planned communities in the United States just outside of Washington, D.C., at Chevy Chase. As part of his plan to sell the property, he organized the Chevy Chase Country Club.

Watching the success of this development, Newlands reasoned that the Burlingame area might be ready for a similar approach. In 1893, he sponsored the creation of the Burlingame Country Club, which attracted some of the leading young men in San Francisco's elite business community.

A year after the club's formation, its members established the Burlingame train station. A small business community emerged around the station to cater to the club's members and their neighbors.

When the 1906 earthquake drove San Franciscans down the peninsula, many stopped at Burlingame because they knew its reputation as a retreat for the elite. In one year, Burlingame's population grew from 200 (1906) to 1,000 (1907).

The incorporated town of San Mateo looked at Burlingame for possible annexation. The people living around the station beat their neighbors to the punch and incorporated their own community (Burlingame) in 1909.

By 1910, both San Mateo and Burlingame were looking west at the country estates surrounding the Burlingame Club for possible annexation. San Mateo had already taken in San Mateo Park in 1901 and Hayward Park in 1910. Burlingame had gobbled up Easton to its north in 1910. So club members banded together to stay out of the clutches of these hungry middle-class towns, to create their own incorporated community—Hillsborough—in March of 1910.

Today Burlingame and Hillsborough remain two of the most attractive communities in the country. Burlingame maintains its quaint atmosphere, especially along its downtown Burlingame Avenue. Burlingame has a population of about 28,000 people. Hillsborough has managed to maintain its country community exclusive feeling. Its population is about 11,000.

Belmont and San Carlos

From San Mateo Creek to San Francisquito Creek stretched the Arguello family's Rancho de las Pulgas. After the Gold Rush began, the Arguellos faced a plague of American squatters on their lands, similar to that which afflicted their neighbors. Coming to their rescue was Simon Mezes, who successfully fought off the squatters in court in exchange for about a fourth of the land grant. This included a large chunk of what we would call Belmont today.

Mezes had come to California in 1850 at the age of 28. Some evidence exists that he had been president of a bank in Puerto Rico. His legal and financial background, plus his ability to read and write in two languages, placed him in a great position to defend the land grants of the old California families, and probably his most valued clients were the Arguellos.

Mezes came to live at Belmont and in 1854 chose to sell a portion of this property to Italian nobleman Leonetto Cipriani, who built a home and lived there for ten years. In 1864, Cipriani's old political ally, Victor Emmanuel, became the first king of Italy, and Cipriani decided to return to his native country. He sold his estate to Morton Cheesman for $5,500. Three days later, Cheesman sold the parcel to famous California capitalist William Ralston for $6,500.

Ralston used part of the Cipriani house for building a huge 50-bedroom mansion. It still stands today as part of the Notre Dame de Namur University campus.

East of Ralston's estate, about 1866, Carl Janke, a native of Germany created Belmont Park, patterning it after a Hamburg biergarten. Huge crowds would make use of the recently built San Francisco–San Jose Railroad, and they came to the park. San Francisco's large foreign-born communities were frequent visitors. Sometimes as many as 10,000 would come for a single organized picnic via half-a-mile-long passenger trains.

Sadly, as the years went by, Belmont Park developed a reputation for drunkenness and brawling. In 1880, a killing took place as a result of fighting between two San Francisco gangs. A little girl names Annie Moonie was kidnapped and was never heard from again. Finally, the Southern Pacific stopped the excursions and, by the turn of the century, Belmont Park closed.

Nevertheless, a small community developed at the railroad tracks. Fearing annexation by burgeoning San Carlos to the south, Belmont residents incorporated in 1927. Today the city has a population of more than 25,000 people.

Inside William Ralston's mansion after his death.

Belmont Soda Works, founded by Carl Janke, made sarsparilla and other drinks. Photograph circa 1890 by James Van Court.

Belmont School for Boys, which became the St. Joseph Military Academy.

It appears that everyone dressed up for this photo at the Emmett Store in Belmont in the late 1800s.

Plane spotting station on Newlands Avenue in Belmont, 1942.

Ralston Avenue with the Southern Pacific Station on the left and Emmett Store in the center in this January 1922 photograph of Belmont.

The intersection of Ralston at El Camino. Photo from the 1930s.

Fred Drake.

San Carlos originated as a dream of successful merchant and politician Timothy Guy Phelps. He bought up 3,500 acres of property along the railroad tracks. In 1887, he had formal plans drawn up and a railroad station was built. Unfortunately for Phelps and his partners, only about a dozen families came to live there. Phleps was killed in a freak accident in 1899 when he was mowed down by a bicycle built for two.

San Carlos continued to grow slowly until, finally, after World War I, skilled promoter Fred Drake came on the scene. Extraordinarily, Drake had suburban San Carlos growing at a faster rate than any other community in California at times during the 1920s. The town was incorporated in 1925. Today it numbers about 28,000 residents.

Redwood City

Part of the land acquired by Simon Mezes, because of his successful defense of Rancho de las Pulgas, was the infant town springing up along the embarcadero at what is now Redwood City. He had this area surveyed and divided into lots that he sold to the American squatters. His block and lot map determined the streets as they are still known in the downtown portion of the city.

The back cover of Sunset Magazine, May 1907. San Carlos at the turn of the Twentieth Century was still a rural community, despite the wishes of real estate speculators.

Of course, the squatters were not thrilled with having to buy their land, and Mezes irritated them still more by calling the place Mezesville. Most of the town's people bought their lots for about $75 each, and on their deeds, some wrote that their purchase was part of the "so-called town of Mezesville." When the post office was established in 1856, they chose the name Redwood City, and Mezesville faded from memory.

Boats prepared for departure from Redwood City by use of the turnaround port. Redwood Creek terminated near current Broadway Street.

Girls baseball team of Redwood City. Two identified people are Roy Cloud, in the center, and Mert Hughes in the front.

Broadway in Redwood City, c. 1911.

The San Mateo County Courthouse in Redwood City, used from 1880–1904.

Redwood City telephone operators in the early Twentieth Century.

As the only town on the bayside in 1856, Redwood City became county seat. Business activity centered around Broadway, and in many ways, the town resembled a typical western community with dirt streets and planked sidewalks. On occasion, Redwood City could be a rough and wild place, especially when loggers were in town.

By the middle of the 1880s, however, the town's character began to change to a more law-abiding, family-oriented community. The metamorphosis was due to the decline in the logging business, which had encouraged the presence of single, transient men, and the rise of agriculture, which demanded the services of a town devoted to farming families.

In 1867, Redwood City became the first municipality to incorporate in San Mateo County (the second, San Mateo, would not do so until 1894). Throughout most of the nineteenth century, Redwood City was the most populous town in the county. It grew from 400 in 1860 to 700 in 1870 and to almost 1,400 in 1880.

Unlike other parts of the bayside that were dominated by estate owners, Redwood City was controlled by the town's businessmen. Into the twentieth century, only South San Francisco had more industrial growth. By World War II, Redwood City had a modern port, tanneries, and cement and salt works. Today, Redwood City numbers more that 76,000 people.

Menlo Park

After the Menlo Park train station was established in 1867, a dozen businesses sprang up around it. The community even incorporated as a town in 1874, but political pressure from estate owners and farmers in the area forced its disincorporation in 1876.

Menlo Park had a rough reputation in its younger years. That reputation convinced Leland and Jane Stanford to found their college, Stanford, south of the county line in 1891.

During World War I, Menlo Park became the site of Camp Fremont, a training center. The military post's history began in 1917, when the Army leased 25 acres and then spent $1,900,000 on improvements. More than 27,000 soldiers were housed at the camp at one time. Many trained at Camp Fremont never served against the Germans, but instead were sent west to Russia's Siberia in a failed attempt to help break up the Bolshevik Revolution. After World War I ended, California political leaders such as Hiram Johnson demanded that this intervention on foreign soil be discontinued.

Menlo Park during World War I. Notice the soldiers on the corner.

Bayshore Highway in Menlo Park. Note the wide open spaces on the southern peninsula in the 1950s.

Not until April 1, 1920, however, were the last of the Camp Fremont troops at Vladivostok finally ordered back to the United States.

After World War I, Menlo Park residents sensed the need to incorporate once again, and this time they wished to include the wealthy area of Fair Oaks. As residents of Hillsborough had done before, the estate owners wished to retain their exclusiveness, so they incorporated as the community of Atherton in 1923. This was a blow to Menlo Park organizers, who finally incorporated their town in 1927.

However, in the post–World War II era, Menlo Park developed into one of the most attractive communities anywhere. Adding to its new suburban reputation, in 1951, the Lane Family moved its *Sunset* magazine and affiliated programs to Menlo Park. Today, the population of Menlo Park exceeds 31,000 people.

East Palo Alto

In 1849, Isaiah C. Woods established an embarcadero at what he named Ravenswood (today's East Palo Alto). This was probably the best location along the south county's bay line to find good anchorage. Nearby were potentially productive farmlands and the logging areas. Ravenswood failed, however, perhaps due to the business practices of its founder and perhaps because of competition from the pioneers at Redwood City.

Ravenswood remained a rural place for all of the nineteenth century and into the twentieth. About the turn of the century, berry farming and Japanese flower growing replaced wheat fields.

In 1909, Charles Weeks established a successful poultry ranch in Ravenswood. He developed a great interest in social reform, and, in 1916, he made 600 acres available to the socialist movement of William Smythe for creation of a colony called Runnymede. This became one of five such communal communities established by Smythe in California. The utopian commune consisted of as many as 900 individuals by 1925, whose main economic activity involved poultry ranching.

Ravenswood residents began dreaming of incorporation during the 1920s. However, others in the community desired that it be annexed to Palo Alto. Still others wished the area to remain unorganized. After a special election, residents agreed to change the name of the place to East Palo Alto, but no move was made for incorporation or annexation to Palo Alto. During the Depression years of the 1930s, Runnymede fell apart. Only a few structures, including some chicken coups, remain from this failed experiment.

Suburban neighborhoods did develop in the 1930s and 1940s. The advent of the Bayshore Freeway, however, changed East Palo Alto in the 1950s. Cut off from other communities physically, the place became one of the few residential areas on the peninsula that allowed African Americans to buy in. Soon white homeowners were moving out, and East Palo Alto began to materialize as a suburban ghetto. Jobs were scarce, business investors were few, poverty increased, neighborhoods deteriorated, and crime worsened.

During the 1960s, trouble erupted at Ravenswood High School (which had been built in 1958). A *home-rule movement* rose up with leaders such as Gertrude Wilkes. In 1983, East Palo Alto incorporated, but went through a period of time when it was known as one of the most lawless communities in America.

Today, with a population of more than 31,000, East Palo Alto has overcome many of its original problems. With land values increasing on the peninsula's bayside, investment dollars have come back to the community, improving its outlook for the future.

Atherton, Woodside, and Portola Valley

South of Redwood City and north of Menlo Park, the estates of the elite dominated the landscape. In 1880, a Chilean hide-and-tallow businessman, the wealthy Faxon Atherton, bought up 600 acres of Rancho de las Pulgas property for his spectacular summer home, Valparaiso. Soon after, prominent capitalists such as James C. Flood joined the Athertons. Until the creation of the Burlingame Country Club in 1893, this

Berrying party at Woodside Store, circa 1880s. Photo by James Van Court.

was the most popular section of the county for the upper classes. When in 1923 the families of this area, which was then known as Fair Oaks, felt the pressure of Menlo Park's dream of incorporation, they beat their middle-class neighbors to the punch by incorporating their own community, Atherton, in 1923. Today, the population of this well-to-do community is about 7,300.

Toward the hills, the Woodside area actually lost population after the logging industry began to decline in the latter part of the nineteenth century. Dr. R. O. Tripp's Woodside Store continued to operate until 1909, but the center of the community shifted to the intersection of Woodside and Whiskey Hill roads. By the 1880s the place had a couple of stores, at least three saloons, and a hotel. The character of Woodside began to change in the early 1900s, when business leaders August Schilling and James Folger established their estates there. Many others followed, of course.

In the 1950s, the elite Woodsiders watched as Redwood City housing tracts began crowding up the hill. To prevent being gobbled up, they incorporated their own town in 1956. Another threat emerged in 1964 when the Atomic Energy Commission and Pacific Gas and Electric desired to bulldoze a lane through Woodside to create underground power lines for the Stanford Linear Accelerator. An early environmental movement emerged to stop the project. Organizers enlisted the legal assistance of Portola Valley attorney Pete McCloskey, who

East Palo Alto in the 1950s. Photo by Gene Tupper.

The Atherton home of Willie Mays. Photograph taken August 23, 1969.

Pete McCloskey.

faced down the giants in federal court. McCloskey became a local legend. In 1967, he achieved a stunning political victory over former film star Shirley Temple Black of Woodside in a Republican primary election for United States Congress. He later became known as one the few Republican congressmen to speak out against the Vietnam War and later to support Palestinian claims against Israel.

Today, Woodside has elevated its status to one of the most desirable places in the country to reside. The cream of the high-tech business community lives there. They can frequently be seen at their "power breakfasts" at Buck's Restaurant. The population of Woodside is about 5,400 people.

South of Woodside, in the Portola Valley, farming and stock ranching predominated until well after the turn of the century. Englishman Andrew Hallidie was the most famous early resident. With his invention of the cable railroad in the late 1860s, he forever influenced the character of San Francisco. In 1883, he bought property in Portola Valley. He donated land for a school and post office, which became the nucleus of a small community. He also continued to experiment with cable transportation here, constructing a model tramway that ran from the Portola Valley floor to the surrounding hillside.

Portola Valley residents sought to become part of Woodside after its incorporation in 1956, but were unsuccessful in this quest. The residents incorporated their own town in 1964. Today, Portola Valley is like Woodside—an extremely desirable place to live. Its population is about 4,500.

Foster City and Redwood Shores

During the nineteenth century, San Mateo County had a substantial maritime industry. However, it did not exist on the coastside, where there were but two whaling stations and not much else. It was on the bayside that important oyster and shrimp industries existed.

The Morgan Oyster Company began operations in 1874. It came to own tens of thousands of tidal acres off San Mateo County, including today's communities of Foster City and Redwood Shores. So successful was the Morgan Company that by the turn of the century the Morgan facilities off San Mateo County had become the sole supplier of market oysters for the Pacific slope of North America, earning about a million dollars a year. Sadly, the polluted conditions of the Bay killed the industry in the 1930s.

About the same time that the oyster business came to the county bayline, so did Chinese shrimp fishermen. After completion of the transcontinental railroad in 1869, hundreds of released workers made their way back to the San Francisco Bay Area to initiate shrimp fishing operations. Utilizing equipment and techniques similar to what they used

T. Jack Foster (on left) points to the model of the proposed developments in Foster City in this February 19, 1960 photograph. Taken with Foster family members. Photo courtesy of the Foster City Chamber of Commerce.

back home, the Chinese, within a few years, completely dominated shrimp fishing in California. By the late nineteenth century, the San Mateo County "China Camps" were providing about 25 percent of the shrimp for the California market.

As the oyster and shrimp industries declined, the underwater properties were bought up by Leslie Salt and the Pacific Portland Cement Company. Both were unique industries. The Bay offers one of the few places in the world where salt can be economically produced through the solar evaporation method. Meanwhile, vast fossilized shell deposits in the Bay make it one of the few places on earth where shell can be used to create cement.

Among the properties of the Leslie Salt Company was an island, dyked by dairy rancher Frank M. Brewer in 1900. In 1958, developer T. Jack Foster decided to purchase Brewer's Island from Leslie in order to create a planned community that he called Foster City.

The new community was designed to house 30,000 inhabit by 1976. The plans were deemed so innovative that in 1963 they were placed on display at the San Francisco Museum of Modern Art.

The first homes went up for sale in 1964 and were an instant commercial success. Originally, Foster City was governed by the Foster family and other investors. Residents of the community decided to control their own destiny by incorporating in 1971. Today (2006), about 30,000 people live here.

South of Foster City a similar project took shape, called Redwood Shores. Back in 1928, Leslie Salt acquired the land. As the demand for peninsula housing increased, in 1959, Leslie decided to get into the residential building business. Leslie proposed that Redwood City annex the property and that it would then create a planned community similar to that of Foster City. The city complied, but the project got off to a slow start for a variety of business reasons. In the meantime, the growing environmental movement began to focus on concerns such as bay fill, water quality, protection of wildlife, and other issues that Foster City had escaped by starting only a few years earlier. As the planning wars raged on, a portion of the property became an amusement park—Marine World—in 1968. In 1973, Leslie sold its holdings to Mobil Oil Estates, which revised the Leslie

Work progress on Hillsdale Boulevard in this 1963 photograph. (Looking east on Hillsdale Boulevard.)

Homes on Flying Cloud Isle were some of the first in Foster City. 1964 photograph.

plans, recognizing the new environmental sensibilities. In 1986, Marine World/Africa USA (the theme park's new name) moved to Vallejo. In its place was built an office complex of circular highrises. Oracle Corporation became the first tenant in 1989. The software giant still occupies the buildings as of 2006.

This billboard stood near the current "Metro Center" developments, in this 1960s photograph of the wide-open land in Foster City.

These photos courtesy of the Foster City Chamber of Commerce.

San Mateo County Historical Association Sesquicentennial Members 2006

Mr. Paul Acklin
Ms. Chiyo Adachi
Mr. and Mrs. Chiyoye Adachi
Mr. and Mrs. Chick Adams
Dr. David Adams
Mr. John C. Adams
Mrs. Mary Frances Adams
Mr. Eric Addicott
AIA San Mateo County
Mr. Larry Aikins
Mr. and Mrs. Steve Aimonetti
Ms. Jane Akizuki
Mr. Rudolph Alfinito
Mr. and Mrs. Thomas Allan
Mr. and Mrs. Edward Allen
Mr. James Walker Allen
Mr. and Mrs. John Allen
Mr. and Mrs. Lloyd E. Allen
Mr. and Mrs. Oliver M. Allen
Mr. Lawrence Allhands
Almond Elementary School
Mr. Richard Alvarez
Mrs. Margaret Amara
Ms. Marie Amaya
Mr. and Mrs. Takeshi Amemiya
American Antiquarian Society
Mr. and Mrs. John Ames
Mr. Thomas F. Ames
Mr. Michael A. Amorose
Mr. and Mrs. Allen Amsbaugh
Mr. Gus Anagnostou
Mr. John Anagnostou
Mrs. John Anderholm
Mr. Terry Anderlini
Mrs. Geraldine G. Andersen
Andersen Family
Ms. Darcy C. Anderson
Mr. Robert Anderson
Ms. Cheryl Angeles
Mr. Ted Angeles
Mr. and Mrs. Peter Angelides
Ms. Edythe Ansel

Mr. and Mrs. Gordon Anthony
Mr. and Mrs. Donald Arata
Ms. Judith Archibald
Ms. Karen Seiko Arimoto-Peterson
Mr. and Mrs. Paul Armstrong
Mr. and Mrs. Thomas Armstrong
Mr. & Mrs. Charles Aronstam
Mr. and Mrs. Kenner Arrell
Mr. and Mrs. Robert J. Arthur
Ms. Helene Ashby
Mr. Kenneth Ashford
Mrs. Frances M. Ashley
Ms. June Athanacio
Mr. and Mrs. Duane E. Atkinson
Mr. and Mrs. Ray Atkinson
Ms. Melissa Atkinson Brazis
Mr. Tom Atwood
Mr. and Mrs. Gerry Aubrey
Mr. and Mrs. Mark Avelar
Mr. and Mrs. Regan Avery
Mrs. Paul Azevedo
Mr. Paul Babwin
Ms. Denise Anne Baccala
Mr. Dennis Bagwell
Mr. and Mrs. Ken Bailey
Mr. and Mrs. Ian Bain
Ms. Kelly Baird
Ms. Diana Baker
Mrs. Dorothy J. Baker
Ms. Jane Baker
Mr. Frank Baldanzi
Mr. and Mrs. Fred M. Baldra
Ms. Norma Baldwin
Ms. Jean Ballard
Ms. Lillian Balliet
Mr. Lee S. Baly
Mr. Robert M. Baly
Ms. Bonnie Bamburg
Ms. Virginia Bamford
Ms. Sheila Bammann
Mr. Philip Bank
Bank of America Foundation

Ms. Carolyn Barbe
Mr. and Mrs. William Bardet
Mr. and Mrs. Jeffrey Barile
Mrs. Joan R. Barkan
Mr. and Mrs. David W. Barr
Mr. and Mrs. Vernon Barr
Mr. John Barrett
Ms. Patricia Barron
Mr. Frank Bartaldo
Mr. Paul Barulich
Ms. Joani Basta
Mr. John Basye
Ms. Nancy Batten
Mr. Gary Bauer
Ms. Marilyn Bauriedel
Mr. Keith Bautista
Mr. and Mrs. Roy Bava
Mr. and Mrs. Joseph Baylock
Mr. and Mrs. Bernard Bayuk
Ms. Beth Beach
Mr. Robert C. Beach
Mr. and Mrs. William Joseph Beall
Mr. Alyn Beals
Mr. Alyn T. Beals
Mr. and Mrs. Irwin Bear
Ms. Kathleen Beasley
Mr. and Mrs. Bob Beattie
Mr. Andrew Becker
Ms. Pat Becker
Mr. and Mrs. Loren Beckley
Mr. and Mrs. William Beeger
Ms. Jeannette Beeler
Ms. Evelyn Behm
Mr. Glenn Behm
Mr. and Mrs. John Beiers
Mrs. Alfred D. Bell
Mr. Christopher Bell
Ms. Lucile G. Benedetti
Mr. and Mrs. August Benz
Mrs. Glade A. Beresford
Ms. Elisa Bernal
Mrs. Pat Bernard

Mrs. Esther Bernardo
Mrs. Jane Bernasconi
Mrs. Betty I. Bernstein
Mr. George S. Berry
Mr. Robert E. Berry
Ms. Virginia Berry
Mr. and Mrs. Paul E. Bettencourt
Ms. Joline Bettendorf
Mr. and Mrs. Richard V. Bettinger
Ms. Carol M. Bickler
Dr. and Mrs. William Bieber
Mr. Richard Bielsker
Ms. Barbara Bigelow
Mr. and Mrs. Albert Bigley
Ms. Donna M. Bischoff
Ms. M. Bjork
Mr. and Mrs. Brian Charles Black
Ms. Pat Black
Ms. Teresa J. Black
Mr. and Mrs. Derald Blackmore
Mr. Dan Blackwelder
Ms. Carmen J. Blair
Mr. and Mrs. Ed Blair
Mr. and Mrs. John W. Blaisdell
Ms. Lisa Blanton
Ms. Barbara Blegen
Ms. Wendy Blinkenstaff
Mr. and Mrs. Ernie Bloom
Ms. Sue Blumenberg
Mr. Robert M. Blunk
Ms. Margaret Lee Blunt
Mr. Joseph Bocci
Mr. and Mrs. Bruce & Elaine Bodnar
Mr. Edward Boehmer
Mr. and Mrs. Robert Boesch
Mr. and Mrs. Ken Bogel
Mr. and Mrs. Edward Bohn
Mr. and Mrs. Carlos Bolanos
Ms. Judith Bolanos
Ms. Beverly Bolt
Mr. Charles Bolt
Ms. Carol Bondy
Mr. Norm Book
Borel Estate Company
Borel Place Associates
Borel Private Bank & Trust Company
Ms. Teri Boucher
Mr. Gary Bower
Mr. and Mrs. Mark Bowles
Mr. and Mrs. Richard P. Bowman
Mr. and Mrs. Ronald G. Boyer
Ms. Norma Boyle
Mr. and Mrs. Russell Brabec
Mr. and Mrs. Lawrence R. Brackett
Dr. and Mrs. Cecil Bradley

Ms. Jane Bradley
Mrs. Mary Sarah Bradley
Mr. and Mrs. Robert Brady
Mr. Robert James Brady
Mr. and Mrs. John Brahy
Mr. Martin Brandfon
Ms. Joan Brant
Mr. Arthur H. Bredenbeck
Mr. and Mrs. Tom Brennan
Mr. Stuart Brickman
Mr. E. A. Briggs
Mr. Claude Brinegar
Mr. Joseph D. Brinzo
Mrs. Don Brockamp
Mr. Geoff Bromfield
Ms. Jennifer A. Brouhard
Mr. and Mrs. Charles Brown
Mr. and Mrs. Clifford Brown
Mrs. Elizabeth Brown
Mr. Joseph A. Brown
Mrs. Kathleen Brown
Mrs. Muriel R. Brown
Mrs. Steven Brown
Mr. & Mrs. Theodore Brown
Ms. Theresa Brown
Mr. and Mrs. Tim Browne
Mr. and Mrs. Lloyd Brownell
Ms. Louise Bruce
Dr. and Mrs. David P. Buchanan
Dr. and Mrs. Stephen Buchner
Honorable & Mrs. Gerald J. Buchwald
Mr. and Mrs. Rosario Bucini
Mr. and Mrs. John K. Buckham
Mr. and Mrs. R. E. Buckingham
Mr. and Mrs. Laurence Buckmaster
Mr. Paul E. Buechner, III
Ms. Dianna M. Buettler
Mr. and Mrs. Chris Buhr
Mr. Roy Bukstein
Ms. Hend Bunni
Ms. Norma Bureau Elias
Mr. Timothy Burkhart
Burlingame Public Library
Mr. Walter E. Burnett
Mr. & Mrs. Harmon Burns
Mr. Leo Burns
Ms. Sheila O'Connor Burns
Mr. and Mrs. Michael Bursak
Ms. Jean Burton
Ms. Ruth Burton
Burton Valley Elementary School
Ms. Jonette Burton-Brockway
Ms. Betty C. Burton-Loop
Ms. Judith Marie Bush
Ms. Sarah L. Bush

Ms. Karen A. Butcher
Mr. and Mrs. Mario Buttignol
Mr. Doug Button
Ms. Maria Elena Caballero
Mr. Steven G. Cabrera
Mr. and Mrs. Pete L. Cacicedo
Mr. Jack Cady
Mr. and Mrs. Gary Cakebread
Mr. and Mrs. Leo Calhoun
Ms. Bess Calic
California History Center
California Security Alarms, Inc.
Mr. and Mrs. Pat Callagy
Mrs. Donna Calles Gustafson
Caltrain
Mr. George Camerlengo
Ms. Connie Cameron
Mr. Ronald Cameron
Mr. William J. Campbell
Mr. and Mrs. Thomas J. Canevari
Ms. Allison Cant
Mrs. Victor B. Carboni
Mr. & Mrs. John P. Carcione
Mr. and Mrs. Joseph W. Carcione
Ms. Paula L. Cargill
Ms. Lourdes Carini
Ms. Elva D. Carle
Mrs. Elsie Carlson
Mr. and Mrs. Jerome Carlson
Mr. and Mrs. Roy B. Carlson
Ms. Adele Carney
Mr. and Mrs. Rod Carpenter
Mr. and Mrs. David Carr
Mr. and Mrs. George E. Carr, III
Carr, McClellan, Ingersoll, Thompson
Mr. and Mrs. Ray Cartwright
Mr. and Mrs. Louis M. Caserza
Mr. and Mrs. John Casey
Mr. Mark Cassanego
Mr. and Mrs. Robert Cassetta
Mr. and Mrs. Jacques Castaillac
Mr. Charles Catania
Ms. Joan Cattermole
Mr. and Mrs. John Cattermole
Mr. Laurence Caughlin
Ms. Margaret Caulkins
Mr. and Mrs. Milton Cavalli
Ms. Mickie Cecchini
Ms. Soo K. Chaing
Mr. and Mrs. James Chalmers
Mr. Gordon B. Chamberlain
Mr. & Mrs. John E. Chamberlain
Mr. Michael Chamberlain
Ms. Florence M. Chan
Mr. Richard M. Chapman

Ms. Rita Chaput
Mr. Todd Chase
Mr. Gene Chasey
Mrs. Carlene Cheetham
Chevron, USA Inc.
Ms. Barbara Chittenden
Ms. Rebecca Christ
Mr. and Mrs. Herman Christensen
Honorable Mark Church
Mr. James B. Church
Mrs. Barbara Cianus and Family
Mr. and Mrs. Eugene Ciranni
Ms. Mary L. Ciranni
City of Belmont
City of Brisbane
City of Daly City
City of San Bruno
City of San Mateo
Mr. Richard S. Claire
Mrs. Jeanne Clark
Mr. Matthew R. Clark
Ms. Rita Clark
Mrs. James Clarke
Ms. Marilyn Clarke
Mr. & Mrs. Stephen Clarke
Ms. Betty J. Clausen
Mr. Jim Clifford
Mr. Tony Clifford
Mr. and Mrs. John Clinton
Mrs. Roy N. Cloud
Dr. Haworth A. Clover
Mr. Dennis Coakley
Ms. JoAnn Cobb
Ms. Helen Cocco
Mr. Fred Coffer
Mr. Melvin E. Cohen
Cohen & Associates
Honorable Melvin E. Cohn
Ms. Sandie Colbert
Ms. Cathleen M. Colgan
Mr. Tom W. Collette
Mr. Andrew Coltart
Mr. Frank Coltart
Mr. and Mrs. Bob Comartin
Comcast Cable
Concar Enterprises, Inc.
Mr. and Mrs. Robert Conlan
Mr. and Mrs. James P. Conn
Mr. Charles Connell
Mr. and Mrs. Earl Connolley
Connolly Family
Mr. Paul Constantino
Mr. and Mrs. Thomas L. Constantino
Miss Odie B. Cook
Mr. & Mrs. Bob Cookson

Mr. and Mrs. David E. Cookson
Mrs. James F. Coonan
Mrs. Michael Coonan
Ms. Sandra H. Cooperman
Mr. and Mrs. George Cope
Mr. and Mrs. Jack E. Corey
Mrs. Zanette A. Cornman
Mr. and Mrs. Joseph Cornyn
Ms. Johanna Corvello
Mr. and Mrs. Craig Corwin
Ms. Britt-Marie Cosgrove
Mr. and Mrs. Harry and Gail Costa
Ms. Louella Costaglio
Ms. Ellen Costello
Mr. Joe Cotchett
Mr. and Mrs. Bernard Cotter
Ms. Margaret Cotton
Mr. and Mrs. G. Bartley Coulter
County of San Mateo
Mrs. Dona M. Cowan
Ms. Ruthmary Cradler
Mr. and Mrs. James Crafts
Mrs. MacDonald Craik
Mrs. D. M. Crawford
Mr. James B. Creighton
Mr. and Mrs. Don Crews
Mrs. Anna Rettagliata Crisafi
Mr. Tony Crisafi
Mr. Arne Croce
Mr. Sue Crockett
Mr. Robert T. Crow
Mr. Dan Cudworth
Ms. Patricia Cuendet
Mr. and Mrs. Alan Culbertson
Mrs. Theresa Cummins
Mr. and Mrs. Joseph Cutts
Cypress Lawn
Mr. Raymond Daba
Ms. Tracy DaCosta
Mr. Daniel Dadoun
Mr. Sam Dafnis
Ms. Claire Daley
Mrs. Jacqueline S. Daley
Mr. and Mrs. Amos Dana
Danford Foundation
Daniel Quan Design
Mrs. Emily Daniels
Mr. and Mrs. Henry Dapkus
Mr. and Mrs. Howard Daschbach
Mr. and Mrs. William Davidow
Mr. Thomas Davids
Mr. Irvin Dawid
Mr. and Mrs. Douglas Day
Mr. and Mrs. Gene De Armond
Mr. and Mrs. Clyde De Benedetti

Mrs. Elizabeth De Benedetti
Ms. Nancy de Ita
Mrs. F. J. De Larios
Mr. and Mrs. Eric De Wild
Rick and Kerry DeBenedetti
Ms. Jeanne Decker
Mr. Vince DeFriese
Ms. Danielle Del Carlo
Mr. James E. Delahanty
Ms. Margaret DeLano
Mr. and Mrs. James Delehanty
Mr. & Mrs. Richard Dellinger
Mr. and Mrs. Richard M. DeLuna
Mr. Shawn DeLuna
Mr. and Mrs. Felix Demartis
Mrs. Lillian M. Dematteis
Ms. Marcia Dempsey
Mrs. Margaret Dennis
Mr. and Mrs. Reid Dennis
Mr. and Mrs. Christopher Der
    Manuelian
Mr. and Mrs. Gary Desantis
Mr. and Mrs. Robert Desky
Ms. Elaine Diani
Dr. Ron Diebel
Ms. Evelyn C. Dietel
Mr. and Mrs. Gary Dilley
Mr. and Mrs. Dan Dobberpuhl
Ms. Helen Dodds
Mr. and Mrs. Richard Dodge
Ms. Carolyn Doggett
Mr. John Dolan
Mr. Lee Dolezal
Mr. and Mrs. Bill Donovan
Mr. Robert E. Dooley
Mr. Laurence Dorcy
Mr. Robert M. Dormoy
Ms. Carolyn Dorsch
Mrs. Pat Doss
Mr. and Mrs. Robert Doss
Mr. and Mrs. Stanley Doten
Mr. Dan Dowling
Mr. David Downey
DPR Construction, Inc.
Mr. Bill Drake
Mr. Edward Drake
Ms. Linda T. Drew
Ms. Gretchen Dryden
Mr. and Mrs. R. L. Dully
Mr. and Mrs. Jim Dunbar
Ms. Anne Dunham
Mr. Arthur Dunne
Mr. and Mrs. George Durfey
Ms. Kit Durgin
During Associates

Ms. Kaia Eakin
Ms. Francesca Eastman
Ms. Mary Eberl
Mr. and Mrs. Louis Ebner
Mr. and Mrs. John G. Edmonds
Ms. Margaret Egan
Mrs. Howard Eisenberg
Ms. Sandy Ekhardt
Ms. Emma Elizabeth Prescott Elfving
Mr. Erik Robert Wisnom Elfving
Mr. and Mrs. John Elfving
Mrs. J. M. Ellis
Marcy and Gene Elsbree
Mr. Richard Elwood
Mr. and Mrs. Jim Engel
Ms. Marian Erdelyi
Mr. and Mrs. Jack Erickson
Mrs. Elizabeth Ervin
Mr. Ralph Eschenbach
Mr. and Mrs. Andy Esteves
Mrs. Audrey H. Etienne
Mr. and Mrs. Jack Euphrat
Mr. and Mrs. Richard Eva
Mr. Arthur Evans and Family
Mr. and Mrs. Edward Everett
Ms. Barbara Evers
Mr. and Mrs. Dean Eyre
Mr. Francis Fabian
Mr. Humberto Fabris
Mr. Neil E. Fahy
Mrs. Louis Falletti
Mr. and Mrs. Eugene Fambrini
Mr. and Mrs. Donald Farbstein
Mr. and Mrs. Michael Farbstein
Mr. Richard H. Farrar
Mr. Bruce Farrell
Mr. Peter K. Fates
Mr. and Mrs. Donald Fay
Mr. Irvin Fegley
Mr. Roland Feldmeier
Mr. and Mrs. John Ferguson
Ms. Rose Marie Ferrando
Mrs. Roy Ferrari
Ms. Jane Ferrero
Mr. James Fetherolf
Mr. and Mrs. Harold A. Fick
Mr. and Mrs. Ronald G. Fick
Fidelity National Title Company
Mr. Duncan Fife
Ms. Rosemary Filippi
Mr. and Mrs. Leslie Filler
Mr. and Mrs. Bernard Finkelstein
Mr. and Mrs. John Finney
Mr. and Mrs. Gene Firpo
First National Bank

Ms. Nancy Fischer
Mr. and Mrs. Jay Fisher
Mr. and Mrs. Ken Fisher
Mrs. Norma F. Fisher
Ms. Helen Fisicaro
Mr. & Mrs. Robert & Margareta Fisse
Ms. Patricia W. Fitzpatrick
Ms. Laura Fletcher
Ms. Marjorie Fletcher
Mr. Terrence Flinn
Mr. and Mrs. Robert B. Flint Jr.
Dr. Thomas J. Fogarty
Ms. Dorene Fong
Ms. Maria Fonseca
Mr. and Mrs. Elio A. Fontana
Mrs. Susan Ford Dorsey
Mr. and Mrs. Curtis Forsman
Mrs. Diletta S. Foss
Mr. and Mrs. T. Jack Foster
Mr. Robert Foucrault
Ms. Eleonore M. Fourie
Ms. Gloria Fourie
Ms. Rosanne Foust
Mr. Mark Fowle
Fox Theatre
Mrs. Marjorie Foyer
Mr. and Mrs. Arthur Francis
Mr. and Mrs. Mike Francis
Mr. and Mrs. George Franco
Mrs. Nancy L. Frank
Franklin Templeton Investments
Mr. and Mrs. Leroy Franzoia
Ms. Catherine Fraser
Mr. and Mrs. Paul Fraser
Mr. and Mrs. Tom Fraser
Mr. Darold E. Fredricks
Dr. and Mrs. William B. Freedman
Mr. George Freisleben
Ms. Helen Fricke
Mr. Robert Friday
Mr. Thomas R. Friebel
Dr. Emanuel Friedman
Ms. Lori Fuchiwaki
Mr. and Mrs. Harold Fuentes
Mr. and Mrs. Katsuyauki Fujimoto
Ms. Arlene Furter
Mr. and Mrs. Toshio Furusho
Ms. Ritsuko Furuya
G. Swanson Construction, Inc.
G. W. Williams Foundation
Mrs. Margherita Gado
Dr. and Mrs. Walter Gaines
Mr. Don Galine
Mr. Donald Gallegos
Mr. Fred Ganjei

Mr. and Mrs. Michael Garavaglia
Mr. & Mrs. Wallace Garcia
Mr. and Mrs. Michael Gardella
Mrs. Irvin B. Gardner
Ms. Ruth Ann Gardner
Mrs. Frank Garibaldi
Mr. and Mrs. Philip Garlington
Mr. Robert Garner
Mr. and Mrs. John Garthoeffner
Mr. David Garvin
Ms. Jeanne Gary
Joann and Heather Gast
Ms. Robin Gates-Quist
The Carl and Celia Berta Gellert
   Foundation
Dr. Patrick Gemma
Genealogical Society of Utah
Genealogy Periodicals
George Family
Ms. Lily Germano
Mr. and Mrs. James Gerstley
Ms. Elizabeth K. Gheleta
Ms. Gloria Giannini
Mr. and Mrs. Roland E. Giannini
Mr. Mike Giari
Ms. Valerie Gibbs
Mr. and Mrs. Ted Gibsen
Honorable Rose Jacobs Gibson,
   4th District
Mr. and Mrs. Daniel Gilbrech
Mr. Patrick Gilbride
Mr. and Mrs. Kenneth Gillespie
Ms. Shelley Gilligan
Mr. and Mrs. Clinton R. Gilliland
Mr. John H. Gimbel, III
Ms. Barbara Gingher
Mr. William Gingher, Jr.
Mr. & Mrs. Sam Ginn
Ms. Janice Giorgi
Mr. and Mrs. John Giosso
Ms. Lorraine Giroux
Mr. Thomas Glanzman
Mr. and Mrs. Edwin Glasgow
Mr. and Mrs. Bruce Gledhill
Mr. and Mrs. Michael A. Glenn
Mr. Vilas F. Gocke
Ms. Karen Gok
Mr. Gary Goldberg
Ms. Jane B. Goldberg
Golden Gate Railroad Museum
Ms. Catherine Goldschmidt
Mrs. Charles Goldsmith
Ms. Leslie Gordon
Honorable Richard Gordon, 3rd Dist.
Ms. Cheryl Gorman

Mr. Lennie Gotcher
Mr. Barry J. Goyette
Mr. Dave Graham
Mr. Edward F. Graham
Mr. Gary Graham
Dr. and Mrs. John Graham
Ms. Nancy Graham
Mr. John L. Grandsaert
George and Margaret Grasso
Mr. & Mrs. Lawrence S. Gray
Mr. and Mrs. Robert Gray
Mr. and Mrs. James V. Grealish
Mr. and Mrs. Kent M. Grealish
Greater Bay Bancorp Foundation
Mrs. J. S. Green
Mr. and Mrs. Ken Green
Ms. Lydia Green
Mr. and Mrs. Joseph Greenbach
Mr. and Mrs. Steven Greene
Mr. and Mrs. George Griffin
Mr. and Mrs. Andrew Griscom
Ms. Carole Groom
Mrs. Claire Sunny Grotsky
Mrs. Joan A. Grover
Mr. and Mrs. Michael Grover
Mrs. Marylou Grunigen
Mrs. Peggy Guccione
Mrs. Francis A. Guido
Mr. Anil Gulati
Ms. Pamela Gullard
Mr. and Mrs. Umang Gupta
Ms. Gloria Gutierrez
Ms. Carol Gutoff
Mr. Donald C. Hack
Ms. Susan-Marie Hagen
Ms. Kathleen Hagiwara
Mrs. Millie Hagstrom
Honorable and Mrs. Dale Hahn
Ms. Ruth N. Hahn
Mr. and Mrs. Robert R. Haight
Mr. and Mrs. Lee E. Ham
Ms. Bette R. Hamachi
Ms. Susan Hamlin
Mr. Andy Hamner
Mr. and Mrs. Mark S. Hanlon
Ms. Linda Hanners
Mr. & Mrs. Frank Hannig
Mr. Ted Hannig
Mr. and Mrs. Paul Hansen
Ms. Patricia Hanson
Ms. Sue Hara
Mr. and Mrs. Martin Harband
Mr. and Mrs. Gary G. Harmon
Mr. and Mrs. Steve Harper
Mr. Walter H. Harrington

Mr. and Mrs. William N. Harris
Mr. and Mrs. Francis Harrison
Tim and Stephanie Harrison
Harry L. Murphy, Inc. Floor Coverings
Dr. Ward L. Hart
Ms. Mary Louise Harwood
Mr. and Mrs. George Haskell
Colma David Hatfield
Mr. Trip Hawkins
Mr. and Mrs. Fred Hawley
Dr. David M. Hayashi
Mr. Andrew Haynie
Mr. and Mrs. Richard Hedges
Mr. William F. Hedrix
Mr. and Mrs. Michael Heffernan
Mr. and Mrs. Walter Heim
Mrs. Eleanor Heinen
Mr. Eugene F. Helfrich
Ms. Joy Hemp
Mr. Robert Henderson
Mr. and Mrs. Robert Hendricks
Ms. Ruth Hendricks Willard
Mrs. June Hendrickson
Ms. Debbie Henken
Mr. and Mrs. Richard L. Hennessy
Ms. Ruth Henning
Mrs. Gladys Heorodt
Mr. and Mrs. Thomas Herlihy
Mr. Arthur P. Herman
Ms. Madonna Herman
Mr. and Mrs. David Hernandez
Mr. Davis Hershey
Mr. Robert Hershiser
Mr. Steven Hibshman
Mr. Harry Higaki
Mr. and Mrs. Naomi Higaki
Mr. and Mrs. Shigeru Higaki
Mr. and Mrs. Kenneth G. High
Honorable Jerry A. Hill
Mr. and Mrs. Richard Hill
Ms. Susan L. Hill
Mr. and Mrs. Thomas Hill
Mr. Ward Hill
Ms. Susan Hiller
Mr. and Mrs. Jon Hillhouse
Mr. Robert Hills
Hillsborough Garden Club
Mrs. Helen Hilton Raiser
Ms. Sharon Himebrook
Mr. William S. Hindson
Mr. and Mrs. John Hipschen
Historical Society of South SF
Mr. and Mrs. John G. Hitchcock
Ms. Patty Hjelm
Mr. Franklin Hoaglund

Mr. and Mrs. Jeff Hoch
Mr. William M. Hodge
Ms. Norah C. Hodgins
Mrs. Dorothea C. Hoefler
Mr. Stuart Hoffman
Dr. and Mrs. William Hofmann
Ms. Alice L. Hogben
Mr. and Mrs. Daniel Holland
Mr. and Mrs. Richard Holm
Ms. Eleanor Holmes
Mrs. Theodore M. Holmes
Mrs. H. J. Holmgren
Mr. and Mrs. Robert C. Hopfenbeck
Dr. Cecilia Hopkins
Mr. and Mrs. Rudolph Horak
Mr. John Horgan
Mr. and Mrs. Albert J. Horn
Ms. Betty Horn
Mr. Donald Horsley
Mrs. Theodora J. Hosfeldt
Mr. and Mrs. John Hosford
Mr. Gary B. Hoss
Mr. and Mrs. H. P. Hotz
Dr. and Mrs. Steve Howard
Ms. Rogena Hoyer
Mr. Alan Huckabay
Mr. Ivan Hudson
Ms. Marian P. Hudson
Mr. James Huebner
Mr. Tom Huening
Mrs. Barbara S. Huff
Ms. Valarie Huff
Mr. Charles N. Huggins
Mr. and Mrs. Don Hughes
Mr. Pete Hughes
Mr. and Mrs. Zachary Hulsey
Mr. Ted Hume
Ms. Dianne Hunt
Ms. Barbara Hunter
Huntington Library
Ms. Lucy Hupp Williams
Hurlbut-Johnson Charitable Trusts
Mr. and Mrs. Robert F. Hutchinson
Hyland-Tsukamoto Painting &
    Decorating
Ms. Gayle Hynding
Mr. and Mrs. Wm. Iver Hystad
IBEW Local 617
Mr. and Mrs. John Inglis
Honorable and Mrs. Jeff Ira
Mr. and Mrs. William J. Iracki
Ms. Nickie Irvine
Mrs. Yasuko Ann Ito
Mr. and Mrs. Satoru Iwasaki
Mr. and Mrs. Luther Izmirian

Ms. Dayna Jabin
Mr. & Mrs. Allen Jackson
Ms. Winifred Jackson
Mr. Nick Jacobsen
Dr. and Mrs. Donald Jaffe
Ms. Mona Jajeh
Mr. and Mrs. John W. Jalonen
Mrs. Helen James
Ms. Jacqueline James
Mrs. Ruth James
Mrs. M. M. Jamieson
Ms. Mary H. Janney
Mr. Wally Jansen
Ms. Margene Janzen
Mr. and Mrs. Paul Jarvis
JB Trophies
Mr. & Mrs. Richard W. Jeffery
Honorable Thomas M. Jenkins
Chris and Mary Jensen
Mr. and Mrs. Ole S. Jensen
Mrs. Barbara A. Johnson
Ms. Carol Johnson
Mr. and Mrs. Charles Johnson
Mr. Charles B. Johnson
Mrs. Charlton Johnson
Mr. Craig Johnson
Mr. Franklin P. Johnson, Jr.
Mr. and Mrs. Greg Johnson
Mr. and Mrs. John Johnson
Mr. Mark Johnson
Mr. and Mrs. Robert Johnson
Mr. & Mrs. Rupert Johnson
Mr. Rupert H. Johnson
Mr. Steve Johnson
Mr. and Mrs. Lawrence Johnston
Mr. and Mrs. Ted Johnston
Mr. Barry Jolette
Mr. Bobby E. Jones
Mr. James Jones
Mr. and Mrs. Jess Jones
Mr. and Mrs. Louis W. Jones
Mrs. Peggy B. Jones
Ms. Angela Jordan
Mr. and Mrs. Mason Kamita
Ms. Ruth Kane
Dr. Harvey Kaplan
Mr. and Mrs. Frank Kappler
Mr. J. Craig Karasky
Mr. and Mrs. Mahmood Karimimanesh
Ms. Carol Karp
Mr. and Mrs. Ronald Karp
Mr. and Mrs. D. Michael Kastrop
Mr. and Mrs. Kiyoshi Katamoto
Mr. and Mrs. Tadashi Kato
Mr. and Mrs. Herman R. Katz

Ms. Antonette Kavanaugh
Mr. and Mrs. Charles Kavanagh
Mr. and Mrs. Norman W. Kavanaugh
Ms. Nancy Kawakita
Mr. Yoneo Kawakita
Ms. Kathleen Kay
KCSM-TV
Ms. Elizabeth Keating
Mr. and Mrs. Stephen Keegan
Mr. and Mrs. Ralph B. Keele
Mrs. and Mrs. Jack Keeney
Ms. Elizabeth Keeting
Mr. and Mrs. Hale Keller
Mrs. Joan R. Keller
Mr. James Kelly
Mr. and Mrs. Kevin G. Kelly
Ms. Lois Kelm-Dully
Honorable Margaret Kemp
Mr. and Mrs. Arlen L. Kennedy
Ms. Kerry Kennedy
Ms. Anne Kenney
Ms. Winifred Kenny
Mr. Adam C. Kent
Mr. George Kerewicz
Ms. Claire Kerr
Ms. Karen Key
Keyston Family Trust
Ms. Joan Kidd
Ms. Joyce Flores Kiefer
Mr. and Mrs. Tom Kieffer
Ms. Alicia Kim
Mr. and Mrs. Thompson Kimura
Mr. E. John King
Mr. and Mrs. John E. King
Mr. William T. Kirby
Mr. and Mrs. Robert L. Kirchgatter
Mrs. Bruce C. Kirkbride
Dr. and Mrs. Bill Kirkham
Mrs. Katherine Kirkland
Mr. and Mrs. Robert Kissick
Ms. Ann Kistner
Mr. & Mrs. Richard Koch
Mrs. D. O. Kocmich
Mrs. Kathryn Koerner
Mr. Frank Kohlweiss
Ms. Anne M. Koletzke
Konditorei
Mr. Les Koonce
Ms. Nancy Koons
Koret Foundation
Mr. and Mrs. David Korn
Mr. and Mrs. Jerry Kosro
Mrs. Elsie Kovac
Ms. Linda M. Kowalski
Mr. and Mrs. Spencer Kowalski

Dr. and Mrs. Robert A. Kraft
Mr. and Mrs. Edwin Krantz
Ms. Leslie Krauss
Mr. John Kreidler
Ms. F. Alene Kremer
Dr. and Mrs. George Kromhout
Mr. Wallace A. Krone
Ms. Suzanne E. Kruger
Ms. Mary Jo Kubota-Arcarese
Mr. and Mrs. John Kuffer
Mr. and Mrs. Yosh Kumagai
Ms. Mary Kunitake
Mr. Philip Kurokawa
Ms. Michiye Kuwahara
Mrs. Keith A. Kvenvolden
Ms. Georgi La Berge
Ms. June La Point
Ms. Denise La Pointe
Dr. Robert LaBerge
Bruce and Carol Lacina
Ms. Lenore Lafayett
Mr. and Mrs. Kenneth Lajoie
Mr. Douglas F. Lambert
Mr. and Mrs. Jack Landers
Ms. Joyce Landry
Mr. and Mrs. Melvin Lane
Ambassador & Mrs. William Lane, Jr.
Ms. Susan Kay Lang
Ms. Kendra Langer
Mr. Mike Lannoy
Ms. Margaret Lanphier
Dr. Rudolph M. Lapp
Ms. Marie Larabie
Mr. Thomas A. Larsen
Mrs. M. Marie Larson
Mr. and Mrs. David Larwood
Ms. Beth Lau
Ms. Susan Lauer
Mrs. Hartley Laughead
Mr. and Mrs. Peter C. Lawrence
Mr. and Mrs. David A. Laws
Ms. Margie Lawson
Mr. and Mrs. Harold Layer
Mr. and Mrs. Edward Leahy
Jason and Brooke Leake
Mr. Charles Ledden
Ms. Elizabeth Lee
Ms. Betty Lee-Kendall
Ms. Suzanne Legallet
Mr. Matt Leipzig
Ms. Sue Lempert
Mr. and Mrs. George Lencioni
Mrs. Nellie W. Leong
Ms. Ellen Leroux
Mr. and Mrs. Andrew Lesser

Mr. Daniel Levin
Ms. Joan M. Levy
Mr. and Mrs. W. Byron Levy
Mr. Dan Lewin
Mr. Chris Lewis
Mrs. Constance Lewis
Mr. David Lewis
Mrs. Judy Lewis
Mr. Rick Lewis
Mr. and Mrs. Donald C. Leydig
Ms. Janet Leyte-Vidal and Family
Mr. Louis A. Liberty
Mr. Martin R. Liberty
Ms. Valerie Liberty
Mr. David S. Liebes
Mr. and Mrs. Sid Liebes
Mr. and Mrs. Stephen Liebes
Ms. Susanne Liedtke
Ms. Frances Liston
Mr. Jacques M. Littlefield
Mr. James Littrell
Mr. Arthur L. Lloyd
Ms. Linda Locatelli
Mr. Peter Locatelli
Ms. Kendra Logan
Mr. and Mrs. Dennis Logie
Mr. and Mrs. Frank Lohmeier
Mr. and Mrs. Wade Loo
Los Gatos Village Printers
Mr. and Mrs. Toni Lozica
Mr. and Mrs. Stephen Lubin
Mr. and Mrs. Francis Ludwig
Ms. Dixie Luebcke
Mr. and Mrs. Lincoln Lum
Ms. Nancy Lund
Ms. Karen Lutke
Ms. Lori Lutzker
Mr. and Mrs. Iver Lyche
Mr. Sandy Lydon
Ms. Robinie Lyhne
Ms. Carolyn Lyon
Ms. Mary Louise Lyon
Mr. Francis M. Lyons
Mr. and Mrs. James Lyons
Mr. Douglas B. MacBlane
MacCorkle Insurance Service
Mr. and Mrs. Steve Machtinger
Dr. Peter MacInerney
Ms. C. M. MacIntosh
Ms. Faith Mack
Dr. Tom Mack
Ms. Anna Maes
Mr. Frank L. Maffei
Mr. and Mrs. Merrill Magowan
Ms. Margo Maguire

Ms. Kathleen Mahany and Family
Mr. and Mrs. Charles Mahnken
Mr. John J. Mahoney
Malcolm Drilling
Mrs. Gwen W. Mallory
Malouf's
Mr. John L. Maltbie
Ms. Anita Maltoni
Ms. Marjorie G. Mandanis
Mr. Robert Mangelsdorf
Mrs. Nat J. Mangini
Ms. Ann C. Mangold
Mr. and Mrs. Neno Maniscalco
Mr. Woody Mansergh
Ms. Barbara I. Mariani
Mr. and Mrs. Conrad Marotta
Ms. Mary E. Marple
Ms. Joan Martel
Mr. and Mrs. Cliff Martin
Mr. and Mrs. Don Martin
Mrs. Janet Martin
Mr. and Mrs. Stanley B. Martin
Mr. & Mrs. Steve Martin
Mrs. Selma Masch
Mr. James K. Mason
Mrs. Louise B. Mason
Mr. and Mrs. Denny Matsufuji
Ms. Karyl Matsumoto
Ms. Jennifer Mattei
Mr. John Matthews
Dr. and Mrs. Dean L. Mawdsley
Ms. Geri S. Mayers
Ms. Lori Maynard
Ms. Jean McHugh
Dr. Roberta McReynolds
Mr. and Mrs. Roger McBride
Ms. Anne B. McCarthy
Mr. Harold McCarthy
Mr. & Mrs. Kenneth McCarthy
Ms. Stephanie McCauley
Ms. Rosalie McCloud
Ms. Marjory McClung Goetz
Ms. Loretta A. McClurg
Ms. Janice McCormick
Mr. and Mrs. George McCown
Ms. Karen McCown
Mrs. Shirley J. McCracken
Mr. and Mrs. Marvin McCray
Ms. Kathleen P. McCrea
Mr. and Mrs. William McCreery
Ms. Mary June McCue
Mr. and Mrs. Ted McDonald
Duane and Marion McDowell
Ms. Carole H. McEwen
Mr. Van McFadden

Ms. Mary Ann McGlynn
Mr. and Mrs. Reginald McGovern
Ms. Kathy McGrade
Mrs. M. Lou McGrath
Ms. Kelly McGrew
Mr. and Mrs. D. Pat McGuire
Mr. Danny McGuire
Ms. Joan McGuire
Mrs. Roderick McLellan
Mr. R. J. McMills
Ms. Mary McMurdo
Michael and Sharon McQueen
Mr. and Mrs. Cristopher McReynolds
Ms. Margaret G. McWilliams
Mr. Edward Medzian
Mr. Tony Melkonian
Ms. Kerry Memole
Mrs. Marion Mendez
Mr. and Mrs. Stanley Mendoza
Mr. James Mengel
Mr. Leslie O. Merrill
Mr. and Mrs. Wallace C. Merrill
A. Metten
Mr. & Mrs. George Christian Meyer
Mr. Henry O. Meyer
Mrs. John C. Meyer
Dr. and Mrs. Basil Meyerowitz
Mr. Dan Meyers
Ms. Cecelia Michael
Mr. and Mrs. Paul Michaelson
Mrs. Robin P. Michelson
Mr. James Mignone
Ms. Diane H. Miles
Ms. Bonnie Miller
Ms. Edythe Miller
Mrs. Jane B. Miller
Jay and Elise Miller
Ms. Mary A. Miller
Mr. and Mrs. Michael Miller
Mr. William A. Millichap
Ms. Constance W. Mills
Mr. James Miraglia
Mr. and Ms. Bruce T. Mitchell
Mrs. Doris Mitchell
Mr. and Mrs. Fred Mitchell
Mr. Dave Miura
Ms. Irene Miura
Mr. Daniel Modena
Mr. and Mrs. Al Molakidis
Kennith and Gloria Molinari
Mr. and Mrs. Kendall Moll
Mr. and Mrs. Lanty Molloy
Molloy's Tavern
Mr. J. Kelly Monaghan
Ms. Angela Mongillo

Mrs. James A. Monroe
Mr. and Mrs. Fernando Montijo
Ms. Julianne Mooney
Ms. Berenice C. Moore
Mr. and Mrs. Clifford J. Moore
Joe & Rondi Moore
Ms. Virginia Moore Neklason
Mrs. B. J. Moran
Ms. Nancy Moran
Mr. Patrick Moran
Mrs. Mary E. Morgan
Mr. and Mrs. Richard K. Morgan
Mr. and Mrs. James Mori
Mr. and Mrs. Takashi Mori
Ms. Toshiko Mori
Ms. June Morrall
Mrs. Janet Morris
Mrs. Willis E. Morrison
Ms. Mary Mortenson
Mr. Harvey H. Mowry
Mr. Marshall Moxom
Mr. and Mrs. Max Moye
MTK Communications
Mr. Allen Mueller
Mr. Bob Mullen
Mrs. Dexter C. Mulliken
Honorable Gene Mullin
Mr. Kevin Mullin
Mr. and Mrs. Tom Mullooly
Mr. and Mrs. Raul Muniz
Mr. and Mrs. Greg Munks
Mrs. Edith Murphy
Mr. and Mrs. John J. Murphy
Mr. Matt Murray
Mr. Vincent A. Muzzi
Ms. Nancy J. Myers
Mrs. Ed Nagler
Mr. and Mrs. Saburo Nagumo
Mr. and Mrs. Mark Naismith
Mr. and Mrs. Eiki Nakagawa
Mr. and Mrs. Albert Nakai
Mr. and Mrs. Don Nakanishi
Mr. and Mrs. Richard Nakanishi
Mr. and Mrs. Harry Nakano
Mr. Jim Nakano
Mr. and Mrs. L. Kei Nakano
Ms. Janice Nakao
Mr. Richard Namba
Mr. and Mrs. Peter Nannarone
Mr. and Mrs. James Nantell
Ms. Joann Nassutti
Ms. Irene S. Neasham
Ms. Cathie Nelson
Mrs. Frances Nelson
Mr. and Mrs. Richard Nelson

Mr. and Mrs. Richard W. Nelson
Mr. Joseph Nespor
Network For Good
Ms. Bette Newberger
Mr. James W. Newell
Ms. Harriet C. Newman
Mr. Henry Newman
Mr. John M. Newman
Mrs. Sally A. Newman
Mr. and Mrs. William Nicolet
Mr. & Mrs. Donald Niederhaus
Mr. Owen Niemann
Ms. Betty L. Nilson
Mr. Stuart Nixon
Ms. Mary Nobriga
Mr. and Mrs. Calvin Noecker
Ms. Linda Noeske
Ms. Betty Nolen
Mrs. Jean Norris
Mr. and Mrs. Arthur Notthoff
Ms. Mary Ann Notz
Mr. and Mrs. J. G. Nourse
Ms. Carol Bauer Nowlin
Mr. and Mrs. Ernest Nusser
Oakland Public Library
Mr. and Mrs. Hank Obayashi
Mr. Cory Obenour
Mr. and Mrs. Dennis O'Brien
Dr. and Mrs. John O'Brien
Mr. Alec D. Obst
Mr. & Mrs. Kevin O'Connell
Robin O'Connell
Mr. and Mrs. Ronald O'Connell
Mrs. Lillian Dickson Odle
Mr. Eugene O'Donnell
Mr. James O'Donoghue
Mr. George Offen
Ms. C. Y. Offutt, Jr.
Mr. and Mrs. Terry Ogami
Mr. and Mrs. Sakaye Okamura
Mr. and Mrs. Minoru Okino
Mr. and Mrs. Kiyoshi Okubo
Ms. Julia Older
Mr. and Mrs. William Oldfield
Mr. Howard A. Oliphant
Mrs. Nancy Oliver
Mr. and Mrs. Wally Oliver
Mr. Lloyd J. Olsen
Ms. Maxine Olson
Mr. Edward K. Onuma
Ms. Maureen O'Rourke and
Mrs. Jean Orr
Ms. Joyce Osborn
Mr. and Mrs. Bob Oster
Mr. Ralph Osterling

Mr. and Mrs. Stephen Pace
Mr. Michael Pacelli
Pacific Partners
Pacifica Historical Society
Ms. Mary Packard
Dr. and Mrs. Peter Packard
David & Lucile Packard Foundation
Mr. and Mrs. Charles Paff
Ms. Sylvia M. Palma
Jim and Marilyn Palmer
Ms. Susanne Pandich
Mr. and Mrs. Rodney Panos
Mr. and Mrs. Mario G. Paolini
Mr. Chris W. Papalias
Ms. Nida Papenhause
Dr. and Mrs. Thomas G. Parker
Mr. Wayne Parker
Dr. Winn Parker
Mr. and Mrs. J. Dean Parnell
Ms. Lois Parodi
Ms. Margaret Parsons
Mrs. Suzanne Parsons
Mr. Guido Pastorino
Mr. and Mrs. Howard Patridge
Ms. Claire Patterson
Mr. and Mrs. Mark Patterson
Mr. and Mrs. Alfredo Paulazzo
Mr. and Mrs. Joseph J. Pausner
Mr. and Mrs. Galdo Pavini
Mrs. Dody B. Payne
Ms. Sylvia Payne
Pea Press
Mr. and Mrs. Ernest D. Pead
Eric and Maggie Pearson
Burgess & R. C. Peck
Mr. and Mrs. Al Pellizer
Mr. & Mrs. Wade Pellizzer
Mr. and Mrs. Kenneth G. Pelllzzari
Ms. Michele A. Pelter
Mrs. Barbara Davis Penaluna
Peninsula Community Foundation
Peninsula Masonic Lodge, #168
Mr. and Mrs. George Pepper
Ms. Judy Pera
Mr. and Mrs. Guido Perin
Mr. Peter Pershing
Mr. and Mrs. Aldo L. Pessagno
Ms. Anne D. Peter
Mr. and Mrs. Michael Peterhans
Ms. Barbara Peters
Dr. and Mrs. W. I. Petersen
Ms. Carol Peterson
Mr. and Mrs. Charles J. Peterson
Dr. and Mrs. Lawrence H. Peterson
Mr. and Mrs. John Petrick

Ms. Marianne Petroni
Mr. and Mrs. Robert E. Pex
Ms. Christine Pezzi
Ms. Margaret C. Phelan
Mr. & Mrs. Max Phelan
Mr. and Mrs. John Phillips
Mr. and Mrs. Lee Phillips
Mr. and Mrs. Ray Phillips
Mr. and Mrs. Samuel Phillips
Mr. and Mrs. Thomas Phillips
Mr. and Mrs. Walter Phillips
Mr. and Mrs. William J. Phillips
Dr. and Mrs. Stephen Pickering
Mr. and Mrs. Clifford Pierce
Mr. and Mrs. Gerald Pierce
Mr. David Pine
Mr. Lee Ping
Mr. Paul Pittenger
Mr. and Mrs. Walter Piulle
Plaza Loan Services
Mr. and Mrs. James Pletzer
Mr. and Mrs. George Plotnikoff
Mr. and Mrs. Michael H. Podell
Mr. & Mrs. Jack Polly
Mr. and Mrs. Jacob Popik
Ms. Lynn Porcedda
Port of Redwood City
Mr. and Mrs. William R. Porter
Pos Card Systems of CA, Inc.
Mr. Bernard Postel
Mr. Conrad Postel
Mr. Donald Postel
Mr. and Mrs. Mitch Postel
Mr. Scott Postel
Ms. Lorna Poston Rollins
Ms. Laurie Prescott
Mr. and Mrs. Ralph Pribble
Mr. & Mrs. Mark Pringle
Ms. Susan Pringle Smith
Ms. Marilyn Proffitt
Progress Glass
Progressors
Mr. Dennis Pustelnor
Ms. Kathryn E. Puterbaugh
Mr. and Mrs. Joseph Putnam
Quent Cordair Fine Art
Ms. Mary Quinlan
Mr. and Mrs. Mario Rabinowitz
Mrs. Dorothy Radyk
Mr. Martin Ragno
Eric and Elaine Raines
Mr. Phillip Raiser
Mr. and Mrs. A. Joseph Rallo
Mr. Eugene Ranghiasci
Mrs. Doris Rankine

Mrs. Martha Rasey
Mr. and Mrs. Donald I. Ray
Mr. and Mrs. Anthony Rebele
Dave and Wendy Redfern
Mr. and Mrs. Jerrold Redford
Ms. Sarah Johnson Redlich
Ms. Peggy Redmond
Redwood City Heritage Association
Redwood City Public Library
Redwood City Redevelopment Agency
Mr. and Mrs. William Rehlich
Ms. Aleth Reilley
Mrs. Elizabeth K. Reinhart
Lynne and Rodger Reinhart
Mrs. Beth D. Remington
Mr. and Mrs. Dale Retherford
Mrs. Shirley Reusch Drye
Ms. Helen C. Reuter
Ms. Janice Rhoads
Dr. and Mrs. Marvin Richards
Mrs. Marguerite N. Richardson
Mr. Will Richardson
Ms. Anne Richter
Mr. & Mrs. Douglas S. Richter
Mr. and Mrs. Bret Ridge
Mr. and Mrs. James M. Riley
Ms. Deborah Rimerman
Mrs. John J. Riordan
Ms. Sue Ritchie
Mr. George Roberts
Mr. and Mrs. Charles W. Robertson
Ms. Renette Robillard
Mr. Walter R. Robinson
Richard and Michael Rocchetta
Rod McLellan Co.
Mr. Joe Rodden
Mr. and Mrs. James Rodondi
Ms. Jeanne E. Roehm
Mr. & Mrs. Harold Rogers
Mr. and Mrs. Nicholas Rogers
Ms. Shelly Rogers
Mr. Edward Rojas
Mr. and Mrs. Roland Rojas
Mr. Kenneth Rolandelli
Ms. Theresa Rolandelli
Ms. Paula Roloff
Mr. Ronald D. Romaine
Mrs. June Romey
Mr. and Mrs. John Root
Mr. Adolph Rosekrans
Mr. and Mrs. Edward G. Rosen
Rosendin Electric
Mr. and Mrs. Edward B. Rosenstiel
Ms. Annette Ross
Ms. Janice Rossi

Rotary Club of San Mateo
Mr. and Mrs. Jack W. Roudebush
Ms. Joanne Rovno
Mr. William C. Rowe
Mr. and Mrs. Henry Rowen
Ms. Susan Blake Rowland
Mr. Randy Royce
Royston, Hanamoto, Alley & Abey
Richard and Janice Rozakis
Mrs. Barbara R. Rucker
Mr. Robert B. Ruff
Mr. and Mrs. Stuart Rumley
Mr. and Mrs. R. J. Rummel
Mrs. Dorothy Rumney
Ms. Marsha Runnele
Mr. Steven Rusconi
Honorable Ira Ruskin
Mr. Alpheus Russell
Ms. Mary Ryan
Ms. Patricia Ryan
Mr. T. J. Ryan
Mr. Donald Sabatini
Mr. & Mrs. Peter M. Sacerdote
Mr. Paul Saffo
Mrs. Harriett E. Saign
Ms. Lisa Sakaguchi
Ms. Misa Sakaguchi
Mr. Scott Sakaguchi
Ms. Jane M. Sakai
Mr. William Sakai
Ms. Julia Salas
Mr. Roy Salvato
Mr. James Salveson
Ms. Sheri Samietz
Sammut Family Foundation
San Bruno Auto Center Inc.
San Bruno Chamber of Commerce
San Bruno Public Library
San Carlos Chamber of Commerce
San Mateo County Library
San Mateo Elks Lodge #1112
San Mateo Public Library
Mr. Henry Sanchez
Mr. and Mrs. Elmo Sanders
Mr. and Mrs. George Sant
Mr. Mike J. Sarikakis
Sarrtori Fine Apparel for Men
Ms. June Sartor
Mr. and Mrs. Arthur Saylor
SBC
Ms. Nancy Scammell
Mr. Paul T. Scannell
Mr. and Mrs. Frank Scarpino
Mr. and Mrs. Victor Schachter
Mr. and Mrs. Robert E. Scharff

Mr. John S. Scheibe
Mr. and Mrs. H. Alton Schich
Mrs. Derry Schillaci
Mr. F. Tracy Schilling
Ms. Betty Schlaepfer
Mrs. Alfred C. Schmidt
Mr. and Mrs. Christopher Schmidt
Mrs. Earl F. Schmidt
Mr. Ozzie Schmidt
Ms. Ruth Schmitz
Ms. Maryannette Schneider
Mr. Bob Schoeppner
Suite 12" Ellis A. Schoichet
Mr. and Mrs. Robert Schonfisch
Mrs. Richard Schotzko
Ms. Cynthia Schreurs
Mr. and Mrs. David Schricker
Mr. and Mrs. John Schrup
Mr. and Mrs. William Schueler
Mr. and Mrs. Richard Schumacher
Mr. and Mrs. Robert S. Schwantes
Honorable John G. Schwartz
Mr. Kenneth E. Schwartz
Ms. Ellyn Schwartzman
Ms. Janet Schwind
Mr. and Mrs. Alfred Schwoerer
Mr. and Mrs. Richard Sciaroni
Mr. Howard R. Scott
Mr. and Mrs. William W. Scott
Mr. and Mrs. Sanford Seaman
Mr. and Mrs. Frank Seebode
Mr. Thomas A. Seeburger
Dr. and Mrs. Gordon M. Seely
Ms. Pamela Segale
Mr. and Mrs. Tom Seivert
Mrs. Shirley Seramin
Judge and Mrs. Aram Severian
Ms. Constance Sevier
Ms. Jeanne Shada
Mr. Wayne Shada
Mr. Hugo E. Shane
Ms. Sandy Shapero
Mr. and Mrs. Allen W. Shelton
Mr. Bruce Shelton
Mr. Paul Shepherd
Mrs. Manuela B. Sherman
Mr. and Mrs. Yoshimi Shibata
Ms. Donna Shimer
Mr. Donald Shoecraft
Mr. John Shroyer
Mr. James Shypertt
Dr. Allan Sidle
Mr. and Mrs. Tom Siebel
Ms. Nancy Siegel
Mrs. Virginia Howard Siegman

Mr. and Mrs. Robert Sies
Mr. and Mrs. Lloyd A. Silberstein
Mr. Carl A. Silveira
Ms. Diane Silven
Mr. and Mrs. Frank Silverman
Mr. and Mrs. John Simonson
Mr. J. Francis Sinnott
Mr. James Sinton
Ms. Marie Slate
Mr. Barry Smith
Mr. Charles J. Smith
Ms. Charlyne Smith
Ms. Chrystine Smith
Mrs. Dem Smith
Mrs. Harry F. Smith
Ms. Helen R. Smith
Ms. Kristine Smith
Mr. and Mrs. Robert P. Smith
Mrs. Roger L. Smith
Honorable Thomas Smith
Ms. Marilyn Snyder
Stanley and Allegra Sockol
Ms. Marion Softky
Leo and Debie Solari
Dr. and Mrs. B. C. Solomon
Mr. Mark J. Solomon, Esq.
Mr. D. C. Sonnichsen
Mr. Keith Sorenson
Mrs. Virginia Soult
Mrs. Berenice Spalding
Mrs. Ray Spangler
Special Library Association
Honorable Jackie Speier
Mr. Bob Spence
Mrs. Robert E. Spence
Mr. and Mrs. Robert L. Spence
Mr. and Mrs. Dirk Spencer
Mr. Ralph Spickerman and Family
Mrs. Evelyn Spiegelman
Mrs. Myrtle Spivey
Spivey Family
Mr. and Mrs. Paul Squeri
Ms. Barbara J. Stafford
Mr. and Mrs. Bill Stafford
Mr. and Mrs. Lee Stafford
Mr. and Mrs. Larry Staley
Mr. and Mrs. Jeffrey Stallings
David and Cindy Stanley
Mr. Peter Stansky
Mr. and Mrs. Albert C. Starr
Dr. Deirdre Stegman
Mr. and Mrs. James Steidel
Mr. and Mrs. David Steinberg
Mrs. Paul Steiner
Ms. Rebecca Stephenson

Marlene and Hank Stern
Mr. & Mrs. Robert O. Stevens
Ms. Lynn Stevenson
Ms. Ina Stewart
Dr. and Mrs. Mark S. Still
Ms. Pamela M. Stine
Ms. Doris E. Stirm
Mrs. Glenn Stirm
Mr. and Mrs. Herbert Stone
Ms. Jean Stone
Ms. Arlene Storm
Ms. Christine Stormont
Mr. Ron Stott
Mr. Marshall Stowe
Ms. Gretchen A. Strauss
Dr. John Stringer
Mr. and Mrs. Robert E. Strode
Mr. and Mrs. Arthur Stromberg
Mr. Bill Stronck
Mr. and Mrs. William Stronck
Mrs. Margot Struble
Mr. and Mrs. Warren Struven
Mr. and Mrs. Dave Stuart
Dr. Thomas Stucker
Mr. and Mrs. Giyojun Sueyoshi
Mr. Dan Sullivan
Mr. Michael Sullivan
Mr. Erik Sundquist
Ms. Chris Surowiec
Mr. and Mrs. Kenneth Sutherland
Ms. Robin A. Sutton
Mr. Michael Svanevik
Mr. Bill Swackhamer
Mr. Greg Sweatt
Mr. and Mrs. Jeff Sweatt
Mrs. Robert C. Sweatt
Ms. Shelley Sweet
Ms. Susan Swope
Mr. James Allen Sykes
Mr. Charles W. Syme
Mr. and Mrs. Chikara Takaha
Mr. and Mrs. Kenge Takahashi
Mr. and Mrs. George Tarleton
Ms. Laura Tarwater
Mr. Chris Tassio
Mr. & Mrs. Geoff Tate
Ms. Joan Tatman
Dr. William Tatomer
Mr. Tad Taube
Mr. Geoffrey T. Tayler
Mr. David Taylor
Mr. and Mrs. Edwin Taylor
Mrs. Jane S. Taylor
Ms. Kathryn Taylor
Ms. Margaret Taylor

Mr. Raymond Taylor
Ms. Donna Teare
Ms. Pat Terman
Mr. Frank Terry
Dr. Arnold Thachray
The Examiner
Mr. Paul E. Thiebaut
Mr. and Mrs. Fred Thiemann
Mr. and Mrs. Harold M. Thiewes
Mr. and. Mrs. Donald Thom
Ms. Eleanor Thomas
Mrs. Irene M. Thommen
Ms. Sally E. Thompson
Mr. Tom Thompson
Mr. and Mrs. Victor K. Thompson
The Thompson Family
Ms. Susan J. Thornton
Ms. Clare M. Thorpe
Mrs. Betty O. Thysen
Ms. Carol Timmerman
Mr. Carlos Tinsley
Honorable Adrienne Tissier, 5th Dist.
Ms. Theresa Titus
Ms. Robin Toews
Mr. Francis Toldi
Mrs. Laurette Toldi
Mr. David Tomatis
Mr. and Mrs. Donald Tomatis
Mr. Evangelos Tonas
Ms. Sharen Topham
Mr. and Mrs. Donald Torburn
Ms. Linda Ruth Torgeson
Mr. and Mrs. Anthony Torrano
Mr. and Mrs. Doug Tozzini
Ms. Nonie M. Tremaine
Ms. Constance Trewin
Mr. and Mrs. Greg Trindle
Mr. and Mrs. Vincent Truscelli
Ms. Suzanne Tschaekofske
Mr. Richard Tsukushi
Mr. and Mrs. Alexander Tuganov
Mr. Tim Twerdahl
Ms. Jean Tyan
Ms. Barbara Tyson Cavalierri
Mrs. Peter Uccelli
Mr. Peter Ulrich
United Way of the Bay Area
University of California Library
Mrs. Margaret G. Utterback
Ms. Lynn Valueff
Mr. and Mrs. Dwight Van Meter
Mr. and Mrs. Thomas Vanden Bosch
Ms. Marilyn J. Vanderplaats
Frank and Glenna Vaskelis
Mr. Meeks Vaughan

Mrs. Sylvia L. Vaughn
Mrs. Harlan Veal
Mr. Michael Verducci
Mr. and Mrs. Walter H. Vielbaum
Ms. Patricia Violette
Mr. and Mrs. Thomas H. Vocker
Ms. Cara Vonk
Tedi Vriheas
Ms. Elizabeth Wade
Mr. Wells E. Wadleigh
Mr. and Mrs. James R. Wagner
Mr. David Waisbein
Ms. Susan Walker-O'Brien
Mr. and Mrs. Kurt Wallace
Mr. Rich Wallace
Mr. Robert Wallace
Mr. Geoffrey Walne
Mr. Matt Walsh
Mr. Bernard Ward
Ms. Helen C. Ward
Mr. John Ward
Mr. and Mrs. Robert Warfield
Mr. George T. Warman
Mr. and Mrs. Philip Warnes
Mr. Deral Warren
Ms. Patrice Warren
Mr. and Mrs. Henry Washauer
Ms. Kay Watanabe
Mr. Robert Waterman, Jr.
Mr. Nick Watry
Mr. Richard Watters
Mr. and Mrs. Robert Way
Mr. and Mrs. Stephen A. Way
Ms. June Wayne
Ms. Ron and Linda Weaver
Ms. Patricia Webb
Mrs. Judith Webster Barton
Mr. Kevin Weir
Ms. Mary Ellen Weiss
Mr. Raymond Weiss
Mr. Theodore Weller
Wells Fargo
Ms. Ann M. Wenner
Mr. Albert Wenzell
Jeanne and Bill Weseloh
Ms. Julie Wesolek
Mrs. Paul Wessel
Mr. and Mrs. Putney Westerfield
Mr. Silas P. Wheaton
Mr. Mark H. Whitman
Ms. Irene Whitmer
Irene & Betty Whittemore
Mr. and Mrs. Douglas J. Wigton
Mr. John Wilkes
Mr. and Mrs. William A. Wilkin

Mr. and Mrs. Robert Wilkinson
Ms. Donna Williams
Mr. and Mrs. Richard Williams
Mr. and Mrs. Robert Williams
Mrs. Marie Jo Willoughby
Ms. Diane B. Wilsey
Mrs. Charles Wilson
Chris and Frannie Wilson
Mr. and Mrs. William Wilson, III
Ms. Joanne Winetzki
Ms. Helen Winsmann
Mr. and Mrs. Jeffrey Winters
Dr. and Mrs. Philip Winters
Wisnom's
Mr. Larry R. Witham
Ms. Sarah Withers Divine
Dr. and Mrs. Irving M. Witt
Mr. and Mrs. Bernard Wolfe
Ms. Pamela Storm Wolfskill
Mr. Ralph Wondra
Mr. and Mrs. Arthur Douglas Wong
Mr. Richard Woo
Mr. and Mrs. Don Wood
Ms. Elinor E. Wood and Family
Woodlawn Cemetery Foundation
Ms. Ardyth Y. Woodruff
Ms. Janice M. Woods
Mr. and Mrs. Larry Woolston
Ms. Judy Worster
Ms. Barbara J. Wright
Ms. Laura Wuest
Ms. Marlene Wuest
Ms. Polly A. Wyant
Mr. and Mrs. Larry Wyman Works
Mr. Richard Wysong
Ms. Susan Yamaguchi
Mr. and Mrs. Aiko Yamamoto
Mr. Kio Yamane
Mr. and Mrs. Ray Yamanishi
Mr. and Mrs. Roy Yih
Mr. Michael J. Ynion
Mr. and Mrs. Seiichi Yoshida
Ms. Helen Yoshii
Ms. Gayle Youlden
Ms. Claire Young
Ms. Pat Young
Ms. Dorothy Yuki
Ms. Vickie Yumoto
Ms. Mari Zachary Lyon
Mr. Christopher Zanoni
Mr. Edmond Zaro
Mr. Dennis Zell
Ms. Gertrude S. Zemanek
Ms. Carol Zim
Mr. and Mrs. Raymond Zinckgraf

Index